Simplified Choices

A Family Memoir of Latvia, World War II and Identity

Anita Spigulis-DeSnyder

Copyright © 2024 by Anita Spigulis-DeSnyder

All rights reserved.

No part of this book may be reproduced in any form or by any electronic or mechanical means, including information storage and retrieval systems, without written permission from the author, except for the use of brief quotations in a book review.

Contents

Preface	xiii
Gathering	1
DIFFERENT	7
1. Half and Half	9
MASTERS OF THEIR BATTERED LAND	25
2. As the Master Commands	27
3. Masters of Their Land	33
4. Kulak Son	43
5. Orphan Girl	55
6. Latvia for Latvians!	65
WORLD WAR II	73
7. The Devils' Pact	75
8. The Year of Terror	85
9. Trading One Master for Another	103
10. Forever No Peace Beneath Latvia's Birches	111
11. Life is a Struggle	123
12. Every Man for Himself	139
13. To Stop Was to Die	149
14. Simplified Choices	159
DISPLACED	169
15. Little to Do But Wait	173
16. Possibilities in Life	185
17. Nothing Left at Home	197
18. Only One Homeland	207

RETURNING 215

19. Return to Latvia 217
20. May the Sands Rest Lightly 229
21. Return to Latvia 231

Acknowledgments 239
Appendix A: Latvian Pronunciation Guide 241
Appendix B: Letters from Arnolds Bērziņš 247
Notes 255
Bibliography 265

In loving memory of my parents, Arvīds and Skaidrīte Spīgulis.

Eastern Europe 1939

LAND
lsinki
Gulf of Finland
Tallinn
ESTONIA
Lake Ladoga
Leningrad
Lake Peipus
Lake Ilmen
ulf of Riga
LATVIA
iga
Dvina R.
Moscow
U.S.S.R.
IUANIA
Kaunus
Vilnius/ Wilno
BYELORUSSIA (BELARUS)
AND
UKRAINE
Kiev
0
150
300 Km
0
150
300 Mi

Latvia 1939

Spīgulis Family Key Personages

Pēteris Spīgulis
Kulak, b.1879, d.1970
Deported to Siberia 1949–57
Returned to Latvia 1957

Kristīne Ārgalis Spīgulis
Wife of Pēteris, b.1891, d.1980
Deported to Siberia 1949–57
Returned to Latvia 1957

Their Children:

Alīne
1914-1990
Remained in Latvia

Arvīds
1918-2019
Auxiliary soldier 1944-45
Baltic University 1946-48
Emigrated to USA 1949

Valija
1927-2013
Deported to Siberia with parents
Returned to Latvia 1957

Skaidrīte Bērziņš
1921-2014
Refugee, Emigrated to USA 1949
Married Arvīds 1951

Arvīds & Skaidrīte's Children:

Maruta   Karl   Anita

Bērziņš Family Key Personages

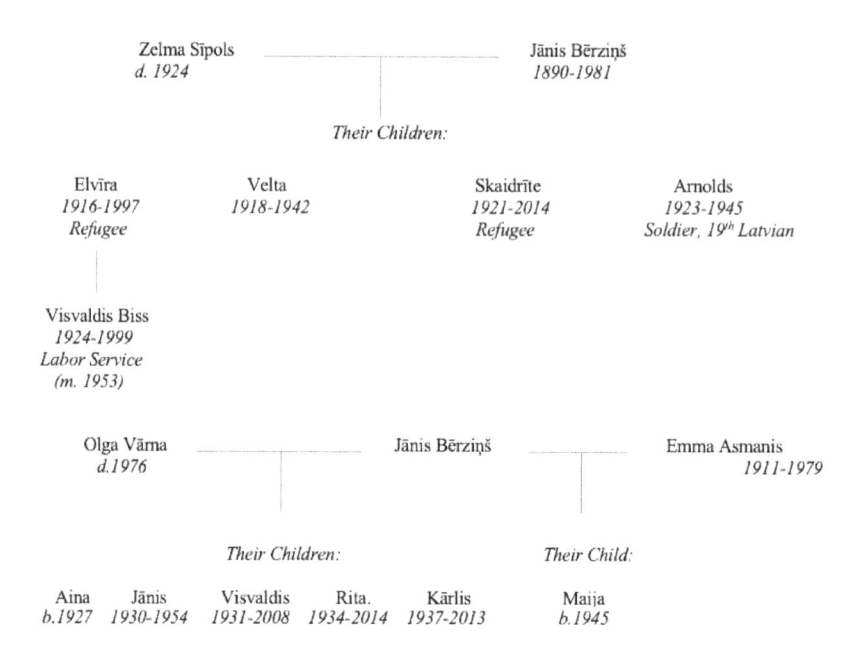

Zelma Sīpols — Jānis Bērziņš
d. 1924 — *1890-1981*

Their Children:

Elvīra	Velta	Skaidrīte	Arnolds
1916-1997	*1918-1942*	*1921-2014*	*1923-1945*
Refugee		*Refugee*	*Soldier, 19th Latvian*

Visvaldis Biss
1924-1999
Labor Service
(m. 1953)

Olga Vārna — Jānis Bērziņš — Emma Asmanis
d.1976 — — *1911-1979*

Their Children: *Their Child:*

Aina	Jānis	Visvaldis	Rita.	Kārlis	Maija
b.1927	*1930-1954*	*1931-2008*	*1934-2014*	*1937-2013*	*b.1945*

Preface

One blistering-hot July afternoon in 1979, I boarded a train in Paris, bound for Avignon, and found a seat in an empty compartment of the second-class section. I was twenty-one. The train was pulling slowly out of the station when a handsome young man slid the door open, smiled, and tucked his backpack up on the luggage rack. As the train gained speed, he sat down across from me and we introduced ourselves. His name was Ari: he was from Israel, traveling on an extended tour of Europe. Conversation was easy. We talked about our travels, university studies, and moved onto our family backgrounds. I shared the fact that my parents were both World War II Latvian émigrés, and that I spoke Latvian; many Americans spoke only English, and I felt this set me apart in an interesting way. Ari maintained his friendly manner, but immediately said, "Oh yes, I know the Latvians. Do you know what your people did to us during World War II?" I was surprised by the question. Stalin had forcibly annexed Latvia, arresting, exiling, or executing thousands of citizens. My father's family had been among those deported, spending eight years in the Gulag. Latvians were among the victims of World War II. Ari's voice remained calm, but as we talked, he mentioned words like Holocaust, concentration camps,

Preface

Nazis—words I did not associate with Latvia. He kept coming back to me with questions about the Latvians' collaboration with the Nazis. My confusion and discomfort grew. Thankfully, he got off a few stops before Avignon. As he left the compartment, he said, "You Americans, you think you know everything. Wake up and find out what the rest of the world goes through. Have a nice trip in France."

It was July 14: Bastille Day. In Avignon, celebratory fireworks exploded everywhere, people bought each other drinks, sang songs, and lurched down narrow streets, arm in arm. Instead of enjoying the party, I was in a fog. What did Ari mean by calling Latvians collaborators? His accusations stayed with me, unshakable. I started thinking about the facts of my parents' lives as I knew them. My father told me that he served in the Latvian Army during World War II. My mother's brother, Arnolds, died on the battlefield, fighting to defend Latvia against the Soviets. Both my mother and father lived in refugee camps in Germany for a number of years before emigrating to the United States. The Latvians of my childhood were decent people: they worked hard, were honest and respectful, certainly not Nazis. But while they shared stories of their childhoods, they never talked about their experiences during the war or their exodus. I never asked. It was as if there was an unspoken agreement between us: don't ask so that we don't have to tell. These are painful memories, best left undisturbed.

On a humid August afternoon, later that summer, my father and I sat on his front porch with a couple of cold Heinekens. The leaves on the trees were perfectly still, the monotone buzz of cicadas droning outside. We sat quietly, drinking our beers. This was my chance. I looked directly at him and asked, "What happened in Latvia during World War II? Did the Latvians join the Nazis? Did you?"

My father sipped his beer, then set down his glass. Condensation dripped down the sides in crooked rivulets. I stared at the droplets as he spoke in a quiet voice.

"The Germans invaded Latvia after the Russians were driven out. You have to understand that we had just lived through 1941, the

Baigais gads (Year of Terror). Thousands of Latvians were tortured, executed or deported by the Russians. When the Germans came in, many of us saw this as trading one master for another, and didn't expect anything good to come of it. But other Latvians thought that the Germans would help us regain our freedom. Some even joined the Nazis."

I drew a deep breath and went further. "When you were in the Army, were you fighting with the Germans or Latvians?"

Again, my father sipped before answering. "I was in a Latvian division that was part of the German Army."

"So, you were on the side of the Nazis?"

My father looked straight at me. "We were drafted by the Germans. It was either serve or be shot as a deserter. When someone points a gun at your head, it simplifies your choices."

My father, my uncle, my family, on the wrong side. It was impossible for me to reconcile with what I knew and loved about them.

Being Latvian was the foundation of my identity, as much a part of me as my fingerprints or shadow. I grew up within the tight-knit Latvian community of Boston. No one knew these people like I did. Or thought I did. The people I knew were certainly not Nazis, and would not have fought under the Nazi banner for ideology. There was more to it than that. There had to be. What had my parents lived through? What happened in Latvia during World War II? What did all of this mean to their identities? To mine? What did it mean to be Latvian?

Those questions remained unanswered for years. Instead, I returned to college, where the shock and discomfort of my father's conversation faded under the pressure of senior year. I finished my coursework, thesis, and graduated. I immersed myself in a job search, found a job, and moved to New York City, losing myself in its maze of people and an exciting new life. I moved back to Boston, got more jobs, fell in and out of love several times. I even traveled to Latvia with my family, a trip spent meeting our relatives, but my real questions

Preface

remained unasked, unanswered. I got married, bought a house, and raised two sons. I earned a master's degree and a black belt.

My aunt died of multiple myeloma. Her husband died of a stroke. My mother was diagnosed with Alzheimer's, spent years in a nursing home, and died. Family friends died. There was always someone to care for, a project to be completed, something to preoccupy me, to push the question back down: what did it mean to be Latvian?

During those years, I would have said that I was too busy to devote time to finding my answers. The truth is that I did not know how to proceed, or where to start. I was afraid of what I might find out. With every illness and every death, the possibility of finding answers to my questions was slowly slipping away.

After three falls, my father landed in an assisted living facility. As his legal representative, I needed access to documents housed in his desk. Before this, I had never looked in his desk without his express permission. The desk was my father's private vault, the first piece of furniture he purchased in the United States, and he guarded it like Cerberus guarded the gates of hell. Glancing through a hanging file labeled "Imort. Dokum."—his abbreviation for important documents—I pulled out a weathered brown mailing envelope, with my mother's handwriting on the upper right corner: *Rita's vēstules*. Rita's letters. Rita was one of my mother's sisters. Opening the envelope, I pulled out four brittle, yellowing papers, covered with a pale spidery penciled script. Written at the top of the first one was, *"Adolf Hitler's 144-9, 1943, 21st November."* They were letters from her brother, Arnolds, the soldier who died in the war.

I couldn't ignore my questions any longer. From a distant time and place, the dead were inviting me to find the answers.

Gathering

My parents' house in Wellesley had a three season porch, with glass casement windows cranked open to admit the breezes in warm weather, cranked shut in cold weather so the solar heat could maintain a comfortable temperature. A mass of climbing vines on either end formed a thick green privacy curtain, shielding us from the neighbors. It was our comfortable space, a space where my parents relaxed enough to talk. Most of the time, it seemed that my parents were working, either at their jobs or at home. My father, an architect, took freelance design projects and worked on them at night to earn some extra money. He called it "moonlighting." My mother worked full-time in a local retail store. On weekends, they tended their vegetable and flower gardens and took care of the house. My sister, brother, and I found after-school jobs as soon as we were of legal age to do so. We were expected to earn and save money for our college educations. Being the youngest, I was responsible for cooking the family dinner beginning in fifth grade. After school, I came home and read my mother's dinner preparation instructions, carefully listing each step on neatly written index cards. After a few months of this, I began planning meals independently.

The porch was not a place for work. It was simply for connection, peace, pleasure. When my parents entertained, their friends who smoked would take their cocktails and cigarettes out to the porch. It wasn't long before the party followed them out there, laughter squeezing through the screens into the yard where I sometimes hid, watching the adults, fascinated. One of their friends French-inhaled, smoke smoothly drifting from her parted lips into her nostrils. I thought it was the picture of glamour. The wicker furniture, the little day bed that served as a couch, and the glass-topped table were infused with friendship and fun. When my parents needed a break from their tasks, they automatically headed out to the porch. In this relaxed mode, I could ask questions about their childhoods in Latvia. My father, the gregarious one, enjoyed recalling his family farm and boyhood antics with great detail. When my Aunt Elvīra and her husband Visvaldis visited, we would sit with a glass of wine while they shared their memories.

My mother's memories came out in a different manner. She would share some stories about her childhood—her mother and sister Velta's death being the ones I remember most clearly. She didn't talk a lot, her boundaries more defined than my father's. When I became interested in capturing their experiences for future writing, I recorded their words with a small tape recorder. My mother answered questions but required a great deal of prompting to elaborate. As her memory declined, my father supplemented her answers with details she had told him over the years. Often, it was enough to keep her going.

Over several sessions, I collected two cassette tapes of material about my parents' childhoods and my father's wartime service. When we talked without recording, I took notes. These recordings, notes, and countless conversations with my brother and sister are the primary sources for the information about my family's experiences.

Our family trip to Latvia in 1989 did not reveal a lot of family history. Conditioned to a life of living under surveillance and the constant threat of repressions, our relatives were guarded and revealed little. Instead, we came away with a first-hand understanding of how damaging the years of Soviet domination were to Latvia. In our hotel, we took care not to speak negatively of the Soviet system, assuming that bugs were placed in the rooms. Anything we said could be used to hurt our family living there. Once back in the United States, my parents spoke openly about how the prosperous country they left in 1944 was destroyed.

My father contributed essays and photographs to volumes about Baltic University and his fraternity Gersicania. His desire to record the past in these volumes shed light on the diaspora Latvian experience among those who pursued an education and camaraderie in the Displaced Persons camps.

After my Aunt Elvīra died, her husband Visvaldis spent his waking hours writing his memoirs. He lived long enough to finish the memoirs and make copies for my siblings and me. His meticulous descriptions of his wartime experiences and subsequent emigration gave me a vivid understanding of his life, and are used in any chapters featuring him.

Once I found Arnolds' letters and began digging, I consulted secondary research to understand Latvian history and its effect on my parents' outlook and identities: what they went through and how it affected their mindset. I hoped to clarify what being Latvian meant to me. I read the history books written by diaspora historians from my parents' collection, but found many to be of limited use, due to the inherent bias (however, reading these works improved my Latvian immeasurably). Several of the books did not mention the Holocaust at all, instead focusing on the Nazis' hostile takeover of Latvia and conscription of Latvian men and women. The few books that mentioned the Holocaust simply stated that the Nazis alone were responsible. Like my parents and their friends, the diaspora authors were silent about the Holocaust and any Latvian role in it. My parents did not own books written by scholars in Latvia at this time, as those books presented an equally biased view that all Latvian nationalists were Nazi collaborators during the German occupation of the former

Soviet republic. This changed after Latvia regained independence and scholars were free to explore historical events without passing them through Soviet censorship. The substantial volume of work produced by the Symposium of the Commission of Historians of Latvia was an invaluable source, and gave me access to the work of current Latvian historians. I have detailed the many excellent sources I consulted in the bibliography.

I hit walls, particularly in piecing together details about my Uncle Arnolds. The Latvian War Museum and Folklore Institute provided information I could not find elsewhere.

Many times I felt that it was presumptuous of me to think that I could recreate what my parents and family had experienced. Could I ever really understand their feelings and thoughts? After my father was in the assisted living facility, my brother, sister, and I were cleaning out his house, getting it ready for eventual sale. One day, as I tackled the basement, I found a treasure trove: pushed to the back of a dusty utility shelf, covered in cobwebs, were old shoeboxes filled with letters. My parents saved every letter they received from Latvia and each other—and here they were, in those dusty shoeboxes. This was my opportunity to learn about my family in their words. Hundreds of hours later, I felt like I knew my grandparents and aunts. Those letters brought them alive to me.

Finally, the trip my sister and I took to Latvia in June 2023 answered several remaining questions. Originally planned for June 2020, the Covid pandemic delayed our trip by three years. It was worth the wait—we had the chance to speak with our mother's sister, Aina, to clear up some questions. We visited my mother's home village, her elementary school, and found the fields and woods where her childhood home had been. Seeing the pastoral countryside where she grew up explained her in a way I lacked while she was alive.

I have included diacritics on Latvian names and words, except where the anglicized versions are well known. For example, Rīga is spelled Riga, and I have used the anglicized names for Latvia's four regions. While Latvians may question this decision, I chose these because Courland is well-known to anyone familiar with World War II military history.

All folk songs have been translated by me, with considerable assistance from my brother and sister. In Latvian, only the first words in titles are capitalized (*Sarkandaiļa roze auga*) unless they are proper nouns (*Dievs svētī Latviju*). For anyone who wishes to hear the folk songs sung in Latvian, simply search the internet for the Latvian name of the song, and you will find several options. Or, find a Latvian and ask them to sing the song for you. We all know them.

DIFFERENT

Chapter 1

Half and Half

From the moment I was born, I knew I was Latvian. Latvian, Latvian, Latvian. It was an inescapable mantra, repeated daily by my parents. The message was clear: we live in the United States, but we are Latvian. For a child figuring out her place in the world and trying to fit in with her peers, this was a hard message to fully embrace. My public life was American: school, friends, activities. My home life was Latvian. Where did that leave me?

My siblings and I knew we were different from our neighbors. Our names were unusually ethnic for Massachusetts in the early 1960s. My sister drew the toughest of the lot: Maruta Silvia (no "y" in the Latvian alphabet). My brother, Karl, landed the most American-sounding name of the three of us, but spelled with a K rather than the highly coveted C of Carl Sandburg, Carl Switzer, and, later, Carls Sagan and Yastrzemski. Never a K, not in those days. My own name, Anita Ingrīda, was the result of my sister's attempt to finally get a real American name in the family. My parents planned to name me Elvīra, after my mother's sister, but once I was born, Maruta announced proudly to her first-grade class that she had a new baby sister named Annette, after Annette Funicello of the Mickey Mouse Club. She whined and cried until my parents caved and gave me the closest Latvian version to Annette they found acceptable. Upon her return home from the hospital, a lovely card from Maruta's first grade class awaited my mother, inscribed "Congratulations to you and little Annette!"

We lived in Dedham in the early years, renting a narrow apartment on Massachusetts Avenue. My mother didn't yet have her driving license or a command of English, so she kept to herself. In my parents' previous apartment, neighborhood women spent the afternoons sitting on the doorsteps, chatting, while they sipped cans of beer, erasing the boredom of their routines. My mother, who didn't drink and had limited English proficiency, chose not to participate, earning the label of "stuck up." She wanted to move out of that neighborhood to a nicer place. In Dedham, our landlord was a "junk man" who lived on the floor above us. He enjoyed his liquor. Periodically, he urinated out of the second-floor window rather than using his toilet, amber droplets falling to the grass below. My mother hated this habit, finding it dirty and foul, but my father simply laughed, saying, "See what a great country America is? A man is free to piss out of his window if he wants!" In 1961, we moved to Wellesley, Massachusetts, into our own home where my mother wouldn't be subjected to the golden shower of freedom.

At home, we spoke exclusively Latvian. My sister and brother spoke almost no English until they started elementary school. This set them apart from the other kids immediately. The teachers kindly assured my mother that they would learn quickly, and seated them in the front row of their respective classes, closer to instruction. However, a different set of rules emerged during recess. My brother was ostracized on the playground. As he told me, "I didn't speak English in first grade. None of the boys would play with me because they said I was 'retarded.' I didn't understand what they were saying, and I didn't know the rules of the games they played. The only kid who would play with me was a fat kid who always had snots running from his nose.

They wouldn't play with him either." Learning English quickly was a matter of playground survival. When Maruta and Karl returned home, they were eager to practice their new language. They taught me, so I became bilingual early on. Our mother responded by fining us a penny every time she heard us speaking English in the house. In Latvia, she said, the Russians were trying to eradicate the Latvian language. Latvians were forced to speak Russian, so it was up to us to preserve the language. At the age of five, I found it difficult to understand how our family could single-handedly save Latvian from extinction, but I didn't want to lose the penny, so I complied—at least until my mother was out of earshot.

Even as a small child, I felt the dual pull of being both Latvian and American. My parents laughed about the time that, as a three-year-old, I heard a dog barking and inquired whether the dog was barking in Latvian or English. Once, when I was about six, a family friend came to call, bearing a bottle of cognac for my father and chocolates for us. We, the children, were expected to present ourselves to the guest and politely answer any questions posed. My sister and brother went first and were already raiding the box of chocolates when my turn came. I stood in front of the gentleman named Thomson, who chose his un-Latvian surname when he immigrated. I shook his hand politely, and waited for his question.

"Are you Latvian or American?" he asked.

I paused for a moment and thought about how to answer this complicated question. I gave the most truthful answer I could: "I am half Latvian, half American."

"Oh, half and half," he said, the beginnings of a smile twitching at the corners of his mouth. "So, which arm is Latvian?"

I raised my right arm confidently.

"Which leg is American?"

I wiggled my left leg. So far, so good.

"And which eye is Latvian, which is American?"

I pointed to my right and left eyes in turn, but I was beginning to

SIMPLIFIED CHOICES

feel like there was a catch to this game. I glanced longingly at the box of chocolates out of the corner of my Latvian eye. My sister had already snagged my favorite, the coconut chocolate crispy one.

The corners of his mouth stretched upwards like putty. "Which nose is Latvian?"

Uh oh. He had me there. I paused and touched a tentative finger to my right nostril.

"And which mouth is Latvian? Which is American?"

I stood silently, smelling the chocolates with my half and half nose.

He laughed amiably. "Ah, you see, child, you cannot split yourself in two. I think you are one hundred percent Latvian!" I nodded in agreement, took a chocolate from the box, and made my escape.

My feeling of being half Latvian, half American continued when I entered school. Every day, it seemed that there were reminders of how I was different, at a time when differences were not celebrated. In first grade, I made friends with Genia. On visiting day, my mother arrived along with the other mothers. I ran to her and gave her a big hug. Standing nearby, Genia stared and asked, "Is that your grandma?"

"No," I responded. "That's my mom."

"She's so old!" observed Genia. My cheeks flushed. I felt both embarrassed and angry about the slight to my mother. It was true; she was forty-one years old, much older than the other mothers milling about the classroom. The war and immigration interrupted her plans to marry and start a family for several years. On top of that, when she spoke, she had a heavy accent. Throughout grade school, when my peers met my mother, they inevitably asked me why she talked "funny." At first, I told them that she was Latvian. This was always followed by, "What's that?" When I explained that Latvia was a country that was taken over by the Russians, they said, "Oh, so you're Russian." Knowing my parents' feelings about the Russians in Latvia, this was horrible. Anything but that! I needed an alternative. I came up with Sweden, land of Ingrid Bergman and other blond beauties, thereby giving my mother a glamour that American children would understand. This became my standard elementary school answer when faced with another dreaded question: what kind of a name is Spigulis?

In Wellesley during the mid-1960s, all children recited the Lord's Prayer at our elementary school assemblies. During the first assembly of the year, my class filed into the gymnasium. Everyone arose and recited the prayer in unison. As the voices began to chant, I was in trouble. I knew the prayer in Latvian. I bowed my head and stole furtive glances at the children on either side of me. Everyone's mouth was moving in synchronicity except for mine. I flapped my jaws as close to the words as I could, but I had no idea what I was supposed to say, hoping my bowed head would disguise my confusion. This continued for a few years until I managed to decipher and commit to memory the English words to the prayer.

I joined Girl Scouts. Every spring, we received our packet of Girl Scout Cookie order forms and went house to house selling the cookies: not my favorite part of scouting. One afternoon, I donned my uniform and took the forms to work my street. I started with our next door neighbors, the Geisels, who were always friendly with my parents, chatting over the picket fence that separated our yards. Hoping this would be an easy order, I rang the doorbell. Mrs. Geisel, an older woman who wore her hair in a loose gray and black streaked bun, answered and invited me in. I stepped inside and, at her invitation, entered the living room where Mr. Geisel sat in his armchair. Taking the forms from me, Mrs. Geisel asked how I liked Girl Scouts and a few questions about me, such as my age and grade. Then, Mr. Geisel spoke up.

"You seem to be a good girl. Your parents seem like fine people."

Why exactly was he saying this? I remained silent and glanced at the cookie order form, still in Mrs. Geisel's hands.

"We've been watching your family," he continued. "Mrs. Geisel and I are members of the John Birch Society. Our job is to watch for Communists. When your parents first arrived here, we watched them very closely. We thought they might be Russian spies or informers." He paused, as if waiting for me to say something. "But we have concluded that they are good people. It's a shame what happened to their country."

By now, Mrs. Geisel had checked off the cookies she wanted. I mumbled my thanks, retrieved the order form, and left the house quickly, my legs shaking. Finding out that your family was suspected of espionage is terrifying. I didn't go to any other houses selling cookies that year, and turned in my form with only the Geisel's order.

I never told my parents about the Geisel's surveillance. The wrongness of the cookie episode offended me. I wanted to protect my parents, my old, funny-accented, foreign parents. I wanted to allow them the comfort of chatting with the Geisels over the picket fence without knowing they were suspected of the worst thing they could imagine: working for the Russians. That was the last time I sold Girl Scout cookies to the Geisels. A year later, I quit Girl Scouts. It was not, however, the last time I felt the need to protect my parents from anti-immigrant biases that periodically came up.

For my parents, it was imperative that my siblings and I knew Latvian language, history, geography, and were culturally literate. Our Latvian education was formalized at the Boston Latvian School. Every Saturday, we piled into the car to drive to Jamaica Plain, thirty-five minutes away, for a full day of Latvian education: reading, grammar, vocabulary, spelling, history, geography, folk songs, folk dance, and half an hour of Lutheran dogma. Our parents faithfully checked our weekly homework assignments for accuracy. It was a love–hate relationship for me; the Saturday schedule meant that I could not participate in any extracurricular activities, such as sports, that required weekend attendance, but I was able to spend the day with my best friend, Nora. We giggled and gossiped our way through nine years of Latvian education. During this time, I learned that Latvia was primarily an agricultural country with a five hundred-kilometer-long coastline along the Baltic Sea, several navigable ice-free rivers, like the Daugava, and that the capital city, Riga, was a historic cultural and trading center. We learned that the Soviets forcibly took over the country in World War II, deported or killed thousands of Latvians, and were trying to erase Latvian national identity through Russification policies. It was therefore up to us, the generation born on American soil, to preserve our Latvian heritage for the day the country would again be free.

There was another benefit to Latvian school. Sundays were our family day. We sporadically attended church, usually forgoing it in favor of walks around Walden Pond or the Arnold Arboretum. We didn't have the scores of aunts, uncles and cousins that our American peers had. Most of our family was behind the Iron Curtain, so our little unit of five was sacred to my parents. Our Sunday outings helped fill the void my parents felt about their missing families.

Although my parents learned English, obtained their citizenship, worked, and made their lives in this country, they referred to the United States as *trimda*[1] (exile) to reinforce the point that their homeland was Latvia. They felt rootless. Officially, we attended the Latvian Lutheran Church of Boston, but everyone simply called it *trimdas draudze* (exile congregation). According to our community of immigrant Latvians, Russians were the devil incarnate who had driven us from our home. No true Latvian endorsed or consumed any Russian products. Smirnoff vodka was a forbidden substance in the bar. Even if my parents could have afforded it, Russian caviar would have been off limits.

Our closest blood relative in the United States was my mother's sister, Elvīra, who lived in Ann Arbor with her husband, Visvaldis. They married late in life and had no children, instead spending their vacations traveling around Europe and the Caribbean. Elvīra and Visvaldis dressed impeccably, and enjoyed fine dining and wine. Most years they spent Christmas with us, and when they arrived, the party began. After picking them up at the airport and situating their luggage in my brother's room, which served as our guest room, my father would take out four highball glasses and ask, "Visvaldis, would you like a painkiller?" They mixed drinks, ate the Latvian appetizers we had prepared, and talked until midnight. For those few days, our house was filled with laughter and the delicious smells of roasting meats and baked goods. I always cried when they returned to Michigan.

For unfamiliar holidays, like Thanksgiving, we sometimes joined our Latvian friends, who I came to regard as my exile family. My American friends all had relatives coming to their houses, bearing side dishes and pies to supplement the feast. In my house, it was just us and maybe my father's cousin, Uncle Ernests, with his wife and two children, or my godparents and their children. My mother had never cooked a turkey before coming to the United States. Lacking the cultural context, the holiday was seen as the day Americans ate turkey, a difficult bird to cook well. My parents and their friends referred to it as *tītaru diena* (turkey day). It was somewhat puzzling to them that Americans would devote an entire day to this bird. Even now, Thanksgiving is not my favorite holiday. To me, it's a lot of work and lacks the meaning of family gathering and tradition that exists in larger American families. The holiday represents my family's efforts to observe an unfamiliar ritual in a foreign land. My husband and I hosted his brother's family for our first Thanksgiving in our new home. Upon arriving, my sister-in-law, a gourmet cook, greeted me with two pies and a kiss, saying, "I can't wait to taste your family stuffing recipe! I love adding traditional recipes to our family collection. " I told her my mother always made Pepperidge Farm stuffing, so that's what I did, doctored up with celery, mushrooms, and onions. She never asked for the recipe.

The Boston area Latvians often got together to celebrate various Latvian holidays. At gatherings, Latvian staples were provided buffet-style by the women. Typical dishes included pickled herring with sour cream, smoked eel, pigs' feet in aspic, potato salad, beet salad, dense dark rye bread, and *pīrāgi* (bacon and onion stuffed pastries). Not fancy fare with sauces and exotic spices, but simple, hearty food, the heritage of a predominantly agricultural society. Latvians did not disguise the source of their food; the eel lay in its shriveled, black, leathery skin, coiled up and sliced on a large platter. You took a slice, pulled out the slight, translucent spine with a fork, and scraped out the meat. Prepared well, it had an oily, smoky, melt-in-your-mouth quality. *Amīši*, (pronounced um'/ee/shĭ) as we called any American who was not of Latvian heritage, were definitely put off by this presentation. For dessert, there were European style tortes leavened with egg whites, filled with fruit preserves, whipped cream, or buttercream frosting. The liquor flowed freely, and once people ate their fill, the songs began.

Latvians love to sing, and there are songs for just about any topic you can think of: happiness, sorrow, love, heartache, good luck, bad luck, drinking, holidays, harvests, rivers, horses, trees, bees, soldier songs, orphan songs, songs about the love of homeland. Songs have played a central role in Latvian history and culture: "Throughout the ages, the Latvian people have been called the singing people. That means that song to the Latvian has always been, and always will be, the most productive means of expressing the state of his soul."[2] My parents' friends followed a public singing protocol: an adult stood and commanded everyone's attention, saying, "*Silentium ad cantum!*" The leader announced the song and started the group off, keeping time with a raised hand, drifting along to the cadence of the song. Each adult had his or her favorites, and we could often tell the progress of the evening by specific songs. We could also tell how much liquor was consumed. I knew when my parents were getting ready to head out as my father would take the floor with the words, "*Silentium ad cantum! Pūt vējiņi!*" (Blow, Breezes), his signature song at these affairs:

> Blow, breezes, drive my boat
> Drive me to Courland.
> A Courland woman promised me
> The hand of her daughter, a miller.[3]

The song is melodic and melancholy, sung with a solemn, sober tone. Literally translating the lyrics, it is about a young man whose fiancée's mother breaks the promise of her daughter's betrothal because of his drinking and gambling. He sings to the breezes to blow his boat to Courland. However, as my father and his friends sang it, the song represented their love and longing for their homeland. In Soviet-occupied Latvia, *Pūt vējiņi* functioned as a surrogate Latvian national anthem during the years that the real anthem was banned. It was in this spirit that my father led the song. After singing all five verses, it was not long until the party broke up. Sometimes my mother, the non-drinker, took the keys and drove home.

My mother had a beautiful voice and loved to sing. In Latvia, she sang in choirs, often performing solos. She did not participate in Latvian choirs in the United States, but was usually singing in the kitchen, as she went about her chores. As children, we learned that the songs she sang were clues to her mood. If we heard a happy song, we knew this was a good time to ask for a playdate or extra snack. Certain songs, particularly if she just hummed the melodies, were a sign to stay away until her mood improved.

My parents were frugal, as were most Latvians. Thrift went beyond mere economy: it was an emotional trigger based on their experiences. We reused tea bags, keeping them in a small dish on the kitchen counter. If you brewed a cup of tea, you simply used several of the bags that had already gone through a pass or two. Nothing was wasted, and it was a punishable offense to leave food on your plate, uneaten. I hated peas but loved lima beans; my sister felt exactly the opposite. We surreptitiously traded our portions of peas and lima beans until my mother caught us and insisted that we each eat our own food. One evening, as I stared at a pile of peas on my plate, I had a brainstorm; I would cut the meat on my plate with a sliding motion, thereby knocking most of the peas on the floor. Surely this would save me from eating those nasty shriveled little legumes. As soon as my peas hit the floor, skittering around under the dining table, my mother gasped. My father glared at me and, in a quiet voice trembling with anger, said, "In the war, we would have cried tears of joy if we had seen even one pea. It is a sin to waste food. You will stay here, pick up every pea, kiss it, and eat it." I sat there stubbornly, tears running down my cheeks, while the rest of the family finished dinner and cleared all the dishes except mine. The dining table doubled as my father's work surface, so he stayed, read his mail and paid bills while I sat there. After one hour, I conceded and began picking up the cold, soggy peas, slowly, kissing each one and gulping it down without chewing. After another hour, I had finished the peas and was allowed to leave the table. To this day, I still hate peas.

My parents also prized formal education and expected us to excel in school. In the 1960s and early 1970s, many parents believed that a college degree was wasted on their daughters, who would become homemakers and raise children. My parents were different. My father impressed the importance of an advanced degree upon Maruta, Karl, and me, saying, "An education is the most important thing you can have. It gives you possibilities in life." He was living proof of this. He began his architectural studies at the University of Latvia, continued them in Pinneberg, Germany at the Baltic University, and, upon coming to the United States, passed his architectural exam, gaining his license to practice. The majority of our family friends also attended the Baltic University. While there, my father and thirteen other students founded the fraternity Gersicania. The Boston-based fraternity brothers met frequently at our house. Meetings took place in our basement, where the cigarette smoke wouldn't bother my mother as much; once the official business concluded, the brothers ate, drank, and sang songs until the wee hours.

My parents periodically received letters from their families and, in response, often put together packages to send back to Latvia. Providing material support was the only way they could show their love and care for their separated families. Typical items were skeins of wool, fabric, and some luxury items, like coffee or chocolate. Sometimes the packages included eyeglasses, shoes, and medicines because of tremendous shortages under the Soviet system. Letters from Latvia often contained the tracing of a child's foot for shoe size, a prescription for eyeglasses, or simply a description of symptoms for medicine. Our family doctor was Latvian, so obtaining medicines in this way was not an issue. People in Latvia were resourceful; given some raw materials, they could knit or sew their own clothing. Items they did not consume were sold on the black market to obtain other goods. Soviet customs agents opened and inspected all packages; theft at this point was a common occurrence. Letters sent to the relatives under separate cover detailed the items sent; once the package was received, the relatives responded with an itemized list so that my parents knew what, if anything, had been taken. Our relatives carefully worded any theft so as not to accuse the Soviet regime of wrongdoing. Something along the lines of, "Thank you for the package. The brown cloth will make an excellent coat. You must have forgotten to include the blue dress material in this package," was the way to simultaneously inform my parents that the package was compromised and avoid retribution.

―――

And then there was "The Fear," so solid and pervasive it seemed to take on corporeal form. Letters from my father's family came addressed to my mother, sometimes containing references to "little Arvīds." My father was a grown man, and my mother had never met his family. Why would they write to her as if he was a child? When I inquired, she explained that they were afraid that Soviet agents would find my father and force him to return to the Soviet Union, where he would be imprisoned or shot as a defector. Even as United States citizens, they still feared the long arm of the Soviet Union.

My mother's Fear was more extreme than that of my father. She was terrified of thunderstorms, often crying or hiding for their duration. She refused to go to the fireworks displays on the Fourth of July; the crack of thunder and the whistling explosions of fireworks forced her to relive the bombings she endured while fleeing the advancing front. One time, she went shopping at a nearby mall with my brother. A fire alarm activated, so all the patrons filed outside to the parking lot, where a construction crew happened to be digging trenches. Panic-stricken, my mother held onto my brother as they exited, sure that they were going to be shot and pushed into the trenches.

There were other differences. My father disliked Franklin D. Roosevelt. In school, I learned that Roosevelt was considered a strong, effective president, steering the United States through the Great Depression, the defeat of Nazi Germany, and setting out the parameters of an international peace organization that became the United Nations. My father, however, merely snorted and said, "He gave away Latvia to the Russians." He was sensitive when it came to humor about Latvia. The Smothers Brothers was one of my family's favorite television shows, until they made a joke about Disneyland having more flushing toilets than all of Latvia. He wrote letters, several times a year, to senators and congressmen in Washington, DC, asking them to support Latvia's independence and denounce the Soviet Union. Beyond these types of things, I never thought much more about my parents' experiences. I was busy getting into college, studying, forming friendships, falling in love: all the usual things that take up a young person's time and energy.

One by one, my sister, brother and I began changing our relationships to our Latvian upbringing. In college, my sister took the nickname Marty, an eminently more pronounceable American moniker than Maruta. My mother disliked it, telling me, "It sounds like martin, that nasty little animal." I suspect the real reason for this reaction was her sadness about her daughter choosing to reject her Latvian name. Karl stayed closer to his roots, using the Latvian pronunciation of Spīgulis (Spee'/gool/ iss). As he said, "No one can pronounce our name anyway. So why not teach them the right way to say it?" He made an excellent point. When I went to college, I used the American pronunciation but, when asked, proudly told everyone I was Latvian. This resulted in a lot of explaining since my classmates, for the most part, did not know anything about Latvia. Although tensions between the United States and the Soviet Union eased during the 1970s, there was still relatively little known about the annexed countries in the Soviet bloc. At this point in our social development, my peers valued individualism more than conformity. With that, my discomfort at being different dissipated. Belonging to a small relatively unknown culture was now interesting. I enjoyed being different and felt it was important to claim my heritage.

The connection to my Latvian upbringing remained strong, and I sought ways to keep my family culture in my life. During my sophomore year, I joined a Latvian sorority in the Boston area: Zintas, founded in Pinneberg like my father's fraternity. We met infrequently, but it gave me the opportunity to get together with other Latvian women, speak the language, and sing the songs I grew up knowing. Latvian sororities and fraternities are quite different from those in the United States. Joining one of these organizations is a lifelong experience and bond. Even after graduating and beginning my career, I attended sorority meetings, as did my other sorority sisters. I joined a Latvian choir, and, later, spent years as a member of the Boston Latvian Folk Dance Group. We performed in local folk festivals, but also traveled to the Latvian Song and Dance Festivals, held every five years in either Canada or the United States. My life was in the United States, and I was an American, but my Latvian heritage exerted an irresistible pull on me. Just like when I was young, facing Mr. Thomson and his chocolates, my identity was still half and half. Until that train ride in France, I did not question what it meant to be Latvian.

MASTERS OF THEIR BATTERED LAND

For an after-dinner dessert, my father often cut a slice of white bread and spread it thickly with butter and jam. He ate it with obvious delight, calling it his ķeizar kumoss (tsar's morsel). When he took a generous portion of food, he referred to this as a ķeizar porcija (tsar's portion). He did not often use the Latvian word for king. Instead, he chose "tsar," a linguistic reminder of Latvia's days under Russian rule that he probably learned from his parents.

When he was angry at my siblings or me, he didn't use curse words. Instead, he referred to us using rural insults: vepris (boar), sesks (weasel), zoss (goose), maita (a dead animal carcass; also a useless person).

Polite versions of rural expressions made their way into his work vocabulary. When things did not go well at work, he was known for saying, "Someday it's chicken, someday it's feathers." The other architects loved it. When he retired, his good-bye card was a caricature of him drawn on a large foam core board, his saying written at the top, with all the employees' well wishes written in the spaces around the picture.

If you listened, you could hear echoes of Latvia's history in his language.

Chapter 2

As the Master Commands

1000 BCE–1900

I am a descendant of peasants and serfs. People of the earth, whose sole reason for being was the land. People of the earth, who served the barons who owned it. People of the earth, whose broken hands tilled it, harvested its crops. People of the earth who survived.

At Latvian funerals, once the coffin is lowered in the ground, mourners take a handful of Latvian sand and scatter it in the grave, saying, "*Vieglas smiltis*" (may the sands rest lightly). Even in the United States, after decades of life outside of their homeland, the dead cannot find eternal peace until they are reunited with Latvian soil. The land is part of the people.

Prior to 1918, the year my father, Arvīds, was born, there was no country known as Latvia on the maps of Europe. Indigenous peoples identified as early Balts migrated to the Baltic coastal region around 1000 BCE. Over centuries, these settlers evolved into five linguistically and culturally distinct tribes: the Livs, Lettgalians, Semigallians, Couronians, and Selians, the tribal names eventually morphing into the names of Latvia's regions. For modern-day Latvians, this history forms the basis of an indisputable claim to their land. They have lived here for millennia. The forests, swamps, fields, rivers, and long white-sand coastline are part of the people, a deep and ancient spiritual connection. The love my father and his friends felt for their homeland was evident as they sang songs and spoke about their childhood villages or farms. In spite of centuries of colonization, Latvia has always belonged to the Latvians. Or perhaps more accurately, the Latvians have always belonged to Latvia. They gain their strength from the land, as the lyrics in the song *Hold Onto the Precious Fatherland* promise:

> Strong roots here keep you secure,
> Like a reed you will be in a foreign land,
> That even a little breeze may harm,
> Hold onto the precious fatherland![1]

For centuries, Latvians took their names from nature. These surnames, often a plant, animal, or natural feature, are still prevalent. My mother's surname, Bērziņš, is a diminutive of "birch," and remains one of the most common in Latvia. Her mother's surname, Sīpols, means "onion," while her stepmother's, Vārna, means "crow." My friend Nora and I used to joke that if we wanted to commit a crime in the Latvian community, we would use an alias with a last name like Ozols (oak), Lapiņš (leaf), or Kalniņš (hill). It would be like searching for a Smith or Brown in New England.

Myth and legend course through Latvian veins. Early Latvians worshipped a pantheon of nature gods and spirits, their polytheistic beliefs inseparable from the land and natural phenomena experienced in daily life. Deities like *Pērkons* (Thunder), *Laima* (Fate/Fortune), *Auseklis* (Morning Star), and *Saule* (Sun) remained important for centuries, appearing in folk songs, literature, and art. *Laima* (also called *Laime*), in particular, is invoked in speech and song. *Mūsu zeme* (Our Land), the patriotic song known by all Latvians of my parents' generation and their children, contains the line, "*Laime par mums lemi, Sargā mūsu zemi!*" (Fortune, rule over us, Protect our land!). The belief that fate and fortune ruled the lives of humans, sometimes cruelly and capriciously, shaped the emotional resignation shared by many Latvians of the World War II generation. My father and his friends often expressed their belief that hardships had to be accepted and endured. Ordinary people, such as themselves, could do little to change events.

Even after the Teutonic knights invaded and forcibly converted Latvians to Christianity in the early thirteenth century, aspects of ancient beliefs lived on. Some holidays, like Summer Solstice (*Jāņi*) and Martins' Day (*Mārtiņu diena*) are still celebrated with vestiges of pagan ritual. Summer Solstice, the longest day of the year, is a time to cleanse yourself using the purifying powers of fire and water. Latvians build large bonfires at dusk, and stay awake, maintaining the fire, until dawn. During the night, the gates to the underworld are open, so staying awake is important. Men and women weave wreaths of leaves and flowers respectively for protection against spirits. My family attended Summer Solstice celebrations every year, held in fields where Latvians would gather, build a large bonfire, sing solstice songs, eat, and make merry until dawn. Martins' Day (November 10) marks the beginning of winter, the time that the earth rests and cannot be disturbed or there will be a poor harvest the following year. Long ago, farmers killed roosters and hens, pouring their blood over the farm animals' feed for protection against disease, after which they ate the slaughtered fowl. Today, the bloodletting is skipped, but the holiday is marked by dressing up in costumes, village fairs, and eating roast chicken. There are a number of harvest-related superstitions repeated on Martins' Day, such as frost on the trees that day portends a good fruit harvest the following year.

Late in the fifteenth century, serfdom emerged in the Baltic area. Multiple invasions periodically changed the ruling powers among Germans, Russians, Swedes, and Polish-Lithuanians, but, like the northern star of misfortune, one aspect remained constant: indigenous Baltic peoples were invariably on the bottom of the hierarchy. Nobles owned the land, and therefore controlled economic power.[2] The feudal system tied the peasantry to the land, so cultural and linguistic differences between the tribes eventually blended. By the first part of the eighteenth century, 78–98% of Latvians were serfs, depending on the area.[3] Life did not change significantly even after serfdom was abolished by Tsar Alexander II's imperial emancipation of 1861. Nobles still controlled the land that they leased or sold to peasants. Peasants either gave up a portion of their harvest as rent or bought land with high-interest loans they struggled to pay off. Landowning nobles maintained the right to hunt, fish, or cut down forests on the land leased to the peasantry, preventing peasants from earning additional income.[4] Unable to own or rent land, many peasants migrated to urban areas, where their success depended on assimilation to German or Russian culture.

Both my paternal grandparents, Pēteris and Kristīne, and maternal grandfather, Jānis, were the children of non-landowning farmers. Although our family tree contains few details and has only been traced back to the mid-nineteenth century, the Spīgulis and Bērziņš families have been closely tied to the land in Livonia for generations. For them, weather, harvests, and rent payments were the real rulers of their lives, not the decrees of the Tsar.

Despite the difficulty of working the land and the need for children to help out, Latvian farmers valued education. My grandparents learned to read and write at the small parish primary schools they attended. They would, in turn, educate their children. There was little free time to play; essential farm chores were completed after school and on weekends, and children were expected to do their share of the work. If necessary, they missed school to help with harvests.

Centuries of foreign domination and serfdom left their mark. Regardless of which country ruled, Latvians survived by keeping their heads down and working. Accepting a turn of fate meant survival. To my father, hard work earned rewards. Negotiating for a raise or promotion was unheard of. As he said, "I don't care if you're a ditch digger, just be the best ditch digger you can be." Implied in this advice was the promise of monetary reward simply on the basis of merit. Latvians did not challenge or question authority. For centuries, to have done so resulted in harsh punishment. Following the rules and obeying authority promoted survival. My friend Nora's mother explained this mentality as *kā kungs pavēl*—as the master commands. For the generation born in the late nineteenth and early twentieth centuries, this was good advice to live by.

Simplified Choices

Every four years, my family watched the Summer and Winter Olympics. My father consulted the newspaper eagerly for which events were to be televised that evening. Dinner was served early, and we rushed to finish it before heading into the living room to turn on the black and white TV set, the regal brass of the Olympic theme announcing the start of coverage. Latvia first participated in the 1924 Olympics. Although no medals were won, it was the first time athletes marched under the newly adopted red, white, red horizontal stripes of the Latvian flag. My parents proudly told us about Jānis Dāliņš, who brought home the silver medal in the 1932 Summer Olympics for the Men's 50 Kilometer Walk. If we walked at a brisk pace, my father might compliment us, saying, You are striding like Dāliņš! After the Soviet annexation in 1945, Latvian athletes participated as part of the Soviet Union team. During those years, my parents scanned the athletes' names carefully and pointed out who was really Latvian.

In 1992, after the restoration of independence, my parents and their friends excitedly awaited the Latvian team during the opening ceremony, carrying the Latvian flag for the first time in fifty-six years. The moment approached, athletes parading in alphabetical order by country: North Korea, South Korea, Kuwait, Laos...commercial break. When coverage resumed, the parade advanced to Lithuania. The Latvians were cut! Furious, my parents and Latvians all over the world wrote letters to the network protesting the decision to cut their team at such a politically significant moment. During the next Olympics, Latvian athletes were shown, anchorman Bob Costas mentioning that CBS received thousands of protest letters from Latvians. To network executives, cutting a small team like Latvia's seemed insignificant. They did not understand the power of freedom.

CHAPTER 3

MASTERS OF THEIR LAND

1905–1922

November 18th was a holiday for my family. Not a celebratory holiday, like Christmas or July 4th, but a somber one. November 18th was sacrosanct: Latvian Independence Day. Every year, we dressed up and drove into Boston for the annual commemorative ceremony, often held at the Boys' Latin School. The auditorium was packed full with Latvians from the entire New England area. We stood and sang the Latvian national anthem, after which speeches about independence, resistance, and the injustice of the Soviet annexation continued long into the night. We also attended the June 14th commemorative ceremonies of the first wave of mass deportations, known as *Izsūtīšanas diena* (Deportation Day). This occasion was even more solemn than November 18th. As we got older, Nora and I negotiated a seat on the balcony, away from our parents, with promises of good behavior. Free to entertain ourselves, we spent our time wandering the halls of the school, unsanctioned and unsupervised, or reading the racy scenes from bestsellers like *Rosemary's Baby*. Given my wandering adolescent attention, I did not realize how long it actually took Latvia to win independence. The declaration was only the beginning of the fight. From an American perspective, it was as if July 4th kicked off the

American Revolution. Since Latvia was part of the Soviet Union, it was up to diaspora Latvians to remember the importance of the date and the long fight that followed.

Land, fate, hard work. Even more than this trifecta, my parents' lives were shaped by Latvian independence. After centuries of working the land and serving imperial masters, ethnic Latvians formed the majority of the population, yet they lacked economic power, political representation, and cultural dominance. There was no constitution, and Latvian was not recognized as an official language. Given the right conditions, it was inevitable that they—former serfs—would fight to win self-determination in the country their ancestors had worked for millennia. My parents' generation was the first to be born in an autonomous Latvia, the first to celebrate November 18th every year. For them, freedom became an inalienable right. And they would do almost anything to defend that right.

At the turn of the twentieth century, Latvia was a Russian territory, ruled by the Tsar. Baltic German nobles owned the majority of land. In 1905, as the Russian Empire exploded with political violence, it spread to Latvia, where peasants burned estates of privileged baronial landowners to protest their landlessness. Workers held strikes and demonstrations that paralyzed cities in an effort to better working conditions. In response, Tsar Nicholas II declared martial law and ordered Imperial Army units to arrest, exile, or execute revolutionaries. Anyone perceived as promoting revolutionary ideas was deemed an enemy of the state. It was not necessary to hold Marxist views; the very act of working for reform was a threat. German landowners participated in punitive sorties, beating and killing peasants as revenge for the earlier violence they endured. Approximately 3,000 revolutionary activists were killed, 7,000 were imprisoned or exiled, and 4,000 fled to North America, among them Kārlis Ulmanis, one of the future founders of the republic.[1] Many of the political refugees were Marxists, working towards their vision of an egalitarian society without class distinctions.

My parents instilled the belief that Communism was anathema to Latvians, so this surprised me. As I dug deeper, I learned that many Latvians at this time, including landless farmers, supported the Marxist vision of complete equality, socially and economically, and wanted a Communist government. I asked my mother about it. When my parents first settled in the Boston area and sought other Latvians, they met some former revolutionaries. There was a deep rift between these Marxists and the new group of post-World War II immigrants, who had seen a considerably less utopian side of Communism. As my mother said, "They could not understand why we were against the Communists. They asked us, 'Why did you leave? You finally got what we fought so hard to accomplish.' After that we had nothing to do with them."

Still, even after the Tsarist repressions, Latvians had trouble shedding the *as the master commands* mentality. On August 1, 1914, Germany declared war on Russia. Latvians sided wholeheartedly with Russians, viewing the war as a chance to settle scores with their longtime German oppressors. In spite of the fact the Latvians had more in common with the Germans than the Russians—culture, religion, centuries of coexistence—the war gave them a chance to vent their hatred of their old land-owning masters. Young men responded to the Tsar's call and volunteered. A total of 120,000–140,000 Latvian men mobilized and fought in East Prussia. There was a naive misconception that the Tsar would show appreciation for Latvia's wartime support by granting the country some form of self-determination.[2] In truth, Nicholas II had no intention of giving up Russian hegemony.

My paternal grandfather Pēteris did not volunteer for military service. During this time, he married Kristīne Ārgalis, who gave birth to their first child, Alīne, in 1914. They remained on a small farm in

Livonia, working the land as the war raged on. For farmers, remaining on their farms was also an act of patriotism, saving Latvian soil for Latvians.

Germany proved a fierce adversary, occupying Courland and a portion of Semigallia, effectively splitting the country in two. In a foreshadowing of their World War II invasion, German occupiers installed a repressive military regime, declared German the official language, and unleashed a police force with unchecked powers. The goal was, as always, to seize the land. The Germans viewed Latvians, along with Jews, Poles, Lithuanians, and Estonians, as inferior people to be moved out of desirable areas. The displaced Latvians would simply be deported to Russia or Germanized.[3]

After the Bolshevik revolution and the Tsar's abdication (March 1917), Lenin, too, disregarded the Latvians' desire for self-determination. He claimed that as a former province of imperial Russia, Latvia belonged to the inceptive Soviet state. By 1918, the Russian Civil War had begun. In order to concentrate on stabilizing the domestic situation, Bolshevik Russia renounced all previous claims to the Baltics, Finland, Belarus, Ukraine, and Poland by signing the Treaty of Brest–Litovsk on March 3, 1918.

As war tore apart continental Europe and Latvian nationalists struggled to end German and Russian claims to their country, Kristīne and Pēteris Spīgulis welcomed their second child, my father Arvīds, on September 20, 1918. The political state of the world had little impact on their daily lives; they rented their land, and rent was due whether or not blood flowed through the fields. Eventually, the war invaded even this area of Latvia; by the end of 1918, German and Soviet military engagements raged across most of the Latvian territory, destroying the land, industry, and creating food shortages and economic hardship.[4]

The Latvian war for independence began when World War I concluded with the General Armistice of November 11, 1918. Latvians, along with neighboring Lithuanians and Estonians, had another two years of war remaining before they could lay down their arms. Terms required German military withdrawal from territories that formed part of the Russian Empire prior to August 1, 1914. With the ink barely dry on the Armistice signatory page, Latvian representatives met secretly in Riga on November 17, 1918. Forty delegates from eight political parties formed the Latvian People's Council (*Tautas Padome*), the antecedent to a national parliament.

On November 18, 1918, as Kristīne milked the cows, churned butter, and rocked her infant son, Latvia officially proclaimed its independence and formed a provisional government. The delegates adopted *Dievs svētī Latviju* (God Bless Latvia) as the official national anthem and sang it for the first time as such:

> God bless Latvia
> Our precious Fatherland,
> Bless Latvia
> Oh, bless it!
> Where Latvian daughters bloom,
> Where Latvian sons sing,
> Let us dance in good fortune there,
> In our Latvia![5]

Germany had not abandoned its plans to colonize Latvia; armed forces still occupied Riga and parts of Latvia in violation of Armistice terms. Lenin and the Bolsheviks still regarded Latvia as territory rightfully belonging to the developing Soviet socialist state. Latvia was of strategic and economic importance to both Germany and Soviet Russia, so it was inevitable that those powers would not give up the prize easily.[6]

In 1919, Latvia became a battleground between the Soviets and Germans as both countries fought to regain lost territory. The Bolsheviks invaded after the revocation of the Treaty of Brest–Litovsk, citing this as a restoration of their pre-treaty rights.[7] They quickly controlled the northern and eastern parts of Latvia, set up a provisional

Soviet government, and began eliminating opposition through arrests and executions. The Germans sent in two Freikorps divisions to oust the Russian Bolsheviks. The British turned a blind eye to the Freikorps presence in the Baltic region; Freikorps units were made up of volunteers, many of them ex-soldiers, who were not officially part of the German Army that was dramatically reduced per terms of the Armistice. Simply put, the British needed help fighting the Bolsheviks. Freikorps recruits were promised ninety acres of Baltic lands for a minimum of four weeks of service. The Latvian provisional government never consented to these terms; however, having little military strength, the Latvians accepted German assistance to eliminate the Bolshevik threat.[8] The Freikorps joined forces with what was left of White Russian forces, and, within a few months, controlled most of the Baltic coastline.

Once the Red Army was pushed back from this area, the Germans set up a puppet government in Riga. During the blood fest following their victory, the Freikorps massacred three thousand citizens in Riga, plus more in other cities. After this, the British provided materiel support to Latvian troops and threatened to reinstate the naval blockade of Germany unless the Freikorps and combined White Russian forces withdrew from the Baltic region. Bolstered by British supplies and naval bombardments, the Latvians and their allies beat back the German forces.[9]

The victory was costly. As the Freikorps retreated, they burned villages, destroyed farmland, and killed civilians. During this time, my maternal grandfather, Jānis Bērziņš, fled from his village in central Latvia to the southernmost portion of the country, along with his wife and their first child, Aunt Elvīra, hiding in forests and abandoned buildings. Prior to leaving, they hid family photographs to save them from harm, an act of desperation that Jānis later referred to as "stupidity." Upon return, the photographs were gone, so no early record of the family exists. Decades later, Jānis wrote to Elvīra, "Those two wars affected me quite painfully. The hardest was during World

War I when the Germans drove us to the Kurzeme area...You were only two. I have never told you how things went then."[10] The remaining Bolsheviks, primarily in Lettgalia, were driven out by partisan units by January 1920.

Latvia's war for independence concluded on January 30, 1920 with a Latvian–Soviet Russia armistice. After the ensuing August 11, 1920 peace treaty, Soviet Russia officially renounced all former territorial claims and recognized Latvian sovereignty, removing one of the major obstacles to international recognition.[11] It was a tough struggle; Britain, France, and the United States refused to entertain the question of Latvia's independence as long as there was a chance that Russia would return to an imperial ruling system under which Latvia would remain a Russian province.

As my father took his first steps on the farm, his nascent nation took its first steps to protect itself from future threats. Latvia applied for membership to the League of Nations. It was denied. European powers and the United States maintained that they could not fulfill League of Nations guarantees in countries that formerly belonged to, and shared borders, with Russia while the Russian Civil War continued. One year after its initial application, Latvia was granted *de jure* recognition as a sovereign state by Great Britain, Belgium, France, Japan, and Italy, followed by retroactive recognition by several other countries. Latvia joined the League of Nations in September 1921. The United States recognized Latvia's sovereignty in 1922.[12]

At last, foreign powers were out. Latvia had no functioning government, no state currency, and no markets for its goods. The population had decreased by 32% from pre-war levels, mostly from deaths. A quarter of its farms had been destroyed by battles, and an estimated 29% of farmland lay fallow, scarred by abandoned trenches. Severe food shortages were widespread.[13] Railways, bridges, and highways were destroyed. Pre-war industry was decimated by the forced removal of over five hundred industrial companies, including equipment, from Latvia to Russia. My grandparents and others like them began the slow, painful process of rebuilding their lives.

Only Belgium sustained more physical damage. Only Serbia lost a greater percentage of its population.[14] Two years after the declaration of independence, Latvians were masters of their battered land. The land they had lived in for centuries was finally theirs.

SIMPLIFIED CHOICES

We had an unusual yard for Wellesley in the 1960s. Our neighbors had lawns with some shrubs, a small flower garden, and a shade tree or two. My parents kept a large vegetable garden, raspberry bushes, a peach tree, an apple tree, and a quince bush that produced hard, inedible sour fruit my mother simmered into delicious jelly, the rows of jars stashed in the coolness of our basement. My mother also planted flowers. We didn't live in a rich section of town; our yard measured just under a quarter of an acre, so on a percentage basis, the square footage allocated to produce was substantial. Gardening was a way of life to them, a means of connecting to their land.

The vegetable garden took up most of the side yard. The previous owners, the Wagstaffs, referred to this as the Victory Garden, so my parents did too. Go out to the Victory Garden, Anitiṇa, and pick a few ripe tomatoes for dinner, they would say. During World War II, American families were encouraged to plant Victory Gardens for their own produce, to ensure that our soldiers had enough food. The gardens were an important domestic part of the American war effort against Germany.

I wonder if my parents ever understood the irony in their use of the term.

Chapter 4
Kulak Son

1918–1934

The barn at Pudas, 1989. Author's collection.

In the early 20th century, farmers were identified by the name of their house as well as their community. My father's birthplace was called Bērzlejas (Birch Valley) in the civil parish of Katvari, Livonia, where my grandfather Pēteris Spīgulis and his older brother, Andrejs, rented a modest house and some land. Their landlord was a Russian general in the Tsar's Imperial Army, who owned a large estate boasting several houses, rented annually to Latvian farmers unable to purchase their own land. The Spīgulis brothers were among the almost fifty-five percent of landless peasants, struggling to meet their financial obligations. Pēteris and Andrejs both lived in the house with their respective families, but each farmed their own portion of the land. Pēteris had a small concern, with only three or four cows and enough land to plant some rye, wheat, and vegetables. He grew food for his family and sold whatever was left over at the market. Selling surplus was the only way for a farmer to earn money, so there was strong incentive to continually increase yield and add livestock.

When my father was two years old, his family moved to another house near the village of Umurga, called Pudas. His maternal grandmother, Anna Eberhardt Ārgalis, worked as the housekeeper of Pudas for years. Her husband managed the farm while she took care of the house and domestic chores. My grandmother Kristīne grew up in the house so, to her, it was home. The owner of the house was an older bachelor uncle of my father's grandmother Anna. When my father was born, Uncle Eberhardt received the honor of becoming his godfather. Eberhardt had another godson as well, named Kreišmanis, who lived in Riga, where he frequently indulged his taste for strong drink. Unbeknownst to my grandparents, Eberhardt made both godsons the beneficiaries of his estate, deeding half of Pudas to each upon his death. By 1920, Kristīne's father passed away, leaving her mother alone to take care of Pudas. The land and animals proved too much for her, so she broached the subject with Uncle Eberhardt, who agreed that Pēteris should take over managing the farm and livestock. The arrangement was an informal one, with Eberhardt telling Pēteris, "You will be the manager. I will oversee it. You take over the place and raise new livestock. Later, you will get to keep the livestock and land." This casual gentleman's agreement left Pēteris feeling uncomfortable. He had no way of knowing whether anything written ensured this agreement would continue after Eberhardt's death. Would he, in fact, have anything to show for his labors some day?

Spīgulis family circa 1922. Left to right: Pēteris, Alīne, my father, Kristīne. Author's collection.

Their luck changed when my father was seven years old. Eberhardt died in the late winter, and was laid out in the barn in his best suit, snow covering the ground. Kreišmanis and several of his relatives from

Riga made the trip to Pudas for the funeral and, more importantly, the reading of the will. After that, there was no room for argument. Seven-year-old Arvīds officially owned half of Pudas. Eberhardt, a surveyor by trade, meticulously split the three hundred sixty acre property. The house was divided in half, as was the barn, with the property line running down the middle of the buildings. My father inherited the southern side, by the road, while Kreišmanis had the eastern, wooded side. The woods and a swamp were divided equally, as were the fields. My father also had a birch grove he loved. Fortunately for my father and his family, Kreišmanis did not want the property, only money to subsidize his love of drink. Pēteris purchased the majority of the land for one thousand *lati* (Latvian currency unit) right after the funeral. They worked out an annual payment schedule for the balance. Kreišmanis made a yearly pilgrimage out to Pudas every summer to collect his share of the payment. While he was visiting, he liked to talk with my young father, who once remarked, "You must really love to drink!"

"Yes, that is true," replied Kreišmanis.

"How much alcohol have you drunk in your life?" asked my father.

"When I was a younger man, I was an inspector for bars. I traveled around Latvia for inspections, and everyone gave me free drinks." Kreišmanis paused and gestured around the room where they sat. "If you put all of those drinks together, this big room and then some would be full of alcohol."

Over the next five years, Kreišmanis would spend all of the money from the Pudas sale on his beloved mistress, alcohol. When he finally died, Pēteris brought my father and the final payment on Pudas to Riga to pay their respects and close out the debt. The payment was just enough to buy a coffin and bury Kreišmanis. This was the first time my father saw Latvia's capital city, Riga. When they returned from burying Kreišmanis, his father Pēteris was now half owner of Pudas. My father owned the other half.

Pēteris was an industrious man who knew how to run a farm. Over time, he purchased additional cows, pigs, and sheep with the money he earned selling the previous years' goods. Eventually the herd numbered over twenty cows, lots of pigs, and several sheep. He also grew rye, wheat, vegetables, and apples. Pēteris hired two men to work for him in the fields, and one or two girls to help Kristīne with the cows. In 1927, another daughter, Valija, was born, completing the Spīgulis family. As the farm thrived, they added a day servant to help with housekeeping chores. Kristīne milked cows and made butter and cheese, for personal consumption as well as selling. For additional income, Pēteris and Kristīne rented out part of the farm. Renters could pay with cash or a percentage of their yield. Paying by percentage was easier; there was no worry that the renter would be short of money, but, as my father noted, "They didn't like it when harvest time came."

My father's farm duties began when he was eight years old. He and Alīne herded cows and sheep in pastures that were fairly far from the house. Beginning in May, when the grass began to grow, the cows and sheep were brought to the field. Herding was tedious work, and the Spīgulis herd was large. My father and Alīne, lacking no imagination, found ways to entertain themselves. There was a frisky, friendly lamb who liked to play with them. One time, they took Alīne's kerchief and tied it to the lamb so that it flapped. The lamb gamboled through the herd of sheep, scattering them as they ran from the flapping cloth. After the initial laughs, my father and Alīne ran frantically to catch him so they could round up the fleeing sheep.

Pudas had plentiful currant bushes that Pēteris used to make wine. He mashed the berries and left them until the seeds separated from the juice. After straining the juice, he added sugar and poured the mixture into a glass bottle for fermentation. After fermentation, the liquid was siphoned off and poured into a clean bottle, ready for consumption. The wine was strong, more like berry liqueur than wine. During harvest time, when Pēteris hired several men for additional labor, he would put a couple of bottles on the table at lunchtime for the workers. One time, a renter's son came over to visit with my father.

Simplified Choices

They found a small horseshoe nail; the wide, flat shape was perfect for poking into a cork. Down in the cellar, my father carefully poked a small hole into the side of the cork, enabling the boys to slowly suck some of the wine out of the bottle. It tasted good. Very good. Over the next few weeks, surreptitiously making trips to the cellar, they drained the bottle. Pēteris eventually caught them when he went to the cellar to bring up the bottle for company. It was empty!

In rural Livonia, school schedules followed an agrarian calendar, with students attending September to early May. Pēteris and Kristīne were literate, and expected their children to complete their education through high school. Pēteris urged his son to study diligently: "Study hard and learn what you want to learn. Don't stay in the country. The life of a farmer is the life of a slave. You work from sunrise to sunset with no rest or relief." My father loved to build towers using stones and sticks, and draw plans for buildings. Watching him, Pēteris would proudly say, "Son, you will be a big builder or engineer someday."

The local elementary school was approximately nine kilometers from Pudas. My father boarded at the school Monday through Friday, sleeping in a boys' dormitory room that provided a cot and small locker for students. During nice weather, he rode a bicycle to school, his rucksack packed with books, a loaf of rye bread and some butter to eat for breakfast, enough to last the week. The school provided one hot meal daily. During winters, his father hitched a horse to a cart and drove him to school on Monday mornings. He walked home on Friday afternoons. Not everyone completed their education. As he recalled, his class was small, with only six or seven students: "There were more students in the beginning, but this is how it was in the country. Struggling students stayed back, then usually dropped out by third grade. They were lucky if they could sign their names by the time they left school. They could not read well either."

He attended the regional high school in the Limbažu civil parish. High school attendance was rare at that time, reserved for the sons and daughters of well-to-do farmers. The school was about fourteen kilometers from Pudas, so my father needed a place to live. Dormitories were not provided as the high school could not accommodate all of the students' needs. Elderly German ladies, or *freilenes* as the students called them, took in high school boarders. Payment was mostly in kind; farmers brought in products needed to feed the students for the year, like potatoes or meat. Pēteris supplied birch logs, all split and ready to use as fuel. My father went home on weekends, weather permitting. As he explained, "I rode my bike. It was pretty far away, and no one wanted to drive that far by horse cart."

My father and his sister, Valija, circa 1932. Author's collection.

In spite of Pēteris' words about leaving the country, my father was heading for a farmer's life until an accident changed his plans. It was a beautiful sunny afternoon, 1933. One weekend, he came home to help his parents get some autumn chores completed, but it was getting to be late in the afternoon, and the sun would soon set. He glanced out toward the apple trees. The winter apples were ripe, ready to be harvested. Winter apples were hard as granite just after picking, so his father buried them in rye grain bins to protect them from freezing, where they remained until Christmas. Over time, they ripened further and became soft and delicious—a real treat over the holidays when fresh fruit was scarce. My father took a large basket and climbed up the tree, hand over hand. He nestled the basket on a nearby branch, balanced himself, and reached for the apples. As he tugged and twisted the fruit to release it, the branch he was standing on suddenly broke. He grabbed another nearby branch, but that snapped off in his hand and he fell to the ground below, still holding the broken branch. Rolling to his side, he tried to stand but became dizzy. He could feel the bones in his left thigh shifting, and pain—sharp pain.

Pēteris came running. He harnessed the horse to his best cart and lifted my father into it. Stabbing pains shot through his leg as the cart bumped over the rutted road. It did not occur to anyone to splint the leg to keep it still. At the local hospital in Limbaži, an X-ray revealed a broken femur. The family doctor met them at the hospital, and prevailed upon Pēteris to hire a car to take my father to the Red Cross hospital in Riga.

"Take him to Riga! They will put the leg back together better than we can. Here, we can fix it, but one leg will be shorter than the other."

That was all Pēteris had to hear. He hired the local veterinarian, who had a big car, to drive my father to Riga. A respected orthopedist wired the femur and put his leg in traction with weights; my father's strapping thigh muscles, well-developed from bicycling, would pull the wiring apart unless it was weighted. The leg was healing satisfactorily until the orthopedist caught pneumonia and another doctor took over. Her name was Sapraša (meaning understanding) but the patients referred to her as *"Nepraša"* (no understanding). She was an internist, who, while accomplished in her specialty, lacked expertise in orthopedics. She left his leg alone to heal. Over time, the wire slipped and the bone mended crookedly so that the ends barely touched, forming a frail bridge between the two parts of the femur. Ten months later, he left the hospital, one leg slightly shorter than the other. Over the years, my father developed a sense of humor about his limp, saying, "See, the doctor makes an error and you have to live with it the rest of your life. I had a professor who said, 'Architects and engineers, your mistakes will bury you but a doctor buries his mistakes.'"

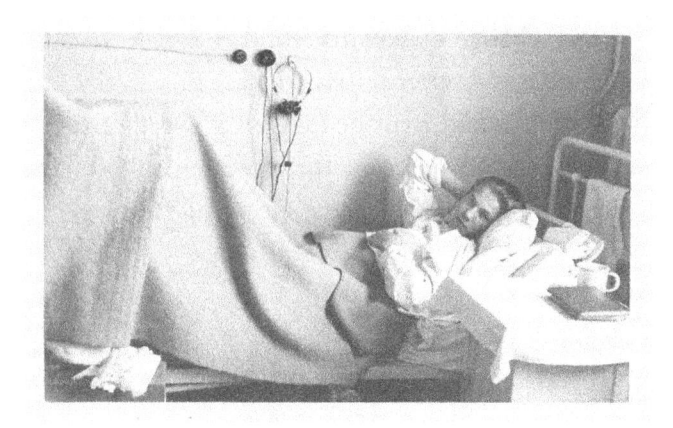

My father at Riga hospital with his leg in traction. Author's collection.

While his leg healed, my father missed an entire year of school. The following year, he advanced to the next class and figured out what he missed. With some self-professed cheating, he got through most of his classes, except languages. He learned German and Latin in earlier years, but his class was learning English or Russian. He struggled through the next two years, only earning a C equivalent in languages. As he said, "I learned a few words in English, but not enough to be of any use later."

His leg troubles weren't over either. That winter, as he skied down a small hill, his ski caught on a buried stick, causing him to fall and break his leg again in the same place. This time, the renowned orthopedist from Riga came out to the local hospital and performed the operation. He grafted a bone to the femur, and it healed, three quarters of an inch shorter than the other leg. My father would limp the rest of his life. The limp, in part, led to his decision to pursue an alternate career to farming. His best subjects in school were drawing and math. When he was bored during study time, he often sketched buildings he had seen on his occasional trips to Riga, so architecture was a natural fit.

At the time, my father didn't know that these unfortunate accidents would change the course of his career and life. Latvia prospered and offered opportunities to sons of wealthy farmers, like him. Likewise, Pēteris and Kristīne did not know that they would be labeled *kulaks* by the Soviets, and therefore "enemies of the state," a steep price for owning and managing a successful farm.

Simplified Choices

Near the end of the school year, my kindergarten class visited the first grade classroom for orientation. The teacher, Mrs. McKenna, had us sit down at desks, our little legs dangling just above the floor, and showed us how to properly grip a pencil. Next, she guided us through the process of drawing a line, two ovals, and three connected lines on a piece of lined paper. She had us draw black dots in the center of the ovals and top them with eyelashes. You wrote the word "look," she said.

It was like someone handed me the keys to a magical kingdom, the most exciting moment in my young life. I could read and write! I consumed books faster than Halloween candy, moving through reading levels quickly. I had always loved stories. My mother read Latvian stories to me every night, both of us sitting side by side on my bed, her arm around my shoulders as I turned the pages. It was our ritual. I couldn't go to sleep without her soft voice reading about animals who talked, or magical creatures like elves living in the woods of Latvia. But once I began to read, I wanted to hear stories in English from the library books I brought home. In second grade, my mother began to ask me to read to her. I love to hear you read, she said. You're getting so good!

It wasn't until my graduate courses in literacy and language development that I realized what had happened. My literacy development outpaced that of my mother's. As I brought home more advanced books, she no longer felt confident reading them to me. Yet, she prized the quiet time in the evening stillness, shared with her youngest child. Mother and child, together, before nightfall separated us.

Chapter 5

Orphan Girl

When my mother died in 2014, my brother, sister and I planned her memorial. Our grieving father could not actively participate. Karl, the most musical of the three of us, was in charge of selecting hymns for the service. He put a great deal of thought into this assignment, and chose a beautiful hymn about love of home and the sacred nature of a mother's love:

> My birthplace, my birthplace,
> Where I, nursed by my mother,
> Took life's first steps.
> I did not know the cares of life,
> You will forever be remembered![1]

We all agreed the hymn was appropriate, given how strongly our mother identified as an orphan driven from her birthplace. Being alone and homeless was part of her self-definition.

My mother, Skaidrīte Bērziņš, was born during a raging blizzard, sometime between December 7 and 12, 1921. The blizzard lasted a few days, isolating her family on their small farm in Nītaure, Livonia. Once the storm stopped, her father, Jānis, waded through the snow drifted dirt road to register her birth in town. Asked to put down a date, he was confused as to when exactly she had arrived. At the church, he wrote December 7, while at the town hall, he entered December 11 as her birth date. Eventually, when my mother was sixteen years old, she applied for her mandatory passport. She chose December 7, and so it became official. The third child of Zelma and Jānis Bērziņš, she joined two older sisters, Elvīra and Velta.

Born in 1890, my grandfather Jānis grew up on a small farm called Laģi. Like most Latvian farmers, his parents rented the land. His mother, Anna, was small, hard-working, and stern, plagued by perpetual leg pain. His father was an elder in the local church. In the Bērziņš family, hard work was a foundational family value; giving up was simply not an option. Years later, Jānis wrote to my mother, "Come what may, my parents taught me to work properly. I inherited perseverance from my mother."[2] Jānis and his five siblings attended school, but the entire family worked long hours to raise enough food for the family, earn some money, plus meet rental obligations. Through his letters, he emerged as a bitter man, angry about the years of working for others with nothing to show for it but survival. He encouraged his children to study diligently in order to better their financial situation.

Jānis had the good fortune to marry Zelma Sīpols, an attractive young woman from a family of means. Her father, Jānis Sīpols, was a successful land-owning farmer. Sīpols obtained a small farm called Kubļi as payment on a bad debt; a fellow named Andermanis had purchased the property, but, unable to repay his loan from Sīpols, forfeited the farm. A fair distance from the road, Kubļi was secluded, surrounded by fields and woods. Upon Zelma's marriage, Sīpols gifted the farm to her and her sister, Milda, where they both lived with their families. Milda Sīpols had two daughters out of wedlock, refusing to marry their father because of his vicious temper. When aroused, he would beat Milda and the two girls. My mother was terrified of the man, and hid whenever he came around.

Zelma Sīpols Bērziņš. Author's collection.

My mother's maternal grandmother, known simply as "Žigurmāte," [literally "mother from Žiguri," the name of her farm] loved to spoil the children. A loving, robust woman, she would encourage my mother to eat, saying, "Eat, my little girl! You will become plump and beautiful!" Žigurmāte took valerian drops dribbled on a sugar cube to calm her nerves. Crushed and mixed with alcohol, and possibly other substances, the valerian roots formed an addictive concoction. As her addiction progressed, my mother recalled hearing her grandmother cry out for more drops.

Jānis Bērziņš had a quick temper and was not the easiest man to get along with. My mother's earliest memory is one of his anger and her mother's protection against it. When she was barely two years old, she was inside the house with Zelma. Jānis had been braiding strands of flax to use as shoelaces, and laid them aside to go take care of the animals. My mother toddled over to the braided flax strips and played with them. When Jānis came in and spotted his young daughter messing up his work, he raised his hand to slap her. Zelma rushed over and scooped her up, saying, "You will not hit my child! If you must hit someone, hit me instead!"

Jānis lowered his hand and backed off.

Jānis Bērziņš. Author's collection.

My mother's younger brother, Arnolds, was born on September 9, 1923. The following year, just before Christmas, Zelma was holding Arnolds when she dropped a fork. As she bent down to pick it up, she cried in pain and clutched her abdomen. Zelma was stricken with a twisted intestine, a potentially fatal condition in which the intestine wraps around itself, cutting off its blood supply. Upon examining her, the local doctor recognized the condition, and instructed Jānis to bring her to the hospital in Cēsis, almost thirty kilometers away, for surgery. That year, there was little snow. Jānis hitched up the horse and wagon. When he lifted Zelma into the wagon, she cried out in pain, so Jānis quickly switched the horse over to a sleigh for a smoother ride over the frozen rutted dirt roads. Arriving at the hospital, they learned that the main surgeon was in Riga for the holidays. The available doctors performed emergency surgery, but discovered that gangrene had already set in. Zelma died that night. Such was life in the country, where doctors were few and far between, and medicines non-existent. Prior to her burial, Zelma lay in state in the barn at Kubļi. Seeing her mother lying down peacefully, my mother held her hand and talked to her, confused by her mother's silence. She asked her father, "Why is Mamma so proud? Is she angry with me? She won't even speak to me!"

After Zelma's death, life changed for my mother and her siblings. On account of the four children, the farm stayed with the Bērziņš. Zelma had bequeathed her share of the farm to her only male child, Arnolds. This stung Jānis' pride. Ashamed that he was not the proprietor of his own farm, he referred to Kubļi as the "orphans' share." Left on his own to manage the farm chores, Jānis hired housemaids to bake, clean, and provide childcare. The maids were more interested in flirting with Jānis than they were in taking care of his children. My mother, her sisters and brother were unwashed, unkempt, and had fleas. Realizing that the situation was untenable, Jānis married the industrious Olga Varna within a year. For Jānis, it was a marriage of necessity, not love. He and Zelma shared a connection. In spite of his harshness and quick temper, they loved and understood each other. If they disagreed, they could talk things over, something that was lacking in his new marriage.

Olga treated Zelma's children kindly. Being young, my mother bonded with her stepmother and called her Mamma, as did Arnolds and Velta. Elvīra, however, grieved her mother and refused to accept

Olga. To Elvīra, her father's rapid remarriage was nothing short of a betrayal. Determined to keep Zelma's memory alive, she harshly reprimanded my mother, saying, "Olga is not your mother. You must not call her Mamma! Our mother is dead and we are orphans!" Elvīra called her stepmother Olga and remained aloof for the years that she lived at Kubļi. Eventually, Jānis and Olga had two daughters and three sons together. My mother, Velta, and Arnolds loved their half-sisters and brothers, feeling as though it was one family. Even Elvīra accepted the children born of this second union. Unfortunately, the marriage was not a happy one, a fact that was not lost on my mother. She once asked Olga, "Why did you marry my father?" Olga replied, "I felt sorry for you children. You needed a mother."

The Bērziņš farm was modest: only a few acres of land, plus some cows, sheep, pigs, and chickens, so money was scarce. Despite endless hours of work, it was a hard-scrabble existence. They grew wheat, barley, and flax for their own consumption, but cows were their livelihood. The grain was harvested and prepared on the premises; stalks were brought into the granary where they were flailed to separate the grains from the chaff. The grains were collected and brought to a nearby mill to be ground into flour. Clothing and farm tools were also stored in the granary, as the house was small. Adding to the discomfort, the sounds of occasional beatings of their Aunt Milda and cousins were clearly heard through the walls.

With Elvīra constantly reminding her of Zelma, my mother identified as an orphan. This sense of losing her mother extended to other areas of her life. When feeling lonely or sad, she would climb to the top of a nearby hill and spend hours singing orphan songs at the top of her lungs. She had a beautiful, clear soprano. Although her father took little interest in the details of his children's education, he once attended a recital at her elementary school, in which she sang a solo: the rhyme, "Karl, Karl, my little brother!" by the Latvian poet, Jānis Rainis, set to music. After the recital, Jānis wiped tears from his eyes, and offered some rare praise, saying, "I never knew you sang so beautifully." My mother continued to sing and act in school plays. On her confirmation day, she performed a solo in the church.

My mother and her brother Arnolds on their confirmation day. Author's collection.

In 1942, the family suffered another loss. Some years before, Velta had been lying outside on the wet grass, enjoying the spring sunshine after a long winter. Velta, a happy, playful girl, contracted rheumatic fever and spent a year in the sanitorium. Although the doctors pronounced her as "cured," the disease left her weakened. In 1942, Velta and her sister, Aina, were sleeping in the hay loft, taking care of the cows and sheep. One chilly morning, Aina awoke and turned to poke her sister awake. Velta was cold and unresponsive. Aina screamed for help, but Velta had died during the night, at the age of twenty-four. Jānis had a particular soft spot in his heart for Velta; once, when she was young, she pretended to shear sheep by cutting the wool out of her father's winter jacket. Given Jānis' temper, it was a miracle that she escaped without punishment. For a lesser offense, Jānis had once whipped my mother across the legs with a horse whip. The death of this fun-loving young girl was deeply felt by the entire family.

Velta Bērziņš on her confirmation day. Author's collection.

My mother attended elementary school through eighth grade, after which she went to an agricultural trade school to learn the business of running a farm. Upon graduation, she became a dairy inspector, traveling about the area surrounding Vaidava, a municipality about fifty-five kilometers from her home town, testing and grading milk according to its cream content. This determined the price local farmers could charge for milk; the higher the cream content, the higher the price the milk would command. She found a boyfriend and seemed destined to have a typical rural life, until the war broke out and she would, once again, find herself feeling like an orphan girl. Alone.

Simplified Choices

My parents had shelves of Latvian books. When the small bookshelf in our living room was full, the overflow went into the basement, where several bookcases were tucked against walls. Books were crammed onto those shelves, vertically first, then horizontally in stacks on top of the other books as space permitted. When Maruta, Karl, and I began the Herculean task of cleaning out our parents' home, we carried armloads of books up to the living room, where we sorted them by category. Books on Kārlis Ulmanis could easily have formed a subcategory to Latvian history. There were three biographies of Ulmanis, all of which presented glowing tributes to the politician and his great work on Latvia's behalf. Tucked in one corner was a tiny book: Redzu jaunu dienu nākam (I see a new day coming). Compiled and printed in Riga 1992 (after restoration of independence), the book is a compilation of Ulmanis' thoughts on Latvia, taken from speeches and writings. What is different is the presentation of Ulmanis himself. Rather than the hagiographies piled on the living room floor, the introduction to this compilation finds flaws in Ulmanis. The editor notes the paucity of thoughts on military and self-defense, a known weakness of Ulmanis that is often criticized in twenty-first century Latvia.

Thumbing through the pages, it is clear why my parents revered Ulmanis. He understood them:

Latvia is for us, around us, within us! The most important is the last, understand! Latvia is within us, our hearts, our conviction, our faith.[3]

Ulmanis knew how sacred Latvian soil was for the generations of Latvians who tilled it. He felt it too.

Chapter 6

Latvia for Latvians!

1934–1939

My Latvian school class was an unruly one. We churned through teachers pretty quickly until Mrs. A. took over. Kind, gentle, and patient, she managed to keep us in line by making us want to behave for her. Until lunchtime one day. Lunches were eaten in the classroom, unsupervised, doors open so the unfortunate hallway monitor could listen for trouble while the teachers took their break. Our classroom was known as the Presidents' Room, on account of the large, imposing portraits of the Latvian republic's four presidents. On this particular day, Eric D. snatched a cream cheese and jelly sandwich from his seatmate and tossed it up behind his back. The sandwich split on the way up, with the sticky cream cheesy half adhering to Kārlis Ulmanis' portrait. Before he could retrieve it, Mrs. A. returned to the classroom. Taking one look at the sandwich slowly sliding down Ulmanis' face, she burst into tears. "How could you? My heart is breaking!" Then she walked out.

Kārlis Ulmanis. Unknown photographer. Downloaded from Chancery of the President of Latvia. Public Domain.

We were mortified. Eric D., and the rest of us accomplices, had done the unpardonable. We desecrated the memory of the man who did more to shape Latvia's history than any other single Latvian politician. Ulmanis' accomplishments were legendary in our history books: one of the founders of the Latvian state, farmers' advocate, prime minister and president of the nation several times, a patriot who elevated the economy and cultural life. We learned that Ulmanis was a political giant who helped create Latvia's representative system of government. What we didn't learn was that Ulmanis also destroyed it in a non-violent coup. Or that Ulmanis admired Mussolini and incorporated elements of Fascism in his political beliefs. This larger-than-life man was an authoritarian leader who dismantled democracy but improved quality of life for many Latvians: a benevolent dictator, if there is such a thing.

My parents and their peers were strongly influenced by Ulmanis, his vision for Latvia, and his particular brand of patriotism. Ulmanis grew up on a farm in Semigallia, and felt the deep connection to the land that my parents did. He believed that the farmer, small farms, and rural life were the essence of the Latvian spirit and heritage; improving the farmers' quality of life would, in turn, build a stronger Latvia. But how had he gotten away with ending representative government? And why did they speak so highly of him?

Ulmanis made his reputation by promoting modern Western European farming techniques that increased productivity. At the time, many Latvian dairy farms were raising cows primarily for manure; milk and dairy product production was fairly low. Ulmanis introduced new techniques to Latvian farmers through his writings and lectures. When he fled the Russian authorities during the 1905 Revolution, he used his time in exile to earn a degree in agriculture from the University of Nebraska. Based on what he learned, he authored articles and books that were published in Latvia, among them *Profitable Pig Farming (Ienesīga cūkkopība)* and *Profitable Dairy Farming (Ienesīga piensaimniecība)*.[1] For farmers like my grandfather Pēteris, increasing yield and finding new markets was the way to build wealth. Ulmanis was their champion.

Upon returning to Latvia in 1913, Ulmanis' fame grew as he continued to promote improved agricultural practices. After World War I, he became a founding member of the Farmers' Union party and co-founder of the Democratic Block. Once Latvia declared its independence, Ulmanis was elected Prime Minister of the provisional government.

Latvia had never experienced democracy. Having had no political representation before independence, giving a voice to all groups became a cornerstone of the new republic. Candidates required only one hundred signatures to secure a place on the ballot, and there was no party membership minimum required to obtain a seat in the parliament, or *Saeima*. This opened the door to tiny splinter parties representing minority interests.[2] The first *Saeima* had twenty parties, the second (1925) twenty-seven, the third (1928) twenty-eight, and the fourth (1931) twenty-five.³ Many parties had one or two elected representatives. With only one hundred members in the *Saeima*, the number of factions necessitated the formation of coalitions to obtain a majority.

Under the skilled leadership of Latvia's first president, Jānis Čakste, the *Saeima* developed and ratified a progressive Constitution. Women were granted the right to vote, and the rights of minorities were specifically protected.⁴ While reaching consensus was difficult, the power of the minority parties in the *Saeima* also protected their rights. By law, ethnic and religious minorities were allowed to open dedicated schools, fully subsidized by the government, with the result that, by 1935, almost a quarter of public schools were dedicated to the instruction of non-ethnic Latvians.⁵ Although this was a sign of the democratic process at work, it rankled those who believed that the Latvian state should represent ethnic Latvians above all other groups.

One of the first challenges the young government faced was landlessness. In 1920, over sixty percent of the population was rural, but most agricultural workers lacked the money to purchase land. The Social Democratic party proposed the solution: seize the land belonging to German barons, many of whom had abandoned their holdings during the war, and redistribute it to landless peasants for free as payback for years of oppression. Ulmanis became deeply involved in the process of land redistribution; it did not go smoothly, as there were far more farmers desiring land than there was land available. He later headed up land reclamation efforts by draining marshes to increase the amount of available land. My paternal grandparents were spared this process, having obtained their land through Eberhardt's will. Maternal grandfather Jānis was technically ineligible as his first wife bequeathed the land to their son, so his family was not landless. For Jānis, the fact that he did not own Kubļi remained a source of resentment.

The ambitious Ulmanis had aggressive plans. In order to increase his influence, he proposed changes to the Constitution centering around significant expansion of presidential powers and a reduction of the *Saeima*. He did not obtain the required two-thirds majority, in part because his colleagues did not trust his motives. According to historians, Ulmanis had already planned the coup before the vote with the help of his allies and the military. The Fascist organization Thunder Cross also contemplated a coup, but lacked the resources to pull it off.[6]

In the wee hours of May 16, 1934, while my fifteen-year-old father slept in the hospital with his broken leg in traction, notices were posted in public places throughout Riga, announcing that a "state of emergency" existed. There was no such thing. Select army, home guard, and police units took over the radio station and secured the Foreign Ministry and *Saeima*. The *Saeima* was immediately dismissed, an illegal action. The press was censored, and all demonstrations and meetings were forbidden, unless prior approval was obtained.[7] Later that morning, Riga's radio station read the Ulmanis declaration of the new government and a defense of his coup:

> Our actions are not against Latvian democracy...The government only wants to create conditions... which unfailingly will return us to the right path and again give us a unified, strong, fortunate Latvia...Latvia, where prosperity for all will rise and our national independent culture will blossom; Latvia where [what is] Latvian will be celebrated and the foreign will disappear...where all Latvian hard-working sons will be equal— the farmer and city dweller, the worker and the official; where there will not be a gap between the people and its native intelligence, the farmer and the worker's son.[8]

The announcement concluded with the Latvian national anthem. Approximately two thousand political opponents were arrested, but there were no deportations or executions. Most terms of incarceration served were one year or less, though surveillance of political opponents continued for years. Ulmanis assumed the role of Prime Minister; there were no elected representatives, only his hand-picked Cabinet who took over all government functions.

Surprisingly, there were no public challenges to Ulmanis. There had been no bloodshed or threats against citizens, yet there were no demonstrations or protests. The president at the time, Alberts Kviesis, did not challenge Ulmanis or defend the Constitutional right to hold a referendum.[9] Why the indifference and lack of opposition to this illegal takeover?

Historians Bleiere et al. point to a political culture that did not support democracy. Latvia had been colonized by foreign powers for centuries; politicians and constituents had short-lived experience with the parliamentary process. For my father's family and other farmers, what mattered most was land ownership, something that Ulmanis understood. In many ways, this essentially was another manifestation of *as the master commands.* Latvia had been a republic for only fourteen years, versus centuries of living by the dictates of Tsars or German nobility. To many, a government takeover and disregard for their new constitution did not seem unusual, given that they still owned their land and maintained their rights as citizens.

Ulmanis adopted the slogan, "Latvia for Latvians" as a rallying cry for ethnic Latvian economic, social, and political power. The slogan was also used by Thunder Cross to promote the removal of ethnic minorities from Latvia. Historians agree that Ulmanis did not use the slogan to give voice to ethnic hatred.[10] In fact, Ulmanis banned Thunder Cross and anti-Jewish propaganda. Yet, post-coup, small policy changes began to reduce the influence other nationalities had in Latvia. After 1934, children of "mixed marriages" with one Latvian parent were required to attend Latvian school, rather than one of the ethnic public schools.[11] While ethnic Latvians comprised over three quarters of the total population, they formed a minority of business owners. Other ethnicities (Russians, Germans, Jews) owned the majority of businesses and factories in which Latvians worked.[12] Ulmanis' policies sought to increase ethnic Latvian ownership through government incentive programs and grants.

Ulmanis supported his vision of a prosperous Latvia built on the backs of successful farmers with a number of agricultural policy changes. Farmers who adapted new varieties of grain or cattle better suited to Latvia's climate, and therefore more productive, earned financial incentives. The government granted low interest loans to farmers buying modern equipment that would increase yield. Ulmanis honored the larger, productive farms, like Pudas; the Spīgulis family and their day servant, Emma, won an award for her years of loyal service, reflecting their status as good employers.

As exports increased and money flowed into the Latvian treasury, the government reinvested some of the returns into Latvian education and culture. Schools improved, literacy rates climbed, unemployment rates dropped, and the government deficit was all but eliminated.[13] The standard of living improved significantly for most Latvians.

Given that he seized power illegally, Ulmanis and his propaganda minister, Alfreds Bērziņš, made sure that the appearance of being universally loved was widespread in Latvia. A quick internet search reveals several grainy pictures of Ulmanis greeted by enthusiastic supporters or posing with children, many bearing flowers. Ulmanis adopted the moniker *"Vadonis"* (Leader), later changed to *"Saimnieks."* In Latvian, *saimnieks* is a nuanced word that can mean several things, depending on the context: farmer, owner of a house/apartment/farm, owner of animals, director or manager, host. It was a shrewd move on Ulmanis' part; most of his constituency self-identified as *saimnieks* or the feminine *saimniece*, so it was another way to present himself as one of the people, looking out for their best interests.

Historically, he remains a controversial figure. Most historians do not consider him to be a true Fascist. Ulmanis incorporated Fascist elements, like the cult of the leader and the sacralization of Latvian soil. However, he sought to maintain Latvia's borders as they were, not expand the territory as did most Fascist leaders in the 1930s. A CIA document dated 5 August 1955 refers to Ulmanis and his government as, "a paternal dictatorship, Fascist on the order of Germany and Italy;

and as the Protector of Latvia from domination of the Soviets." His propaganda minister Bērziņš fared worse, described in the same document as "the most dangerous Fascist in the United States."[14] Historian Edgars Dunsdorfs raised the difficulty of accurately assessing overall popular approval of Ulmanis and his government: no vote or poll was held to examine public opinion, and the façade of support could be created by staging photo opportunities.[15]

Among diaspora Latvians of the World War II generation, Ulmanis is generally popular due to his connection with rural people and the improved standard of living he brought about. Not many people complain when they have achieved their dream of owning land, when there is food on the table and a roof over their heads. Latvians lived for centuries under the yoke of foreign nobility. They experienced a republican form of government for only fourteen years. To my father and his friends, Ulmanis was the leader of their Latvia from their teenage years onward. To them, Ulmanis was not a dictator; he was the *Saimnieks* who brought Latvia into a new period of prosperity. To them, the dismantled democracy was a price worth paying. In fact, they hardly thought about what they had lost.

WORLD WAR II

Simplified Choices

As a child, I spent two weeks each summer at our church camp. Piesaule (which translates to "by the sun") is located in Bradford, New Hampshire, on three hundred sixty acres of wooded land purchased by our church in 1954. Over the years, Latvian families purchased small plots of land around the main campus, and built summer homes. The camp activities were unlike those of American camps my school friends attended. Those camps had sports like tennis, sailing, and waterskiing. Our conditions were rustic, and the activities were simple, the main objective being fresh air and exercise. We hiked and participated in track and field events, like shotput, long jump, and high jump. There was no actual track for these activities; we used flat areas in a field. We swam in a man-made pond that had leeches at one end and water snakes at the other. During afternoons, we learned Latvian handicrafts. Every night, the campers and counselors gathered by a bonfire, performing skits and singing songs until it was time for bed.

Piesaule also hosted large Summer Solstice celebrations. Wearing crowns of flowers and oak leaves, attendees gathered in a procession and visited several of the summer houses, where we stopped and serenaded the owners with solstice songs. The owners would then treat everyone to food, like "solstice cheese" (a homemade mild caraway cheese), pīrāgi, and beer. After the homes were visited, the celebrants would return to the bonfire ring for the lighting of the fire, which burned until dawn.

To the Boston area Latvians, Piesaule was more than a summer camp and get-away location; it was a cultural center, a place where the flames of tradition and Latvian identity could burn. The Soviet Union did not permit traditional celebrations tied to a particular ethnic identity; it was supposed to be one great family, eradicating ethnic or cultural differences, in the name of the Soviet state. But it is impossible to eradicate an identity as ancient as that of the Latvians.

Chapter 7

The Devils' Pact

Whenever diaspora Latvians gathered—in the United States, Canada, Australia, England, or anywhere else—it wasn't long before they started singing. Invariably, they sang *A Beautiful Red Rose is Growing*. I grew up knowing the words and haunting, melancholy melody by heart:

> A beautiful red rose is growing
> By the side of a busy road
> It grew, it bloomed
> It taunted the boys.
> Why do you grow, why do you bloom?
> Why do you taunt the boys?
> I am free to grow, free to bloom,
> Free to taunt the boys.
> Free to taunt the boys
> Throughout the entire summer.[1]

On the rare occasions that my American friends asked me to sing a "typical" Latvian folk song, I chose this one. A thinly veiled metaphor, the rose represented Latvia, taunting the powers around it with its beauty and freedom. At no time was the metaphor more appropriate than 1939, when two former enemies collaborated to strip Latvia and its neighbors of their freedom, setting in motion events that began World War II.

In 1989, I attended a gathering in our church function hall. As I milled about, greeting people I hadn't seen for a while, I bumped into a friend who recently returned from a trip to Latvia SSR. Her first words to me were: "Have you heard of the Molotov–Ribbentrop Pact?" I had not, and, at the time, had no recollection of who Molotov and Ribbentrop were. She explained: they were foreign ministers of the Soviet Union and Nazi Germany, the two men whose signatures were on a secret agreement that ended Latvia's independence in 1939. She had not been vacationing in the homeland; she had traveled to Latvia to protest the pact, the existence of which Gorbachev had only recently acknowledged.

My parents came of age during Latvia's first years as a republic. Even after the Ulmanis coup, with the representative government dismissed, Latvia still belonged to Latvians. The state protected the rights of all citizens, regardless of ethnicity or religion. In 1939, the course of their adult lives changed forever. A one-page secret document destroyed the Latvian state and any protections for its citizens: the secret protocols of the Nazi–Soviet Non-Aggression Pact, known to most Latvians as the Molotov–Ribbentrop Pact. My parents and the diaspora Latvians were intimately familiar with the Soviet annexation of their country: they had lived it. What they did not know was that Stalin and Hitler had negotiated a secret agreement that carved Europe into what was referred to as spheres of influence.

The Nazis destroyed the original documents. After World War II ended, the Germans turned over a microfilm copy to the British and

Americans. Still, for decades the protocols remained unknown. In an era of no internet, no linked databases available to the public, and thousands of sealed World War II documents, it was almost impossible to learn of the secret protocols without some kind of high level clearance. The Soviet Union denied the existence of the protocols until August 13, 1989.[2] As mainstream press, like *The New York Times*, reported on the agreement, Latvians informally referred to it as "the devils' pact." It was proof of what Latvians had always known; the Soviet annexation of Latvia was illegal and pre-planned, a strategic decision made by Stalin and Hitler.

Latvia's land, so beloved and honored by its people, has one particularly striking feature: its long coastline. Geographically only three times the size of Massachusetts, Latvia's coastline stretches over five hundred kilometers along the Baltic Sea. The country also has deep-water harbors, port cities, and ice-free rivers. Latvia is one of the small countries situated between the Soviet Union and Germany, along with the much larger countries Poland and Ukraine, that historian Timothy Snyder refers to as "bloodlands." Lands that, by the misfortune of their location, experienced political mass murder because they were central to both Stalin and Hitler's plans. Given that, it was inevitable that Stalin and Hitler would destroy those countries.

For Latvia, independence depended on strong alliances, and so it joined the League of Nations in 1922. While the League guaranteed the security of its member countries,[3] it proved ineffective. The United States, an essential partner for international security obligations, did not join; following World War I, the possibility of foreign military engagements was extremely unpopular with the public and would have meant political suicide for elected officials.[4] Conflicts over disarmament, problematic relations among member countries, and the lack of a military presence were among the issues that caused the League to ultimately fail.

In our Latvian school history classes, I often wondered why the three Baltic nations had never worked together to prevent foreign occupation. In fact, they unsuccessfully attempted to create a trilateral defense pact several times. Latvia, Lithuania, and Estonia are culturally, linguistically, and historically distinct from one another; these differences plus their individual histories of oppression proved insurmountable. The biggest obstacle was the role of Poland. In 1920, Polish armed forces invaded and occupied Lithuania's capital city, Vilnius, citing historical territorial rights. In the early 1930s, Baltic diplomats discussed possible alliances: one limited to Latvia, Lithuania, and Estonia, and an expanded option that included Poland and Finland. Poland possessed the greatest army of the five nations, but the occupation of Vilnius made this a non-starter for Lithuania. The most the three nations managed to achieve was the Baltic Entente of September 1934: a neutrality pact that made the three Baltics plus Poland a neutral zone between the USSR and Germany.[5]

Lacking a trilateral agreement, the Baltic nations individually considered how best to protect their sovereignty. In February 1932, Latvia—along with the other Baltic nations, Poland, and Finland—signed non-aggression agreements with the Soviet Union. The signatory nations agreed to refrain from aggression against each other, either independently or with other powers. Baltic diplomats continued to seek mutual self-defense pacts with other Eastern European nations, but none were strong enough to give assurances to border inviolability.

By 1934, as Europe's political situation became increasingly volatile, Latvia's British ambassador sought guarantees of Latvia's independence from Great Britain. He was rejected: Britain would sign any League of Nations declaration, but offer no direct military support. The Latvians also unsuccessfully approached Finland for an alliance; Finland's security concerns were limited to its shared border with the Soviet Union and did not involve Germany.[6] Following these unsuccessful attempts, the Ulmanis government chose neutrality as Latvia's best means of defense.

Stalin believed that Hitler would use the Baltic nations and Finland as strategic bases from which to launch an attack on the Soviet Union.

In spite of the existing non-aggression pact signed in 1932, he viewed the Baltic nations' neutrality as a direct threat to Soviet security.[7] In April 1939, as concerns about Hitler's intentions grew, the Soviets pursued border security with Latvia and Estonia by proposing guarantees of their independence; Ulmanis rejected these outright as a *de facto* protectorate. In May 1939, Stalin replaced Soviet Foreign Minister Maxim Litvinov with Vyacheslav Molotov, a teetotaling vegetarian fiercely loyal to his boss. This staffing replacement signaled a shift in Soviet foreign policy. Litvinov had sought collective security agreements with Great Britain and France. From now on, Stalin dictated foreign policy decisions, always with the goal of creating border states between the Baltic and Black Seas to serve as a buffer to German military action.[8]

While Stalin changed foreign ministers, my father prepared for his final exams and subsequent graduation from the Limbažu regional high school. He had exciting plans for his future: attending the School of Architecture at the University of Latvia.

Graduating class, Limbažu High School. My father is second from the left, back row. Author's collection.

With thriving herds, acres of grain, and hired workers to help with the crops and livestock, the Spīgulis family achieved the prosperity Ulmanis envisioned with his land reforms and agricultural incentives. Pēteris and Kristīne had the luxury of sparing their only son as he pursued higher education. In June, as he helped Pēteris work the farm and looked forward to beginning his studies, the Latvian government signed a non-aggression pact with Germany, a move Stalin interpreted as hostile.[9]

Stalin needed to protect Soviet borders from German military action while he built up Soviet military strength. At the same time, Hitler planned his invasion of Poland with a target date of August 26 and could not sustain a war on two fronts. Both Stalin and Hitler wanted the same thing—a guarantee there would not be an armed conflict between them at this time.

Stalin instructed Molotov to draft a non-aggression pact and invite Hitler's Foreign Minister Joachim von Ribbentrop to come to Moscow. Hitler, determined to stick to his invasion timetable, demanded an earlier meeting. Ribbentrop arrived on August 23 and met with Stalin himself, Molotov in attendance. Terms were direct and simple: no aggression against each other and no support for any party attacking either Germany or the Soviet Union. Any disputes between the two countries would be settled through diplomacy, not armed conflict. The agreement would be active upon signature, not ratification, and in effect for ten years.[10]

Publicly released to the other powers, this portion of the pact made headlines around the world the following day. The second portion—the secret protocol—was the real reason for the meeting. In it, Germany and the Soviet Union carved up Eastern Europe into spheres of mutual influence. There were a few points of negotiation. Germany demanded Lithuania and Latvia up to the Daugava River, including Riga, with the rest of Latvia, Estonia and Finland going to the Soviet sphere. Stalin refused these terms, largely out of his fear of a German attack on the Soviet Union launched from the Baltics. He insisted on having Latvia in its entirety, citing the Soviet need for Baltic port cities. Ribbentrop secured Hitler's approval for this change within three hours. The draft was edited to reflect the alterations and signed by both Molotov and Ribbentrop.[11]

Then they drank. The collegial atmosphere surrounding what both parties believed to be a good deal belied the real import: an unconscionable and illegal step that directly preceded and made possible the beginning of World War II. After receiving news of the signed pact, Hitler reportedly ordered champagne for his staff. As the toasts were poured, he pounded both fists on the wall, shouting, "Now Europe is mine. The others can have Asia."[12] A later addendum, signed on September 28, 1939, would give most of Lithuania to the Soviet Union. According to historian Zara Steiner, this later addendum signaled another shift in Soviet policy. Stalin's need for security drove the original protocol; the addendum was about territorial acquisition.[13] Stalin's objectives in the Baltics had evolved.

Following the signing of the pact, Hitler invaded Poland on September 1. Knowing the Soviet plans, he called for Baltic Germans to renounce their Latvian citizenship immediately and return home.

Known as *Heim ins Reich* [back home to the Reich], the policy was in effect since 1938, urging ethnic Germans to leave areas not under German control; this was the first time it was directly applied to Latvia and the other Baltic nations. Over the next months, about 51,000 Baltic Germans repatriated to Germany and Poland.[14] Latvians felt mixed emotions about the German repatriation: relief at the departure of this controlling minority as well as concern that the repatriation stripped away protection against Soviet aggression. As long as there were Germans living there, Latvians believed that Hitler would not allow the Soviet Union to have free reign.

With no reason to fear Hitler's interference, Stalin proceeded quickly. The Red Army's military strength vastly outnumbered that of the three Baltic nations. Estonia was forced to sign a "mutual assistance" treaty on September 27. Latvia was next; Molotov summoned Latvian Foreign Minister Munters to Moscow where he signed a "mutual assistance" pact on October 5, 1939, allowing the Soviet Union to station 25,000 Red Army troops in Latvia, west of the Venta River.[15] By October 10, Lithuania signed a similar agreement. For the Latvian government, capitulation was the best option; Molotov had made it clear that the troops would be stationed in Latvia, regardless of whether the government allowed it or not.

As bad luck would have it, the winter of 1940 turned out to be bitterly cold. The German blockade in the Baltic prevented Latvia from exporting goods or obtaining raw materials. Factories idled and widespread unemployment affected all Latvians. Coal was virtually unavailable. Unemployed workers formed fuel task forces and chopped green wood in nearby forests, of limited use since it could not be immediately burned. When spring finally arrived, the fruit trees had small, black, withered buds, the harbingers of hunger. Farmers referred to the spring of 1940 as the *melnais pavasaris* (black spring).

In May 1940, the Soviets accused Lithuania of shielding an undercover cell working to recruit Red Army agents for their secret service, along with other anti-Soviet acts. The charges were false, a pretense to justify an invasion of Lithuania. On June 15, Red Army units, without any provocation, attacked a border guard station in Latvia. The Soviet government followed up the attack by falsely accusing the Latvians of hostile acts in violation of the mutual assistance pact, setting in motion a full-on invasion.

The League of Nations provided no support or protest. Following Hitler's attack on Poland, France and England were now at war with Germany. Latvia was alone. With no allies to help, Latvia's first occupation of World War II began.

SIMPLIFIED CHOICES

Latvians celebrate two independence days. November 18th commemorates the original declaration of the sovereign state of Latvia in 1918. May 4, 1990 is known as the Latvian Republic's Restoration of Independence Day. On that day, the Supreme Soviet of the Latvian SSR declared its independence from the Soviet Union. Moscow was not yet ready to accept this, but the foundation of the regime had crumbled. Latvia's independence was internationally recognized in 1991. The original November 18, 1918 declaration was made over a year before de jure international recognition, but that didn't stop the Latvians from honoring that date. Similarly, Latvians consider 1990 the official date of their restoration of independence, not the year the international community recognized the dissolution of the Soviet Union.

On the first Restoration of Independence Day, my husband and I were on our honeymoon in Sonoma wine country. I must confess that I did not pay much attention to world news that week. When we returned to Boston, my parents eagerly filled me in on the momentous event. To them, it was the answer to their dreams. Had they ever doubted or lost hope? If they had, they did not share it with me.

The fact that the Latvians call May 4th Restoration of Independence Day is significant. The Soviet Union stole their country and punished those who fought for it. Although Latvians lost their independence, they did not truly become Soviet citizens. Contrary to Soviet doctrine, they did not lose their Latvian identity. In their hearts, Latvians were always free; it just took forty-five years for their oppressor to collapse, and the rest of the world to right the wrong. The master would no longer command them.

Chapter 8

The Year of Terror

June 1940–June 1941

In 1940, my father left Pudas and matriculated at the University of Latvia's School of Architecture, fulfilling Pēteris' prediction about his son's future career. He found a small room to rent and settled into his studies. Old Riga, the medieval heart of the city, was a step into past centuries with its brightly colored buildings and narrow cobblestone streets. Beyond the old city center, Riga's Art Nouveau masterpieces, famous among architecture students, stood tall, featuring scrolled columns, stained glass, and statuary characteristic of the style. Plentiful restaurants and nightclubs promised a lively social life to a young man from the countryside.

My mother completed her vocational school training, left home, and was working as a traveling dairy inspector, a fairly typical life for a Latvian farm girl.

But the peace they knew was about to end. June 17, 1940 marked the beginning of the *Baigais gads* (Year of Terror), a year of arrests, deportations, and executions—crimes against humanity committed on orders of the Communist Party. My parents rarely spoke of it. When I asked them about what happened, my mother teared up and simply said, "Those were terrible times." She refused to say anything more. My father, huffing with rage, talked about beatings, nighttime disappearances, and executions. It was in these moments that his absolute hatred of the Russians, as he called them, was most evident. To him, the finer distinctions of party affiliation did not matter. Even though there were plenty of Latvian Communists, he categorized the invaders as Russians. He was not alone in this sentiment. The psychological impact of the Soviet campaign of terror against Latvian citizens is impossible to overstate. It produced a collective national case of trauma and absolute fear of the Soviet Union. As a result, many Latvians would do whatever was necessary to prevent another Soviet occupation.

My uncle Visvaldis' memoir opens with a meticulous description of his experiences during the Year of Terror. The first-hand observations I write about come largely from that memoir, as well as extensive interviews with my father. My mother's voice is missing, her pain too great to put into words.

June 15, 1940

Summer nights are short in Latvia. The knowledge that long nights of darkness are only a few months away makes warm weather celebrations all the more special. As my father attended his first year of university, his future brother-in-law, Visvaldis Bišs, graduated with a chemical engineering degree from the Riga State Technical School.

Visvaldis Biš, 1940. Author's collection.

The students possessed a naive confidence in the Latvian government, born of their patriotism for the young country. Regardless of international unrest, the government knew what was best for its citizens and would keep them safe. Visvaldis believed in Ulmanis, the *Saimnieks*.

That evening, the graduates took a postal bus out to a classmate's house for a celebration. The group ate, drank, and sang patriotic songs until dawn's first rays of light appeared in the sky. The following morning, Visvaldis arose early to catch the first bus back to Riga. He arrived at 06:00, caught a streetcar to the Torņkalnu stop, and returned to the apartment he shared with his sister, Zelma, near the western bank of the Daugava River. Zelma was completing her night shift at the Children's Hospital nearby. His other sister, Marta, and her husband lived a few doors down on the same street. Visvaldis let himself into the apartment, washed off the dust from his bus ride, then climbed into bed to catch up on his sleep.

He awoke to Zelma's agitated voice calling, "Wake up! Why are you sleeping? Do you know what's happening?" As Visvaldis struggled to rouse himself, Zelma elaborated, "The Russians are invading! The government has resigned!"

Visvaldis popped upright in bed, stunned. It was impossible. Throwing aside the bedclothes, he dressed quickly and went down to the street. Before he opened the door, he heard the grinding sound of iron. Along the street perpendicular to his, dusty, dirty tanks rolled, one after another. People lined the street, silent, somber, watching the Red Army's arrival. Visvaldis went to Marta's apartment, where they read a brief, official notice in the newspaper: the Soviet Union denounced the Latvian military conspiracy against them and demanded the resignation of the current Latvian government. The treachery resulted in an unlimited presence of the Red Army in all of the Baltic states. Although the accusations were false, the government accepted the ultimatum and all current ministers submitted their resignation letters to President Ulmanis. Visvaldis and Marta turned on the radio, hoping for more news. Only music played, meaning that control of the station was now in the hands of the occupying forces.

THE YEAR OF TERROR

*The first Red Army tanks enter Riga, June 17, 1940.
Courtesy of the Latvian Occupation Museum.*

*Crowds in Riga observing Soviet occupation, June 17, 1940.
Courtesy of the Latvian Occupation Museum.*

SIMPLIFIED CHOICES

Stalin struck quickly. After the June 15 attack on the Latvian border patrol, Soviet soldiers crossed into Latvia. The following day, more Red Army troops mobilized and crossed into the interior of Lettgalia. At 14:00, Ulmanis received a telegram from Molotov accusing the Latvian government of a conspiracy against the Soviet Union. In order to fulfill the terms of the mutual assistance pact, Stalin demanded the resignation of current leadership in favor of one the Soviets trusted. The Red Army would enter Latvia and station troops without resistance. If Ulmanis refused these terms, the Red Army would invade Latvia and force capitulation. Ulmanis and his advisors were given just nine hours in which to reply.[1]

Ulmanis and his advisors faced a difficult situation with no easy choice. Resistance would incur the might of the Red Army, likely killing thousands of Latvians. Ulmanis hoped that accepting the ultimatum would save lives, and enable him to keep the government secretly intact until Latvia regained its independence. A few hours later, another telegram from Molotov clarified the situation: any mobilization of Latvian troops would result in the immediate bombing of Latvian cities.[2] Ulmanis accepted the ultimatum unconditionally and refrained from any diplomatic protests. The London ambassador received no instructions to invoke emergency powers, so he did not petition other nations on behalf of Latvia's sovereignty.

Latvian scholars are divided in their judgment of Ulmanis and his rapid surrender. Some believe that by conceding to the Soviet Union, enough Latvians survived to eventually form a new nation in 1990. Stalin would not hesitate to kill Latvian civilians, particularly young men who could have mobilized against the Red Army. Others believe Ulmanis missed the opportunity to resist while the motivation to fight for Latvia was at its highest. The lives lost by resistance perhaps would have been fewer than those lost due to executions, purges, deportations, battles, and the subsequent Nazi invasion and Holocaust. Latvians like my father and his friends agreed that Ulmanis was left with two bad choices; he chose the only viable option.

My father recalled the day of the government's resignation: "It was very sudden, overnight. Suddenly the tanks appeared. They were everywhere, rolling down all of the major streets. We were shocked and confused, and didn't know what to think or do. We just went on as usual."

The Red Army took over the newspaper, radio station, postal and telegraph offices, severing contact with the rest of Europe. Soviet Deputy Foreign Minister Andrei Vyshinsky arrived in Riga to set up a Soviet puppet government. Augusts Kirhenšteins was installed as the new Latvian Prime Minister, along with Soviet-designated ministers. Vyshinsky left Ulmanis as the nominal head of state, under house arrest, to prevent organized opposition to the Communist Party and lull residents into a false sense that life would remain relatively unchanged. Vyshinsky also wanted to mask the Soviet takeover of the Baltic republics to international powers and create the illusion of an orderly transition. It worked: foreign powers, including the United States and Great Britain, sent congratulations to Kirhenšteins on his new role as Prime Minister of Latvia.[3]

Elections were the next step in the Soviet annexation plan. Purported to be constitutional elections demanded by Latvians, Kirhenšteins declared the Communist Party to be the only political party in Latvia. Voters could select candidates from a single list of the Latvian Working People's Block. Kirhenšteins arrested leaders of opposing political parties.[4] Elections for this new *Saeima* were held on July 14 and 15, after which the Kremlin announced that nearly ninety-eight percent of Latvians voted in favor of the candidates. Communist officials counted the ballots in secret. They announced the percentage of votes cast in favor of the Communist candidates before voting stations closed; it exceeded the number of citizens who actually voted at that time.[5]

One week after the elections, the now expendable Ulmanis was imprisoned and deported as an enemy of the government. Two years later, Ulmanis died on the date of my father's birthday, September 20, in the Krasnovodsk prison hospital.[6]

When the Communist government met for its first *Saeima*, representatives declared Latvia a Soviet Socialist Republic and voted to petition the Supreme Council of the USSR for acceptance into the Soviet Union. On August 5, the Supreme Council accepted the petition, and Latvia became the 15th republic in the Soviet Union. The sovereign state of Latvia no longer existed.

———

The Soviet Union never acknowledged that the July 1940 elections were illegal and fixed. The Russian Federation continues that denial today. Soviet historians portray the July elections in the Baltic states as three spontaneous socialist revolutions, and refuse to acknowledge that the Baltic republics were forcibly occupied, or that crimes against civilians were committed on Party orders. Instead, the Russian Federation cites its role in defeating Hitler and attributes the crimes committed in the 1940–1941 period to Nazi sympathizers.[7]

———

The United States and Great Britain took over a month to respond, at which point both countries condemned the action and did not recognize the annexation of Latvia. The condemnation became worthless once the Allied powers formed an alliance with Stalin; the Allies tabled any formal protests to avoid straining Soviet relations. At the Tehran Conference, President Roosevelt met secretly with Stalin on December 1, 1943. During this private meeting, Roosevelt reassured Stalin that "he fully realized the three Baltic Republics had in history and again more recently been a part of Russia and added jokingly that when the Soviet armies re-occupied these areas, he did not intend to go to war with the Soviet Union on this point."[8] In return for Soviet military cooperation, the United States would not block the re-annexation of the Baltic nations after World War II. This *quid pro quo* formed the source of my father's contempt for Roosevelt.

Reading Roosevelt's words, I shared my father's outrage. They brought home the duplicity of the United States government: stopping one murderous regime while appeasing another. Clearly, Hitler had to be stopped. The United States, Great Britain, and France needed the Red Army to defeat the Nazi forces on the Eastern Front. Yet it shocked me to read the words of our president joking about giving up the freedom of three tiny countries. By doing so, he condoned the forceful annexation, loss of freedom, and repressions that occurred in the Baltics. The United States demonstrated a naiveté when it came to assessing Stalin, who was voted *Time Magazine*'s Man of the Year in the January 4, 1943 issue for "long-neglected recognition of his abilities by nations outside the Soviet borders."[9] For all of the talk about defending democracy and being the leader of the free world, the United States willingly sacrificed Latvia and its Baltic neighbors to decades of oppression. Only some countries, it seems, were worthy of democracy and freedom, depending on whether or not they aligned with United States' interests.

The new Communist government went to work dismantling Latvia's infrastructure and economy. Officials fired influential economic and political appointees. The state seized personal property, businesses, levied exorbitant taxes, and took over distribution of goods. The *ruble* replaced the Latvian currency, the *lat*, resulting in an astronomical increase in the cost of living and the complete loss of savings for many people. Groceries shot up to three times the price of just a few months before, and kept going up. Goods like butter and beef were shipped to Russia, resulting in shortages. For the first time since gaining independence, Latvians received ration cards for food and clothing. The sudden changes destroyed the prosperity Latvians experienced prior to the annexation. The Telegraph Agency of the Soviet Union, known by the acronym TASS, expelled foreign correspondents and controlled all news sources. The Ministry of Education, a propaganda agency, assumed control of theater, opera, books and films, removing approximately four thousand volumes of Latvian history, politics, and religion from bookstores and libraries. Plans for mass collectivization of farms proceeded a bit more cautiously. Anticipating resistance from Latvia's large rural population, Soviet officials needed time to set up the regime and eliminate its most likely opponents.[10]

In the autumn of 1940, my father found a changed Riga when he arrived at the university. Soviet officials appropriated choice living quarters, displacing residents and causing a housing shortage. A new ordinance allowed only nine square meters of an apartment's width per person. For space exceeding that limit, residents had to take in tenants or pay three times the rent. Initially, my father rented a room but was not getting along well with his landlord. His friend Vilnis Zirdziņš invited him to move into his family's apartment to meet the terms of the Soviet ordinance. Vilnis' older brother was serving in the Latvian army, and his absence meant available space. My father gladly accepted the offer and moved in, joining Vilnis, his parents, and an engineering student who was also renting.

As his semester began, the repressions shifted into high gear. Stalin deployed his secret police force as the engine of terror and repression across Latvia. Known by its acronym, NKVD (renamed the KGB after Stalin's death), the force wasted no time arresting and deporting anyone considered a threat to the new Soviet order: members of political parties; clergy; military officers; high-ranking civil servants; industrialists; large landowners; and anyone with foreign ties. On November 16, 1940, the mandated Criminal Code gave authorities the right to punish Latvian citizens according to Soviet laws for their activities during Latvia's time as a sovereign nation, prior to annexation.[11]

The NKVD assumed the headquarters of the former Latvian Ministry of the Interior. The building came to be known simply as *Stūru māja,* or Corner House. Latvians spoke of it in whispers, knowing full well that anyone taken there did not return. Today, the building is a museum preserving the memory of the Year of Terror. The NKVD converted the ground floor and cellars to interrogation rooms, torture chambers, and cells. Cells that were built for two or three people typically contained as many as forty, with the temperatures kept intentionally high to make conditions even more wretched. Those used for solitary confinement were equipped with wiring that enabled high intensity lights to be turned on prisoners. Once a week, prisoners were taken to a tiny internal courtyard for exercise. They stayed just long enough to breathe some fresh air, making the return to their cells as cruel as possible. Executions took place in a special chamber, the walls still riddled with bullet holes. A truck idled nearby while executions took place, the engine covering up any noise. Afterwards, bodies were placed in the truck for disposal without attracting too much attention.

The Soviet repressions opened one of the most troubling chapters in Latvian history. Latvian Jews were generally supporters of the Soviet occupation. For many, it was a choice between the lesser of two evils: they hoped the Red Army would prevent the Germans from invading Latvia. As historian Ben Cion-Pinchuk writes, "Pogroms and Nazi terror, not enthusiasm for Communism, were the dominant forces that drove the Jews towards the Soviets."[12] Older Jewish citizens, in particular, often owned industry or businesses, and therefore resisted the idea of Soviet state ownership. As Soviets fired ethnic Latvian workers, Latvian Jews often replaced them; the Soviets needed people with experience and knowledge of former Latvian institutions to keep the country running. Active supporters of the regime joined the Red Army, or were placed in charge of NKVD punishment forces, prisons, and served as members of the NKVD police force. Young Jewish men comprised close to half of membership in the Communist Youth League.[13] The visibility of the positions some Jews occupied, particularly in the military, positioned them as facilitating violence directed against Latvians by Soviets. The first warden of Corner House was V. G. Zevin; while he was almost the only Jew working there, his high position fueled rumors that all Jews were working for the Soviet State forces, or *chekists* as Latvians typically called them.[14] These associations eroded the previous tolerance that existed among Latvians.

Arrests and deportations always occurred at night. Government officials fired Latvian policemen, who harbored nationalist loyalties, and replaced them with a militia, described by my father as "Russian sympathizers with guns." My father vividly remembered the night he had a close call with deportation. As he recounted, one night he awoke from a loud banging on the apartment door. He heard his landlord, Mr. Zirdziņš, open the door. Four militia members and a translator burst into the apartment:

They said, "Get ready. You have twenty minutes. You are being deported." Suddenly, there was a soldier with a gun, who kept watch over us while we went to get dressed quickly for deportation—me too! I was going to be deported with them! I got dressed. What could I do? You cannot do anything when you have four soldiers standing there with Turks [guns with bayonets].

The militia's arrest list identified the Zirdziņš family as the parents and two sons. They assumed that my father was one of the sons, to be deported with his family. As they searched the apartment, they discovered the other tenant, the engineering student.

The militia shouted, "Who is that?"

"That is the engineer, our renter."

"Do you have someone else here?"

"Yes," replied Mr. Zirdziņš, "We have the student Spīgulis."

"What are you talking about?" demanded the militia. "That is your son!"

"No, our son is in the army."

Upon hearing this, the militia entered my father's room and demanded his documents. They took the papers, shoved in the engineering student, and locked them both in the room: "We were terrified...I had some illegal leaflets against the Russians on the table that they could have prosecuted me for. I thought, 'If they look at those, I am in Siberia too.'"

The two students waited anxiously. Nothing happened. After what seemed an eternity, a militiaman unlocked the door and let them out. The militia directed Zirdziņš to designate someone to liquidate their personal belongings. Mrs. Zirdziņš turned to my father and asked him to perform this duty, saying, "Do what you think is best." Knowing that they were being deported, they gathered some clothes and a few belongings. My father gave them the butter and ham he had brought from Pudas so that they could eat. As they said their goodbyes, my father shook his friend's hand, saying, "See you, Vilni." The Zirdziņš spent fourteen years in Siberia. It would be fifty years before Vilnis and my father saw each other again.

My father was indeed fortunate that the leaflets in his room were not discovered. Student leaders urging resistance to the Soviet occupation were deported to Siberian labor camps, where most of them died. Arrests, deportations, and executions increased on a monthly basis, with people disappearing in the middle of the night. Charges were vague, often simply stated as "struggle against the revolutionary movement." The scope of criminal conduct broadened to tearing down posters of Soviet slogans, laying flowers at the Freedom Monument, or even telling jokes about the Soviet Union.[15] The result was an effective terrorism campaign: Latvians were terrified of leaving their homes, but equally terrified of staying.

Visvaldis, also in Riga, was preoccupied with finding a job. He went on job interviews, where the first question invariably asked was, "Are you a member of the Communist Youth Organization?" When he replied no, he was dismissed with no further questions. Eventually, he found a position in the state-run sugar factory. A camaraderie developed among the Latvians employed in his division. One evening he and his colleagues went to a basement restaurant, known as *Jāņu pagrabu restorāns* (John's basement restaurant), a place where you could eat dinner and drink a beer for short money. The restaurant was crowded, but they managed to find a table near a window. As they drank their beers, they began singing a song that was popular at the time: *The Bear Slayer Song* (*Lāčplēšu dziesma*). Lāčplēsis, the Bear Slayer, is a mythical Latvian folk hero featured in an epic poem written by Andrejs Pumpurs. Lāčplēsis, who is part man, part bear, defends his homeland from invaders by ripping apart bears by the jaws with his bare hands. Visvaldis and his friends got as far as the first verse of the song:

> Together here, we colleagues, who were not doomed to die
> We can row the lifeboat further.
> Those who can still greet a new sun each day,
> Can work and dream and still accomplish much.[16]

Suddenly, a blue uniformed man appeared before their table: a *zābaks* ("boot") for the NKVD. He demanded their documents immediately. They produced the papers and identified themselves as state workers. After an impromptu interrogation, he said that he would not report them. The Boot explained that the song was popular during Ulmanis' time, but was now regarded as anti-Soviet. Visvaldis knew he was saved by dumb luck; his next encounter with a Boot might not end so well.

In May 1941, the head of the NKVD presented Stalin with a plan called "An Operation to Cleanse the Lithuanian, Latvian, and Estonian Soviet Socialist Republics of Anti-Soviet, Criminal, and Socially

Dangerous Elements." The plan contained details of how mass executions and deportations would be implemented.

Riga buzzed with rumors: freight yard workers were altering hundreds of boxcars, cutting holes in the floors and mounting bars on windows. The NKVD was preparing deportee lists. Worried, confused, and anxious, Latvians barely concentrated on their jobs. On the eve of June 14, word got out that mass arrests were imminent. Visvaldis and his friends at work decided not to go home that evening. Instead, they hid in the basement archives room of the sugar factory. After work, Visvaldis and his friends went down to the storeroom and their colleague, the archivist, quietly locked the door. They spent the night perched on dusty file boxes, listening to the grinding sound of heavy trucks driving up and down the street above them. The next morning, not having slept a wink, they reported to work at the normal time. Their supervisor came in a couple of hours late; he, too, had been hiding.

That night, NKVD operative teams deported an estimated 15,424 ethnic Latvians. That number does not include other groups deported, such as Jews, who comprised a disproportionately higher percentage of the June 14 deportees than they represented in the population of Latvia. Historian Irēne Šneidere notes that ethnic Jews occupying high positions in the Commissariat of the Interior and National Security endorsed the majority of resolutions on the deportations, essentially sentencing Jews and ethnic Latvians alike to deportation.

The teams arrested the people on their list, making no effort to list specific charges, and confiscated their personal belongings. In some cases, notes on arresting files indicated that no reason for deportation was found. The arrested persons were moved to designated loading stations, where men were taken from their families and locked in separate cars.[17]

Taking into account the arrests, deportations and executions that were ongoing since June 17, 1940, it is estimated that a minimum of 20,000–21,000 Latvian citizens were arrested without charges, given no trial, and either executed or deported to Siberian Gulag forced labor camps. This figure reflects only the documents stored in Latvia, and is therefore considered to be lower than the actual number of victims. It does not include files that may be housed in what is now the Russian Federation or civilians who were executed by Red Army units without the creation of a case file. Most of the 1941 deportees were sent to camps in Siberia or the Northern Urals. The majority died from the scarce food, disease, harsh living conditions, and relentless labor. According to the state archives, there were 3,441 known deaths in the camps, but the actual number was certainly higher. International law classifies the mass arrests without trials or adequate charges, deportations, torture, and execution as crimes against humanity.[18]

Seventy years later, our family friend Astrīda is still moved by the memory of the deportations. Over lunch at her home, she recalled Deportation Day vividly:

> I remember it like it was yesterday. We were terrified. You have no idea how terrifying it was. School was out for the summer, so we were on vacation. My best friend must have had a premonition that something awful was about to happen because the day before the deportations, she came to me and gave me a little ceramic pig. She said, 'I want you to have this.' The next night her family was sent to Siberia. We somehow escaped because we were not on the list. I don't know why. Maybe we did not have enough money. When we left Latvia, I took the little pig with me. I still have it today.

On June 22, 1941, Hitler tore up his short-lived Non-Aggression Pact with Stalin and began Operation Barbarossa, his massive assault on the Soviet Union. Hitler had taken over Austria, Czechoslovakia, and Eastern Poland. Now it was time to take on the Soviet Union.

Simplified Choices

My father impressed the importance of voting upon my siblings and me. Local or national, it didn't matter; once he obtained citizenship, my father voted in every single election until the year before he died. He voted for politicians who took a strong stand against the Soviet Union and, after its dissolution, supported the countries that regained independence. As I came of voting age and began to develop my political beliefs, we occasionally locked horns over who we thought worthy of our vote.

In 1986, news of the Iran Contra Affair went public. I remember debating my father about then-president Reagan. I was criticizing Reagan for illegally selling arms to Iran and using proceeds from the sale to covertly support the Nicaraguan Contras. My father defended Reagan. I pressed him on the issue. Reagan broke the law, lied, and betrayed the trust of the American people. How could he support him? My father replied, Did it ever occur to you that, where I come from, people got shot for speaking out against the government?

I had nothing more to say.

CHAPTER 9

TRADING ONE MASTER FOR ANOTHER

JUNE–JULY 1941

After the shock of the deportations, Visvaldis took a few days off to regroup in the pastoral Brunava Parish, about eighty-four kilometers south of Riga. He learned of the German attack on the Red Army over the radio, and recalled this as good news. Finally, Latvia would get rid of their Russian oppressors! Over the next few days, he saw Red Army soldiers across the Nemunēlis River, digging trenches. Vacation over, he rode his bicycle to Bauska, a small town nearby, where he waited for the bus from Riga. It never showed up. The crowd waiting for the bus began to dissipate, and Visvaldis decided to bicycle to Riga. As he crossed a bridge, a Russian soldier stopped him to inspect his documents and let him pass. The road to Riga was increasingly filled with Red Army soldiers, all fully armed. Approaching Iecava, a town forty-five kilometers south of Riga, he began to encounter more civilians fleeing: families, single people, many of them Jews—terrified, desperate, fleeing the Germans, looking for passage across the Daugava. Visvaldis rode further to the nearby township of Ķekava, thinking that he would spend the night with some friends. When he arrived in the township, he learned that they were no longer there. He rode out of Ķekava, and found himself alone on the road. Suddenly, he heard the sound of an airplane, followed by machine gun fire nearby. He dismounted, threw his bicycle and himself into a roadside ditch, and lay still until the airplane passed. Thirsty, he turned into a nearby house to ask for some water. The woman who answered his knock gave him water, but urged him to go to Riga, where her relatives reported that all was calm. She clearly did not want him staying any longer. Visvaldis thanked her for the water and resumed his ride.

Just beyond the house, he spotted a small Red Army unit and heard another airplane overhead, but this time the plane dropped bombs on their position. He dove for cover on the ground, and saw the water woman running towards him. She explained that her husband took their children to a neighbor's house deep in the forest that morning. She stayed behind to guard the house from looting. Would he please help her harness the horse and pack some items in the cart? He would be welcome to stay with them; they would provide him with food. He took her up on the offer and, running toward the barn, helped her hitch up the horse. When they arrived at the large house in the forest, they met several people besides the homeowner: the woman's family, the homeowner's relatives from Riga, and several neighbors whose houses were close to the fighting. Visvaldis, the water woman, and her family were given the sauna as their quarters because the rest of the house was full. They heard several gunshots nearby, then a small band of Red Army soldiers came out of the woods in small groupings, looking exhausted and starving. The soldiers explained they were sent to stop the Germans with only one large artillery gun. When Germans approached, they shot once and then sought cover in a ditch because the Germans had more and larger guns. Their commander threatened to shoot them with his pistol if they did not return to their posts, so they fled.

Unbeknownst to him, Visvaldis pedaled right into the German offensive to take Riga. Led by Colonel Otto Lasch and a regiment from the 1st Infantry Division, the Germans were in the process of pressing northeast toward Riga, capturing and securing bridge crossings at

Ķekava and Iecava before the retreating Red Army could destroy them. The Baltic region became the Northwest Front. The Wehrmacht's Army Group North had three other offensives happening simultaneously to capture Latvia's major cities: Liepāja, Daugavpils, and Krustpils. Caught by surprise, the Red Army was now scrambling to defend its position or, failing that, to retreat. It was complete chaos.

Visvaldis and a few men decided to venture out to see what was happening on the road to Riga. Before leaving, they prepared several small white flags for surrender, in case they were fired upon. As they left the forest, they could see soldiers in the distance. Soviet or German? They walked carefully along the road, keeping their white flags at the ready. As they drew closer, they saw that the soldiers were German. One of them came closer, speaking perfect Latvian: a repatriated Baltic German. He asked details of the skirmish Visvaldis witnessed, and informed the men that, as of that morning, Riga was in German control. The German occupation of Latvia was swift. The Wehrmacht entered the western part of Latvia on June 23. By July 8, the Red Army was driven back and Army Group North's occupation of Latvia's territory was complete.

Visvaldis and his group returned to the large house, telling everyone that Riga was liberated from the Russians. In the house, the refugees were listening to the radio. Trembling with emotion, the female radio announcer called out, "Latvians, our nightmare has ended!"

She could not have been more wrong.

———

Visvaldis spent another night at the forest home. The following day, thanking his host and hostess, he mounted his bicycle again and began pedaling toward Riga. The road was filled with other returning refugees who were hiding from the Soviets. Upon entering his apartment, he saw dirty dishes still on the kitchen table, the traces of sudden flight. Collecting them, he began washing and wondering about his family's whereabouts. A little later, his sister Marta appeared; she spent the days of the German invasion in the basement of her workplace, the sound of bombs and gunfire outside. After hearing her story, he went outside and walked around the city. St. Peter's Church spire was bombed to rubble. Most of the buildings in central Riga were piles of bricks, timbers, and debris. He found it difficult to orient himself as the old landmarks were gone. Bridges across the Daugava River were blown up, and boats were ferrying people across. He walked a few streets over to check on his former workplace. Miraculously, it was still standing. On his return trip to his neighborhood, it began to rain heavily, a downpour. People stopped in the streets, soaking wet, smiling at each other, calling, "Let it rain! Wash away the traces of the Communists!" He passed some farmers heading into the city, carts laden with food and supplies for the Latvian Army. Everywhere he heard talk of freedom—Latvia would be independent again now that the Soviets were gone.

The Germans had different plans. There was never an intention of allowing Latvia, or the other Baltic nations, to regain independence or any degree of autonomy. Hitler held a conference on February 3, 1941 to assess the progress of Operation Barbarossa planning, during which he stated, "When it is carried out, it must be remembered that the *main aim* is to gain possession of the Baltic States and Leningrad." Hitler opposed autonomy or self-government for occupied territories; the goal of *lebensraum* was to create areas for German settlement. Any people who could not be "Germanized" were to be removed or eliminated:

> The objective of a *Reichskommissariat* [administrative entity in occupied territory headed by a government official] for Estonia, Latvia…must be to strive for a form of German protectorate, and

then through Germanisation of racially acceptable elements, colonization by German people, and deportation of unwanted elements, to turn this region into a part of the Greater German Reich.[1]

Latvia and Estonia were designated for complete colonization within twenty to thirty years. Only fifty percent of Latvians met the criteria for Germanization; the rest would be transferred to Russia and Belarus. The relocation idea was not original: Hitler modeled his ideas about how to deal with undesirable local ethnic populations on the settlement of North America and the colonists' treatment of its indigenous peoples. Latvia was to be incorporated into the occupied territory known as *Ostland* (Eastern Territory), comprising Latvia, Lithuania, Estonia, and part of Belarus. If the Latvians hoped the German occupation would result in their independence, they were tragically mistaken. The Germans exploited that misguided hope to recruit support for their regime.

From the start of the occupation, the Germans treated Latvia as a hostile territory with the intention of eradicating any vestiges of nationalism. The Nazis imposed martial law immediately and ordered citizens to surrender all weapons, observe a curfew, and disband all national and political organizations. In order to efficiently rule the occupied territory, the Nazis created a local civil administration called the *Pašpārvalde* (Self-Administration). This administration was to keep the occupation regime running smoothly by appointing local officials. The Self-Administration was a political eunuch, relegated to following Nazi orders with no decision-making power or authority of its own.[2]

The executional details of Rosenberg's *Generalplan Ost* depended on the populations involved. For Jews, the plan was complete extermination. Slavs, considered *Untermensch* (sub-human), were to be starved, deprived of medical care, and sterilized in order to achieve eventual elimination. On the National Socialist racial hierarchy, Latvians and Lithuanians fell between the Slavs and German Master Race (*Herrenvolk*): fit to serve but unfit to receive full benefits of citizenship.[3]

The Nazi regime functioned similarly in all of the occupied territories. As soon as the first military units entered and strategically secured an occupied territory, they were followed by the *Einsaztzgruppen*, known as mobile killing units. *Einsatzgruppe A*, headed by SS Brigadenführer Walter Stahlecker, followed Army Group North into Latvia. Once the Soviets were driven out, Army Group North was deployed to Lithuania to continue their takeover mission. *Einsatzgruppe A* went to work swiftly, beginning the Latvian Holocaust.

Simplified Choices

Silences. Silence to my parents, particularly my mother, meant burying pain: what they witnessed, what they felt, deep inside, kept from light and air in an effort to smother it, as if it was a weed. Silence about the war. Silence about the Holocaust. Silence about leaving Latvia. Silence about their pain. Perhaps they talked to each other, perhaps not. I didn't witness it. Did it work? Did the silence fade the pain, make it wither and die? Or did they simply not heal?

By watching them, I learned silence. When pain arose, I learned to bury it, to deprive it of light and air, just as they did. It cost me. When my husband and I encountered problems fairly early in our marriage, we did not speak about them. His reasons for keeping silent were different than mine, but the result was the same. Things got worse. Our marriage fell apart. We eventually picked up the pieces and put them back together, but it was a long, painful process—one we almost did not make it through. The seductive power of silence is the promise of avoiding pain. Instead, silence betrayed me. It was supposed to keep the pain away. It didn't.

Chapter 10

Forever No Peace Beneath Latvia's Birches

June 23, 1941–1944

The Latvian Holocaust.

The first I heard of it was on that Paris-bound train in 1977 from Ari, the young man sharing my compartment. At the time, I was in disbelief. Yet, later that summer, when I drank that Heineken on the porch with my father, I did not ask him directly about the Holocaust, and whether or not one had occurred on Latvian soil. I already knew the answer, without having consulted any history books. Instead, I asked him if Latvians joined the Nazis—and more specifically, if he had fought on their side. He began his answer with the words, "You have to understand…" That opening sentence spoke volumes. To me, it confirmed that there was a Holocaust in Latvia. It confirmed that my father had served on the Nazi side, though he did not share their ideology. And it confirmed that my father was not proud of this history.

But it also asked for understanding. And understanding is what I sought as I began my research. Understanding begins to answer the questions "Why?" and "How?" I cannot speak for all Latvians, only

SIMPLIFIED CHOICES

the people I know, particularly my father. Since the past cannot be changed, understanding the why and how are all we have left to learn from, to avoid repeating the past.

Sane human beings who value and respect life find it difficult to comprehend the atrocities that occurred. For anyone wishing to learn more, I recommend Andrew Ezergailis' excellent book *The Holocaust in Latvia*, as well as more recent works published by the Symposium of the Commission of the Historians of Latvia. For context, here are the major facts to provide the scope of what occurred in Latvia.

Latvia was the first occupied territory to have mass killings that began only a week after the Germans arrived. The Germans invaded in mid-June 1941. By the end of December 1941, approximately ninety-one percent of Latvia's 66,000 Jews were killed. Formerly historians believed there was an interregnum, an extended period of a power vacuum, between the withdrawal of the Soviets and the establishment of the Nazi regime, during which Latvian nationalists attacked Jews and any Soviet Communists they could find. More recently, researchers have discovered evidence that this was not the case. Upon arrival, the Nazis tried to spur ethnic Latvians into violence against the Jews, referred to at the Nuremberg Tribunal as "self-cleansing." It did not work. Spontaneous violence against the Jews proved difficult to instigate as ethnic Latvians were generally unresponsive. A quicker solution was required to meet the Nazi goal of eliminating the Jewish population in its entirety.

Most of the Latvian Jewish population was killed in two phases. The *Einsatzgruppen phase* lasted July–October 1941, during which the entire rural Jewish population of about 24,000 was killed. This was an organized process. First, district police chiefs took a census of their area, after which Jews were ordered to report to a designated location. They were either shot on the spot or transported elsewhere to be killed. Latvian Auxiliary Order Police performed the killings under orders issued by the German security police and *Einsatzgruppen A*.[1] Members of these local forces were carefully selected: "When attaching

Lithouanian and Latvian detachments to the execution squads, men were chosen whose relatives had been murdered or removed by the Russians."[2] The Nazis looked for angry men who sought revenge and misdirected that anger against innocent people.

In the larger cities of Riga, Daugavpils, and Liepāja, Jews were registered and incarcerated in ghettos and used as laborers. Biķernieki Pines (Mežaparks) was the site of the first Riga mass killings. In addition to Germans, Latvian police battalions and the Arājs Commando were involved. Arājs men and police arrested the targeted people, brought them to Riga Central Prison for a few days, then drove them by truck at night to Biķernieki Pines, where they were shot in pits dug by Russian POWs. The pace was too slow for Himmler. He dispatched Friedrich Jeckeln, commander of the *Einsatzgruppen*, to Latvia.

The second phase began with Jeckeln's arrival—the man who planned and organized the mass executions at Rumbula Forest. Today, the Rumbula train station is an unassuming whistle stop, surrounded by tall pines. Just a kilometer away is the Rumbula Forest Memorial, a peaceful wooded park that witnessed the most grotesque, inhumane behavior possible. Quiet paths lead the visitor through the pines, stones engraved with the victims' names, and grassy mounds where shooting pits were located. This is the site of the largest massacre in Latvian history. Not only that—except for Babi Yar in Ukraine, it was the biggest single atrocity during the Holocaust.

On November 8 and December 8, 1941, 25,000 Jews were shot. Jeckeln developed a system in Ukraine that was employed in Latvia. To kill more efficiently, different stages of mass murder were assigned to a designated group of men: getting victims from the ghetto, marching them at a fierce pace to the killing site, stripping them of clothes and belongings, and shooting them. Even seasoned killers in the *Einsatzgruppen* were reportedly shocked at the barbarous manner of shooting: "sardine packing," a method where victims were first driven into the pits, ordered to lie down, then shot with a bullet in the back of

SIMPLIFIED CHOICES

the head. The second wave of victims was then driven into the pits, ordered to lie down on top of the previous victims (many of whom were still alive) and shot. The killing went on for hours. Besides the Germans, an estimated 1,000 Latvians took an active role in the slaughter: the Arājs Commando, the Latvian ghetto guard, and precinct police drove the Jews out of their homes, marched them to the site, and maintained order prior to execution, making sure no one escaped. A precinct policeman later testified that they were told that the Jews were being marched to Rumbula for resettlement to a labor camp. Perhaps this is true. However, anyone reporting for duty on the second day of the massacre, December 8th, knew exactly what was going to happen.[3]

The inhumanity did not stop at Rumbula. There were other actions. With most of the Latvian Jews killed, the Nazis transported Jews from other occupied areas to Latvia to newly opened camps. Gas vans arrived in Latvia in 1941 after most of the killing was done, though it is unknown as to whether they were ever used. Besides Viktor Arājs, other Latvian names live on in infamy: Mārtiņš Vagulāns, Herberts Teidemanis, the local police chiefs. During the Nazi occupation, a total of 70,000 Jews and 18,000 ethnic Latvians were executed in Latvia. There were also approximately 2,000 Roma and 2,271 civilians with mental health issues killed.[4]

How could this have happened in Latvia? I turned to historical research and my father to understand.

History changes. Facts are interpreted by people, sometimes according to a narrative they wish to present to the world. The responsibility for the Latvian Holocaust is no different; over the years, the interpretation has changed. The second Soviet regime (1945–1991) firmly put the blame for the mass killings on Fascists and Latvian nationalists. In the 1970s, a series of KGB pamphlets accused ethnic

Latvians of killing thousands of Jews prior to the German occupation. Historian Ezergailis points out that the pamphlets largely contained false information but the perception of ethnic Latvians as initiating killings took hold among historians in the West.[5] It is likely that Ari was familiar with these pamphlets when he confronted me on that French train. However, there is no evidence that supports the claims made therein. Besides containing false information, this interpretation ignores Stalin's role. The preamble to World War II was the collaboration between the Soviet Union and Nazi Germany: the secret protocols of the Molotov–Ribbentrop Pact in which the two powers agreed to divide and annex certain territories. This non-aggression pact made it possible for Hitler to invade Poland. Historian Timothy Snyder points out that Stalin later revised the Soviet Union's role in World War II as the "Great Patriotic War" that began in 1941. To have done otherwise would have assumed some of the blame for what happened in the annexed territories.[6]

When writing about the German occupation, diaspora authors from the 1960s–early 1980s consistently put responsibility for the Holocaust squarely on the Nazis and did not examine the role of the Latvians. The reason that Latvians tolerated the Nazi regime was directly attributed to the brutality of the 1940–1941 Soviet repressions. In this viewpoint, Latvians were not collaborating with Nazis; they were doing what they had to do in order to rid the country of Communists and regain Latvia's sovereignty. Many diaspora communities embraced this line of reasoning.

This position is defensive and inaccurate. Some Latvians participated in the killings, either directly or indirectly: the Arājs Commando, other Latvian SD units, and local police units. Contemporary historians estimate that number to be relatively small, no higher than a few thousand. Others were Nazi collaborators, directed by German supervisors, working in low level administrative positions, and signing new laws: not arresting or shooting, but performing duties to help the Nazi regime run. Some Latvians tried to save Jews; historian Marġers Vestermanis has compiled a list of about four hundred Latvians who saved Jews, assisted by hundreds of others.[7]

The majority of ethnic Latvians fall into a category described by some historians as bystanders: not actively involved in killing or saving Jews. They did not support the Nazi philosophy and refused to participate in pogroms, nor did they risk their lives to save their Jewish neighbors. My father belonged to this category.

When an occupying power takes over, local residents are forced to adapt to sudden changes: who holds power, new governing structures, new laws, and, most importantly, how to survive. What will keep their families safe? The Nazi occupation was Latvia's second during World War II, immediately following the Soviet occupation. For obvious reasons, Latvian Jewish citizens preferred the Soviet regime over the Nazis. While many Jews were deported along with ethnic Latvians, the Soviets did not target them for extinction as did the Nazis. For ethnic Latvians, who had their lands stripped from them and collectivized, who had watched family and friends arrested, deported, or executed, the ousting of the Soviets was a welcome relief. Many Latvians, like Visvaldis, initially welcomed the Germans as liberators, ridding them of Soviet oppressors. As it quickly became clear, the Germans were hostile to any Latvian aspirations for regaining sovereignty. In my father's words, most Latvians came to see the Germans as another occupying regime—but it was one that did not directly target them. Again, the *as the master commands* mentality surfaced; they feared Nazi retribution against anyone protesting the changing order. Others still believed the Germans would restore Latvia's status as a sovereign state. And, of course, there were Nazi sympathizers.

Historians agree that the Nazi invasion resulted in the Latvian Holocaust. Prior to this, there is no evidence of organized violence in Latvia against Jews. Equal rights were guaranteed to minorities by the 1922 Latvian Constitution; there were no anti-Jewish laws. After World War I, Latvia was the first European nation to enshrine equality for Jews in its Constitution. While there was anti-Semitism, particularly among urban intellectual groups like Thunder Cross, the general population was not heavily anti-Semitic. When I asked my father about anti-Semitism where he lived, he replied, "We got along pretty well with the Jews. There weren't that many of them where we were." Demographically speaking, he was correct; most Jews lived in urban areas, like Riga or Daugavpils, not the country. The 1935 Census shows no Jewish households in his home town of Umurga so his contact would have been limited to larger centers, like Limbaži, where he attended high school.

During his dictatorship, Ulmanis banned anti-Semitic writings and kept the Latvian border open to Jewish refugees fleeing Poland longer than other countries, including Sweden. However, Ulmanis shut down ninety-five percent of the Latvian press, including twelve Jewish newspapers. This created a vacuum that was easily filled by Nazi propaganda during the occupation. Ulmanis also forbade press coverage of German atrocities in Poland or the Winter War in Finland, an ill-advised effort to keep the peace between Latvia, Hitler, and Stalin.[8] Had Latvian citizens been aware of the anti-Jewish violence in Poland, perhaps they would have seen the Nazis for what they truly were before the occupation.

How much did Latvians actually know? As the Nazis initiated mass killing actions, they took care to keep them secret. In criminal case files, Arājs Commando members stated that they were forbidden to speak of the massacres after the fact.[9] Most of the killing took place in the early morning hours in secluded locations to prevent witnesses from reporting what was happening. People who knew about the killing actions most likely had connections to the police or SD members. The exception to this was the Rumbula massacre; as the area was suburban, residents witnessed the columns of Jews being beaten or shot if they could not keep up the pace of the marching column. When interviewing diaspora Latvians, Ezergailis found that a surprisingly large number of Rigans did not know about Rumbula or other actions.

My father matriculated in 1940 and studied at the University of Latvia until 1944; he witnessed both the Year of Terror and the Nazi occupation while he was in Riga. The University of Latvia is within walking distance of the Moscow suburbs, site of the first Latvian ghetto. Ezergailis discovered that about half of the diaspora Rigans he spoke with did not even know that the Riga ghetto existed. I find it difficult to believe that my father was among them; certainly he knew about the anti-Jewish laws that forbade Jews from purchasing goods or non-Jews from purchasing the goods on their behalf. These were widely publicized in Riga and other locations.

After the occupation, the Nazis sought to generate anti-Jewish sentiment among the local population by manufacturing a connection between Jews and Bolsheviks. While it is true that many Jews, particularly the youth, were members of the Communist Party, it is not true that all Jews were Communists. Plenty of ethnic Latvians were Communists who had supported the Soviet regime. As mass graves of victims from Soviet executions were discovered, the Nazis displayed the mutilated bodies in plain sight, claiming that the Jewish *chekists* were responsible for the atrocities. They were not, but the traumatized population seeing the bodies did not question this.

My father was certainly exposed to Nazi propaganda linking Jews with Bolshevism. Almost immediately, Nazis imposed complete control over the Latvian press. Newspapers were the main source of news and, hence, the primary vehicle for distributing propaganda. The Nazi newspaper *Tēvija* was published on July 1, 1941. A day later, *Tēvija* was distributed to all districts. Other regional papers were published as well, with the objective of establishing a false connection between Jews and Communist repressions, particularly those committed by the *cheka*. The term "Bolshevik Jew" was frequently used. Radios were common in the cities, less so in the country, so they were of limited use in disseminating propaganda. My maternal grandfather only obtained electricity and a radio in 1970.

A photo book called *Baigais gads* (*The Year of Terror*), published in

1942, featured disturbing photographs of atrocities committed during the first Soviet occupation with text emphasizing the close collaboration of Latvian Jews with the Bolsheviks and their role as repressors of the Latvians. My father mentioned this book as a documentary of the first Soviet occupation. He did not have a copy so I looked online; the Nazi propaganda was evident to me immediately, but I had the benefit of current knowledge. What would someone living in Riga, bombarded by pictures, newspaper articles, posters, and exhumed bodies have thought?

The same year, a documentary film called *Sarkanā migla* (*The Red Fog*) was produced to achieve the same end. Shot in black and white, the film features dramatic background music while graphic images of torture, such as corpses with tongues or eyes gouged out flash across the screen. The narrator labels Jews as Bolshevik torturers while German soldiers are described as "liberators" fighting to eliminate Bolshevism across Europe so all people can coexist peacefully. Historian Arturs Žvinklis notes that by the time both the book and film were distributed, most of the Jews in Latvia were already dead.[10] Still, both the photo book and the film had a powerful effect on public opinion.

Some historians observe that the Ulmanis authoritarian regime did not encourage independent thinking or free speech against the government.[11] My father and his peers came of age during this time, and did not question the powers that ran the country. Obedience to the state was expected, another example of *as the master commands* mentality. The Nazi regime was militaristic and oppressive, not friendly and cooperative. My father felt the danger of the new order. He kept his head down, his mouth shut, and concentrated on his studies. My father also had a tendency to think in black and white terms. I could see this in his anger at Russians, for example. The Bolsheviks who annexed Latvia in 1940 were Russians. Therefore, to him all Russians were Bolsheviks. The connection between Jews and Communists was made repeatedly in the press, so there was no reason to question. The narrative fit.

I was raised believing I was a Latvian because I was culturally literate. I spoke, read, and wrote Latvian, could prepare the food, dance the folk dances, and sing the folk songs. I had a clear understanding of how Latvians suffered under the Soviet regime. I was raised to be a defender of Latvian culture against the ethnocide Stalin began, the eradication of Latvian identity that continued until independence was regained in 1991. This is what my parents and their peers chose to teach me and other Latvian Americans in my generation.

We missed a big part of what it means to be Latvian. To be a Latvian is to recognize, learn about, and understand what our fatherland went through during World War II. Including the Holocaust. Understanding is not the same as excusing, something the diaspora authors in the 1960s and 1970s did. Almost the entire Jewish population of Latvia was killed in one year. The Holocaust is part of our history, our identity. I wish we had learned that in Latvian school. To me, it is a lost opportunity. I understand the pain caused by the Soviet occupations. What is missing is an exploration of the pain caused by the Nazi occupation. What did my parents and their friends feel as the Nazis arrested and killed Jews? How much did they really understand about the Nazi goal of total elimination of Jews? Reading about it now, I feel the pain of being Latvian in a more complete way. I wish my parents had been willing to talk about it more openly with me. We should have commemorated the dates of the Rumbula massacre, just as we commemorated the dates of the Soviet deportations. Our collective folk memory holds a great deal of pain from centuries of serfdom, wars, occupations, repressions, killings. We hear it in our folk songs.

The land knows. The land has always known. The land will not forget. There is a Latvian folk song, *Forever Blue are Latvia's Hills*, that comes to my mind when I think about the pain the Latvian people—all of the Latvian people, not just ethnic Latvians—lived through during this time:

> Forever blue are Latvia's hills,
> Forever no peace beneath Latvia's birches,
> Forever the kokle weeps over Latvia's hills.
> Broken are our forefather's sacrificial vessels,
> Lost in mists are the fields of our homeland,
> In the forest under the ancient branches
> There is no peace for the shades of our forefathers.[12]

The peaceful land at Rumbula tells the truth. There is no peace beneath Latvia's birches.

Simplified Choices

One night, my husband and I were having dinner with some friends. Among us, we had a history buff, a social studies teacher, and a high school English teacher—all educated people with a solid knowledge of history. At this time, I had just begun researching my uncle's experience as a legionnaire. As I explained that the Latvian Legion was subordinated to the Nazi forces, I could see the shock registering on their faces, similar to my initial reaction of realizing my uncle fought on the wrong side. Even these friends, educated as they were, did not know how many troops fought under the Nazis. They did not know that the Nazis treated any country they invaded as a hostile territory and conscripted men to fight on their side. I explained my father's viewpoint of "simplified choices," the weighing of difficult options and choosing the one with the greatest chance of survival for him and his family.

What would you do, I asked them, if you knew the Nazis would either shoot you or send you to the front anyway? What if they punished your family? What would you do if you and your family could be killed or sent to a concentration camp for aiding Jews?

Every one of them admitted that they probably would do everything in their power to protect their families. When the choices are between wrong and wrong, the one that offers the best chance of survival usually wins. When people choose to be on the wrong side of history, there are reasons. But they are still wrong.

Chapter 11

Life is a Struggle

Arnolds Bērziņš. Author's collection.

I knew very little about my Uncle Arnolds. As with other painful subjects, my mother did not talk about him, other than saying that he died fighting for Latvia. She had only two pictures of him: one of their mutual confirmation day (see Chapter 5) and the one shown here. His physical resemblance to my oldest son, particularly his eyes, touched me. We were connected by blood. I wanted to find out as much as I could about him, to make him more alive, to create a memory. He lived a short life and left a light footprint upon the earth. I would have to do some searching.

Most of the information I had about Arnolds came from the four letters I found in my father's desk drawer, given to my mother by her sister, Rita, in 1989. The letters revealed some of his personality and a little information about his wartime experiences, but I sought more. To that end, I contacted the Latvian War Museum that maintains a database of the men who served in the Latvian Legion. With their assistance, I learned of Arnolds' mobilization date, his training, and gained an approximate idea of his unit's assignments. By combining the information from the museum, Arnolds' letters, and information about the Latvian Legion's engagements, I was able to flesh out his wartime movements. Slowly, my uncle was becoming real to me.

In Latvia, the Nazi occupation entered another phase on January 23, 1943, when Hitler issued orders to form a voluntary Latvian Legion. The term "voluntary" was a matter of semantics, disguising the violation of the 1907 Hague International Convention; Article 52 specifically prohibits an occupying power to "involve inhabitants in the obligation of taking part in military operations against their own country."[1] When they first entered Latvia, the Nazis confiscated citizens' weaponry, including hunting rifles, and forbade formation of any national groups that might resemble armed forces. The order to form the Legion was needs-driven; the war was not going well for Germany and more soldiers were required.

My parents kept a collection of Latvian albums, recorded by diaspora musicians. They played them repeatedly, wearing down the grooves until you could hear the crackle and catch of a well-loved piece of music between songs. One of my father's fraternity brothers formed a trio that recorded my parents' favorite albums, often featuring songs I did not know. Most of my knowledge came from singing lessons in Latvian school. The songs on these albums dealt with mature topics, like love, exile, or war. This was one of my personal favorites, dealing with the foregone conclusion of the conscription:

> You have no luck in life,
> So said the fortune teller,
> Just sorrowful memories and goodbyes.
> Do not tell me anymore about my fate,
> For I know that my path is in the East.[2]

Conscription in Latvia began in March 1943 with the *Musterung*, a physical screening of eligible men. All men born 1919–1925 were ordered to report for the screening and, if they passed, were drafted. Local police prepared lists of eligible men. This was not optional; anyone avoiding service would be punished as a deserter, by execution or imprisonment. The Nazis rejected few draftees; the physically suitable fought on the Eastern Front, with those not meeting Nazi standards funneled into civil labor service.

I assumed that Arnolds was drafted, like the majority of Latvians who served in the Nazi armed forces. Only fifteen to twenty percent actually volunteered for service. When I spoke with Aunt Aina in 2023, I learned that Arnolds had, in fact, voluntarily enlisted, though not for his political views or any shared ideology with the Nazis. For Arnolds, the war offered a chance to escape a bad family situation. His father, Jānis, had begun an affair with a local woman. Nītaure was a tiny village, so there was no way to discreetly see her. The entire village undoubtedly knew what was going on. Arnolds, the legal owner of the family farm Kubļi, enlisted, saying, "I am ashamed of such a father. I won't stay here any longer." He also believed, as did most legionnaires, that he was defending his homeland from another Soviet occupation. Enlisting was not about fighting for the Nazis; it was about fighting for Latvia. At the time, Arnolds planned a future: he attended the vocational school of the State Electrotechnical Factory (*Valsts elektrotehniskā fabrika, or VEF*). Being a healthy 20-year-old, country-boy strong, he was selected for the Latvian Legion, mobilized on November 3, 1943, and sent to Liepāja.[3]

There, candidates were evaluated for the formation of a Zenith anti-artillery unit. An artillerist needed mathematical knowledge in order to operate the cannons with accuracy. To his relief, Arnolds passed the evaluation, reassuring Aina that it was safer than infantry positions. He received his assignment: Second Brigade of the Zenith Artillery, First Battery division.[4]

His first letter, dated November 21, 1943, was hastily scribbled from Riga on his way to Germany. At this point, Arnolds had completed training in Liepāja and was heading out for specialized artillerist training: "Things did not go badly for me in Liepāja and they will not go badly in Germany either… The service there will be tough but after that when I return, I will have more free time." The damp climate of Liepāja gave him a case of laryngitis, but otherwise he felt fine. Thanking his sister for a package she sent, he noted that he still needed soap as that had not been distributed. Arnolds also foreshadowed some of the difficulties soldiers would experience: "Too bad that my suitcase cannot be packed full with food because that will be harder to get in Germany. But all has to be overcome. Life is a struggle."[5] There were no letters from him for another year.

In spite of Arnolds' positive attitude, the division was far from combat-ready. The soldiers slept on wooden bunk beds, with a portion of the recruits sleeping on straw mats in the corridor due to a shortage of rooms and beds. Although they had uniforms, the coats were ill-fitting, often too small or long. There was a lack of winter clothing, particularly new sweaters; the warehouse had only old, threadbare sweaters requisitioned from citizens. Footwear posed an even bigger problem; most of the boots provided were too small or in need of repair. The soldiers received guns, but no target practice had occurred yet as there was no ammunition. The unit also had a mix of anti-aircraft cannons, designed to be attached to tractors or heavy trucks.Those vehicles had not yet arrived, so the unit was incapable of movement. There was much to learn before the battalion was fully prepared for combat.[6]

Following his unit assignment, Arnolds transferred to Schongau, Germany near the Bavarian Alps for *Flugmelder* (flight detector) courses. He also attended a course in aircraft recognition from November 26 — December 17, 1943, completing it with a "Very Good" rating.[7] Arnolds was now an aircraft spotter, using a telescope to locate and identify enemy aircraft. He worked in a battery that operated four 88 mm anti-aircraft cannons, the backbone of German aircraft defense. These cannons were known as Zenith because the muzzle of the gun was often aimed nearly vertically. The 88 mm guns were powerful and accurate against both aircraft and armored vehicles. An apocryphal story often attributed to a United States infantryman describes the 88 mm anti-aircraft guns as "anti-everything."

Returning from training, Arnolds and his unit deployed to support the Second Latvian SS Volunteer Brigade, renamed the 19th Latvian SS Volunteer Division in January 1944, that was attached to the German VI SS Army Corps. Due to the lack of surviving documentation about the specific activities of the 19th Latvian, I made some assumptions about where Arnolds and his unit were based on what is known about the Latvian Legion's military engagements. The map herein covers the movements of his time in Russia.

SIMPLIFIED CHOICES

THE VOLKHOV FRONT AND 19TH LATVIAN MOVEMENTS

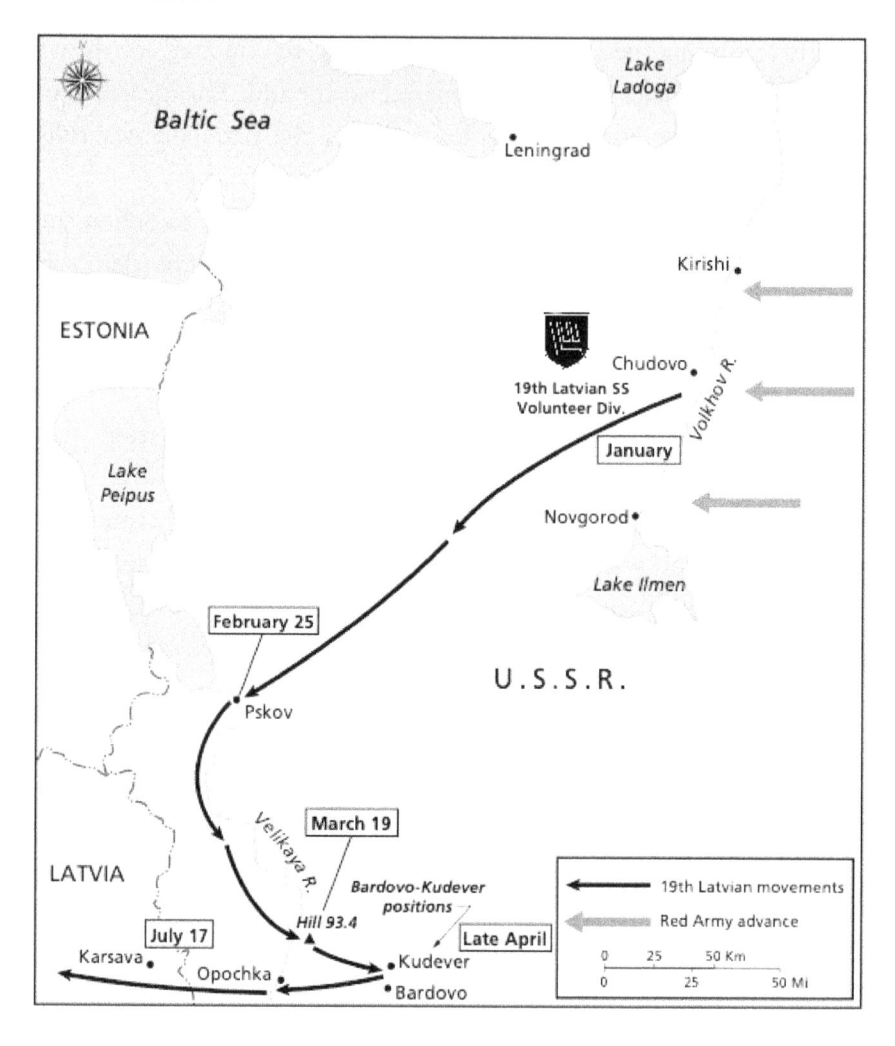

Arnolds' specific unit, the Second Brigade of the Zenith Artillery, supported the 19th Latvian in all major battles. During January–February 1944, the 19th Latvian fought along the Volkhov River, south of Lake Ladoga. It was a frozen, miserable slog. Deep snow, no roads, swamps, and almost constant engagements with the advancing

Red Army forced their retreat southeast to the Pskov area by the end of February.[8]

The 19th Latvian moved to the Velikaya River, where it fought a series of bloody engagements throughout March defending Hill 93.4, a critical defensive position on the river's east bank.[9] In spite of daily battles, there was little territorial gain by either side. In mid-April, a new challenge appeared: the arrival of spring, when the frozen ground thawed into deep mud. Heavy equipment like the artillery Arnolds manned sank into the mire and was almost impossible to move. With great difficulty maneuvering the artillery, the 19th Latvian and its accompanying German VI SS Corps retreated to Bardovo–Kudever, where they fought through June.

On June 23, 1944, the Soviets began their massive offensive, Operation Bagration, along multiple points on the Eastern Front. Unable to fight off the attacks, German high command ordered a retreat from Bardovo–Kudever on July 9. Leaving under cover of a thick fog, the Latvians and Germans crossed the Velikaya to the western shore. Only one bridge near Opachka was intact. Many men waded, swam, or crossed on jury-rigged rafts. By July 17, the entire VI SS Corps, including both Latvian divisions, crossed the Latvian–Russian border east of Karsava, Lettgalia.[10]

The fighting now shifted to Latvia. Arnolds was back in his homeland, though not under the circumstances he hoped for. The fight to hold the Volkhov area resulted in heavy losses. Exhausted and in desperate need of reinforcements, the men did not even get a chance to bathe and delouse themselves. The Red Army pursued the retreating German forces westward during the dry weather. Eventually, autumn rains would begin and they would be bogged down in the swamps and woods of Latvia. Undermanned and lacking ammunition for the artillery, the Latvians were pushed back further west into Livonia by the beginning of August, retreating under constant fighting.[11]

By mid-September, Arnolds and the 19th Latvian found themselves fighting in the area surrounding his village, Nītaure. Arnolds' second letter, dated January 13, 1945, mentions passing through Nītaure on September 26 looking for news of his family, but the village was empty. He wrote a message on the windowsill of a village house in hopes that his family would learn that he was alive and safe. With the fighting advancing deeper into Latvia, this detour posed a significant risk. Happenstance intervened: while leaving the area, he met a boy along the road who told him that his division had already moved on, retreating westward toward Courland. He rushed to join them to avoid capture by Red Army soldiers, who undoubtedly would have shot him on the spot. The area, once so familiar, bore the scars of warfare: "From Zavadas looking toward Laġi was like looking at a palm [of a hand] because the forest between them was chopped down and trenches dug along the swamp's edge. I cannot believe that Laġi [his father's birthplace] remained intact, because the front was there for about a week."[12] Cutting down forests was common practice among the Germans and Latvians; the thick trees offered advantageous cover to the Red Army.

By now, with military engagements occurring daily, many Latvian civilians packed a few belongings and fled westward—on foot or in horse-drawn carts—to avoid getting trapped in Soviet controlled territories. They had good reason to fear the Soviets; as areas of Latvia were "liberated," young men were conscripted into the Red Army. Women were frequently raped by Soviet soldiers. What little food remained was requisitioned. Most of all, the Latvians feared a Soviet takeover, still recalling the arrests and executions of The Year of Terror. As refugees flooded the roads, the soldiers anxiously scanned the crowds, looking for a familiar face that might have news of their families.

With the Red Army pressing in on Riga, the Germans announced complete evacuation of the capital city. The order did not reflect concern for civilians; rather, the Germans wanted to make sure the able-bodied could not be conscripted by Soviet occupiers for either labor or military duty. Codenamed "Donner" (Thunder), it was a scorched earth retreat. The Germans burned or blew up any structures that could be of value to the Soviets. By midnight, October 12, after the last members of the German military had left the area, German engineers blew up two bridges over the Daugava River. The Red Army occupied Riga on October 13, declaring its liberation from the fascist Nazi powers and its re-occupation by the Communists. The last phase of the war on the Latvian Front began: the defense of Courland.[13]

Depending on the source, this portion of the campaign has different names: the Courland Pocket, the Courland Kettle, Courland Fortress, or the Courland Bridgehead. Latvians typically refer to it as the Courland Fortress (*Kurzemes cietoksnis*), which I thought referred to Hitler's standing order to fight to the last man. Historian Edgars Dunsdorfs offers another explanation. After the retreat to Courland, Germany was no longer accessible by land. The word *cietoksnis* has multiple meanings, one of which is "place of imprisonment." Hence, in his explanation, Latvian soldiers knew they were trapped until the war ended.[14]

The 19th Latvian and other German divisions fought a total of six battles in Courland, all with the objective of keeping the port city Liepāja from the Red Army. Other divisions of the Waffen SS, including Swedish, Belgian, Dutch, and Italian troops, joined. Courland's damp climate brought on heavy rains, dense fog, and swampy soil that filled any freshly dug holes with water soon after the shovel hit the earth. Soldiers lined bunkers with wood to keep from sinking. During the first battle, Arnolds' battalion was pressed into service for targets other than aircraft, shooting anything large enough to warrant the power of the 88 mm cannons. The Red Army discontinued attacks on October 22, ending the battle.

For most of November and December, the area of Courland where the 19th Latvian dug in remained relatively quiet. Under the slate-gray winter sky and the handful of hours between dawn and dusk, a sense of calm—even boredom—settled in among the men in the bunkers. Christmas, beloved by the Lutheran and Catholic soldiers alike, was

SIMPLIFIED CHOICES

coming. The 19th Latvian looked forward to a Christmas celebration, that, in soldier parlance, meant they had obtained some vodka. Men wrote letters home and made playful bets with each other about which of the lucky ones would receive Christmas packages from loved ones. They filled spent cartridges with yellow fat to use as candles, decorating small evergreen trees they cut in the nearby forests, dreaming of past holidays.[15] Many of the soldiers were teenagers, spending their second Christmas away from home.

The Red Army had other plans. Instead of playing cards, singing carols, and enjoying a stiff drink, the Latvians found themselves in one of the most intense engagements of the Courland Fortress. Arnolds wrote, "For us here, Christmas was spent during fierce battles, so understandably it was impossible to have the holiday spirit. All ended fortunately, although the entire time was spent in bigger or smaller battles. We were all prepared to celebrate the holidays, but those cursed Russians began their attack on December 23rd."[16] The attack began with a heavy artillery barrage along the entire 19th Latvian sector. Legionnaire Alberts Eglītis described the start in his diary: "Suddenly, the entire woodland border was dancing [with light]. Dark red streaks of flames, countless heavy caliber roars, countless mortar batteries bursting. The great silence was gone. Only whining explosions, whistling iron shards, and clods of flying earth. Every light in the bunkers was extinguished. The burning air blew the men's clothes and boiled their blood."[17]

There were an estimated five hundred aircraft actively bombing the sector. During one battle on a particularly swampy piece of terrain, the 506th and other artillery units became the only means of defense against the Soviet airborne assault that ended December 31. Although accurate accounts are difficult to obtain, one source cites the Zenith Artillery as shooting down one hundred twelve aircraft during this time.[18]

For Latvians, the greatest tragedy of the Christmas battles was the result of the Soviet conscription of many young Latvian men as they occupied Livonia. Regardless of which side they were on, Latvians fought their own countrymen, in some cases, literally their brothers. The weather turned bitterly cold, adding to their discomfort. Arnolds wrote, "We spent New Year's in a stable because if you do not want to freeze to death on the field you have to get used to that kind of living. I am lucky that I was safe and healthy and able to greet the New Year."[19]

By January 12, 1945, the Red Army entered Germany. Seven divisions left Courland to go to the homeland's defense, weakening the forces left in Latvia. A mere ten days after Arnolds wrote the previous letter, the 19th Latvian engaged again. Liepāja and the surrounding towns were now overrun with refugees from the eastern parts of Latvia. The loss of this critical port would be disastrous. Given the constant fight-retreat cycle, the 19th Latvian and other units must have known the end was near, but they continued to fight and repel the Soviet assaults. Once again, Mother Nature intervened with the arrival of spring weather in the beginning of March. Frozen ground turned to the familiar soft brown sludge, trapping vehicles and boots, so the battle ended March 14.[20]

At some point during a lull in the fighting, Arnolds penned another letter to his sister, dated March 1st. Written from the bunker, he apologized for not having written sooner: "I could not answer right away because we were plagued by fierce fighting. Now everything is quiet and calm again. There were pretty wild days, but all the same, everything went luckily. This commotion, compared with Christmas, was a cinch!" He expressed his fear that the rest of his family may not have escaped from Livonia before the Soviets crossed the border: "I think that many did not get out of that corner. Fate is dreadful but we cannot do anything about that. Let us hope that, in the end, it will not be that horrible..." This letter was more reflective of Arnolds' emotional state, and voiced a common fear among the young men forced to make war a way of life:

I am also satisfied with the life of a soldier. It is not pleasant, but all the same, it has its own beauty and attractiveness. Sometimes thinking about the old peacetime life, after this kind of life it would be difficult to get used to the old life again. Living here, we have gotten spoiled, like soldiers do. We are no longer used to work. Personally, I cannot imagine that I could work like I used to work back home.

Arnolds also departed from his previously upbeat letters in which he sought to reassure his sister that all was well. He described a gruesome sight he witnessed during the recent battle:

A few days ago we forced the Russians back in one place and some horrible sights were revealed. We found seven women and all had gunshots to the head. After this sight, our hatred for the Russians increased. You cannot imagine the feelings we had seeing all of that.[21]

Although he does not specifically call it out, the women were undoubtedly raped, as was the common practice. By now, his sister had seen her share of wartime brutality, so there was no innocence left to protect. He closes the letter by reporting that he was awarded the Iron Cross, Second Class, on January 30. Records show that the date of the ceremony was actually January 26.[22] The Iron Cross, Second Class was awarded for bravery in combat; it was likely given to Arnolds for the artillerists' relentless stand during the Christmas battles.

Pressure from the Red Army did not subside. Remarkably, the Latvian legionnaires continued to exhibit their determined fighting spirit in spite of the obvious defeat just ahead of them. Many surviving legionnaires have stated that, during the war, they believed the United States and Great Britain would never allow the Soviet Union to annex Latvia again. They were determined to spill their last drop of blood for Latvia's freedom, to save their ancestral lands.

On March 14, Arnolds wrote his final letter to his sister, in which he expressed optimism and pride in his unit: "I am sure you will have heard and read a lot about our 19th division. Our commander has said that the Kurzemes [Courland] soldiers are the best in the world, and we are the best in Kurzeme, in other words, the best of the best. Therefore, sister, you can be proud that your brother is fighting here." Hardships continued to plague the soldiers, but Arnolds appeared to have accepted them with stoic grace. He and his fellow soldiers learned to survive under the current conditions, finding warm lodging in a stable or foraging for food:

> During the days, it is nonstop work, and the nights are spent under the open skies or in a stable if we find one. The last several days were very cold and that is why I did not want to write. Now I am back in the fighting region, now it is calmer, but things could flare up again at any moment...food is also very good because we have the chance to look for something ourselves.

In conclusion, he reassured her, "Do not be afraid for me, sister, I am very sorry for everyone else." He signed the letter, "Until we meet again."[23]

The Red Army captured Liepāja on April 4, 1945. There were no more battles on Latvian soil. It was over. Hitler ingested cyanide and shot himself in the head on April 30. On May 8, 1945, General Alfred Jodl, Chief of Staff of the German Army, unconditionally surrendered to the Allies at General Dwight D. Eisenhower's headquarters in Reims.

The legionnaires and their commanders hoped to surrender to the British or Americans, but that did not occur. Some escaped into the nearby woods, hiding out and joining partisan bands that would fight the Soviet occupiers for years to come. Others committed suicide rather than surrender to the Soviets. Approximately 14,000 were arrested and sent to Gulag labor camps, where most of them perished under the harsh conditions. Many were executed on the spot by the

Red Army. In all, the Nazis mobilized about 110,000 men during their occupation of Latvia. Of these, roughly 52,000 served in the Latvian Legion. The majority did not survive the war. [24]

Arnolds was one of them. For years, the Bērziņš family had no news of him; they assumed he died on the battlefield, but knew none of the details. In his first letter to Aunt Elvīra, dated June 10, 1957, my grandfather Jānis wrote, "Arnolds died on the battlefield, it seems beyond doubt, though for nothing." My father told me that Aunt Aina had written that he was killed near Remte, Courland, but the circumstances were unknown. The Latvian War Museum did not have his name listed among the dead or missing legionnaires. They suggested that perhaps he had been sent to the Gulag as a POW, where he undoubtedly perished.

———

I thought that was the end of Arnolds' story. Like countless other families, we would never know what happened to him. One day in 2023, I was sorting family letters from Latvia when I came across a large brown envelope filled with old pictures of my children. My mother's organizational skills deteriorated for years prior to her death from Alzheimer's, so these never made it into a photo album. On a whim, I dumped the pictures out and rifled through them. There was an envelope addressed to my mother, no return address or date. Curious, I pulled out the letter—it was from one of Arnolds' classmates, Leonīds, who served in the same Zenith Artillery. Leonīds fought with Arnolds during the March battles, and witnessed his death near the town of Remte on March 22, 1945. My mother, it turns out, had never stopped trying to find out what happened to her brother. Here, shoved in amongst old snapshots, was the story of my uncle's death, never shared with me or my siblings, her pain buried in silence. Arnolds, the trained aircraft spotter, was scanning the skies with his telescope:

It was a sunny afternoon. In our area there was this period of silence. Then, suddenly, there was an explosion. It turned out that a Russian tank had crept up very close to our position and, as we thought, had observed the telescope's lens reflected in the sun, and shot a direct hit. Arnolds was struck with a fragment, right in the head. And so, his heart stopped beating that moment, without any suffering.[25]

Leonīds wrote that the survivors found a coffin in a nearby house and buried Arnolds in the Zantes cemetery, where he lay with other legionnaires who perished during the battles. Years later, another war colleague returned to the cemetery, but the area was overgrown with trees and new graves with tombstones were placed in the same location. Perhaps this answer to Arnolds' fate provided some measure of comfort to my mother and her family. As Leonīds wrote, "I feel your pain, Skaidrīte, but it is also fortunate to eternally sleep in the sands of your homeland. I was horribly afraid that I would remain in Siberia's barren lands. When I returned to our homeland, I no longer feared death."

Arnolds was reunited with Latvian soil. *Vieglas smiltis* Uncle—may the sands rest lightly.

Visvaldis and Elvīra were the glamorous members of our family. When I moved to New York City after college, they flew out from Ann Arbor and visited me for a long weekend. They took me to expensive French restaurants like Lutèce, so far out of my price range I could barely stand to look at the menus. They treated me to the Metropolitan Opera. We went to museums and the Rainbow Room for dancing.

On weekends, they were always well-dressed. Once, when I visited them, we went to walk near the dunes of Lake Michigan. When we returned to their apartment, they both showered and changed into their usual weekend garb: a skirt, silk blouse, and nylons for Elvīra, a suit and tie for Visvaldis. As he emerged from his dressing room, freshly shaven, adjusting his tie, he remarked, At last! Now I feel like a person again.

I had a different dress code for weekends. For me, that was a time to put the nylons aside and wear jeans. But then, I hadn't fled my homeland during war with only the clothes on my back.

Chapter 12

Every Man for Himself

March 1943–1945

After his physical screening and mobilization in March 1943, Visvaldis was presented with a choice: go into the army or industry. Mobilization orders stated that conscripts should be able to choose between military service or civil labor, but, in reality, this choice was seldom offered. No fool, Visvaldis chose industry and was instructed to report to the Riga shipyard the following day, renamed Rigaer Werft. The Nazis planned to build a military harbor; Visvaldis was put to work designing railroad tracks.

Simplified Choices

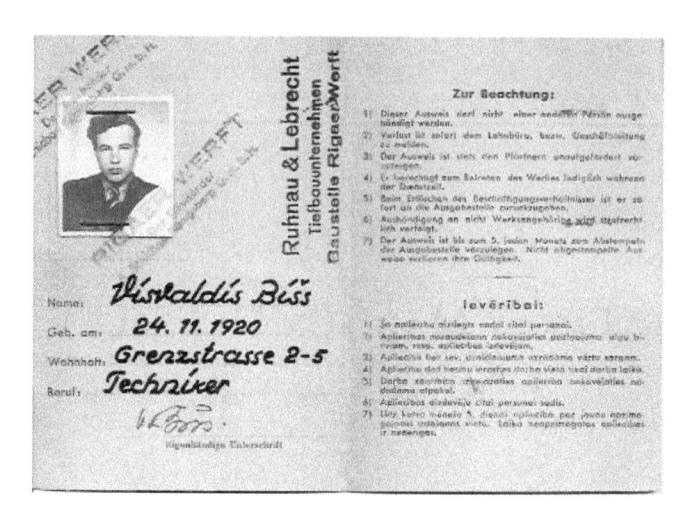

Visvaldis' work pass. Author's collection.

When it comes to surviving war, never dismiss the role of luck. Visvaldis had luck—sometimes disguised as misfortune—plus a survivor's instinct that kept him alive. In any difficult situation, he used his wits and charm to ease his way. First, he received the choice to work instead of fight. Some months later, good fortune appeared in the form of a cough that began in early winter and grew progressively worse. In February 1944 he was diagnosed with tuberculosis. He immediately reported to the sanatorium in Īle, housed in a former landowner's large Courland mansion.

Visvaldis spent his days convalescing, quietly sitting on the grounds or reading, in spite of the war raging only kilometers from the border. Before antibiotics were available, a tuberculosis patient was prescribed rest, fresh air, and food. Given what the rest of Europe was experiencing, Visvaldis drew a winning ticket.

The peace of the sanatorium was disturbed in June 1944, around the summer solstice celebration *Jāņi*, when the staff got word that the Germans were retreating. The fighting grew closer to Latvia's borders. Then word came that the Red Army crossed the southern border with tanks. Patients and staff needed to leave to avoid capture by the

Russians. Ever the charmer, Visvaldis employed his social graces and developed friendly relations with the sanatorium's two doctors. It paid off; the doctors invited him to leave with their families. They had two horse-drawn carts. Visvaldis, a recovering tuberculosis patient, walked but at least he could stash his suitcase on a cart. The group headed east for the port city of Liepāja. They came to a large house, where the proprietress invited them to eat some porridge. As they ate, she promised to call ahead to a neighbor's house to arrange night quarters for them and their horses. That house was only a few kilometers away. When they arrived, they found the proprietor surprised—and displeased—to see them. The porridge lady lied, simply to get them out of her house. The neighbor at this house begrudgingly agreed to let them stay in the barn, but would not allow them to graze their horses. When they tried to sneak some food to the animals, the proprietor drove them out in anger.

A version of this story repeated itself over several days. By now, the roads were increasingly flooded with refugees. Residents with houses and food drove the refugees from their doors, intent on protecting what they needed for themselves. After days of walking, Visvaldis was dirty, sweaty, smelly—hardly the dapper Riga resident of months before. He had taken food for the journey from the sanatorium, but his supply was running out. One day, he found an old net and decided to try his luck catching fish in a nearby stream. Visvaldis was a city dweller, not a fisherman. The fish he caught were small, bony, and inedible. While he fished, he removed his shirt. A nearby cow wandered over and began chewing it. By the time Visvaldis intervened, the shirt had large holes in it and was useless as apparel. He managed to find a kind woman in a nearby house. Laughing, she exclaimed, "These fish are not fit for cat food!" but accepted the meager fish in return for a voucher to buy a new shirt. She also invited him to dinner. Splashing some water on his stinking body, he cleaned up as best he could. The woman prepared a feast with meat and potatoes, and her husband even produced a bottle of vodka he shared with Visvaldis. The following day, he rejoined his travel companions on their journey. Unfortunately, a cart wheel broke, requiring the services of a blacksmith. Visvaldis donated the voucher slated for the shirt as payment for the blacksmith.

Rumors ran rampant in the countryside; the Germans were winning, they were driving the Russians back, Latvia would soon be liberated! By now, it was August 1944: harvest time. In exchange for food, Visvaldis helped a farmer and his wife bring in the harvest. During that time, he learned the military outlook for Latvia was actually quite grim. He needed to get to Liepāja to plan his next steps.

Taking a train from Aizpūte to Liepāja, his first stop was the People's Aid Office, where fleeing citizens sought relatives or passage out of Latvia. Visvaldis was dismayed at the transformation of the port city: parks were jammed with refugees, grazing their horses silently. The word on the street was "every man for himself." Food was scarce, lodging even harder to come by, no jobs, and no way to get money. Luck intervened once more in the form of a friend, who had an apartment in the city and invited Visvaldis to stay with him. The friend directed Visvaldis to a nearby bakery to buy fresh bread, but without any connections, it was unavailable. He stayed in Liepāja for a few days, going to the People's Aid Office once daily for a hot meal. While there, he saw notices stating that previous military service exemptions were no longer valid. All men were to register immediately or be punished with the full might of the military court as deserters, the same mandate that resulted in my father's conscription. Upon hearing this development, Visvaldis boarded a train for Riga to obtain a medical waiver from the tuberculosis center that diagnosed him in February. Waiver in hand, he reported to a registration center where he was told that health evaluations were no longer performed; anyone showing up was immediately sent to a military division. Thinking quickly, Visvaldis harnessed the power of a well-timed cough, explaining that he had arrived from a sanatorium. It worked. He left the center with a pass on military service until March 1, 1945. He also confirmed that, indeed, the Red Army was close to encircling the capital city. Once that happened, it would be almost impossible to escape.

Visvaldis set out for Liepāja. Along the way, he met up with a friend from the Īle sanatorium. They conferred and agreed that their best bet was to go to the sanatorium in Vaiņode, where there was food and room for patients. The two men stayed there for a few weeks. One night, they heard the unmistakable rumbling sound of heavy trucks driving by. The following morning, the patients learned that the Germans had retreated. Visvaldis and his buddy left, stopping by a nearby house. The talk was all about escape. They headed out—seven adults and two children—in a horse-drawn cart, many refugees joining them along the way. By Rucavas, the road turned and entered a forest. The staccato report of nearby machine gun fire was heard. Shortly after they entered the forest, a group of German soldiers came by and warned them of Russian soldiers ahead. Panicking, the refugees turned around and began running. Hearing reports of the encroaching Red Army along the way, the group made its way to Liepāja by picking narrow roads going through dense forest, where it would be unlikely that Russian tanks could get through.

As they approached Liepāja, they saw fires in the distance; the Soviets were bombing the city. Pausing until the bombing stopped, they finally arrived in Liepāja, which was overrun with refugees seeking passage out. Some were waiting for weeks, unsheltered, cold and hungry. The word was that authorities were not yet releasing tickets for Latvian citizens; only people with connections were getting out. While some people decided to take their chances and return home, Visvaldis stuck it out. After several days, he and his group obtained tickets for passage to Germany on the *Lapland*, headed to Gotenhafen [now Gdynia, Poland].[1] Someone they knew took the horses.

Visvaldis embarked on the *Lapland* on October 10, 1944, the same time that Arnolds retreated to Courland, three days before Riga fell to the Red Army. As the ship left the port under nighttime cover, the refugees on board sang the Latvian national anthem, weeping openly, as they watched the outline of the harbor quickly fade in the darkness.

Unable to find a place to sleep, Visvaldis walked the upper deck in the chilly dark; the *Lapland* was sailing with no signal lights to avoid detection. Noticing that people had life jackets on, Visvaldis obtained one for himself, wondering, had the ship already been sighted? Were they about to sound an alarm?

The following morning the *Lapland* arrived in Gotenhafen harbor, where the refugees collected their baggage and were doused with insecticide powder. After disinfestation, they boarded trains. Visvaldis and his traveling companions chose the one headed to Breslau [now Wroclaw, Poland], the largest city east of Berlin. Upon arrival, authorities directed the passengers to an area surrounded by barbed wire. He became apprehensive: what kind of a place was this? As they funneled into an empty barracks with no chairs, beds, or furniture, it became clear to Visvaldis; this place was one of the camps for "eastern workers." After a few tense days of waiting, the refugees were released with no instructions or place to go. One of Visvaldis' companions knew a woman in Zerbst with an apartment. Perhaps she could help them find lodging and jobs? A small group of them agreed to try their luck in Zerbst, about four hundred forty kilometers away. They needed rail tickets.

Once released from the camp, the group discovered that they could not get their baggage or necessary documentation without bribing the station clerk. Bribing officials was illegal, so, of course, everyone did it. The group reserved a bottle of brandy for this purpose; Visvaldis, having the best command of the German language, was unofficially elected to be the chief briber. He had never bribed anyone before. Should he openly shove the brandy in someone's hand or wink, smile, and do it secretly? Entering the station office, he saw several tables where workers appeared to be very busy doing something with papers. Looking around, he saw one worker catch his eye and smile, as if inviting him to come to the table. Visvaldis approached, explaining that he was traveling with a group who had relatives living in Zerbst, with living space and jobs for them. The worker nodded, and explained that, as Latvians, they were free to go wherever they wished in Germany. He then fell silent and smiled, as if something was missing. Visvaldis surreptitiously pulled the bottle out of his pocket and handed it to the worker, who quickly put it in his desk drawer. He then handed over documents and train tickets from Breslau to Zerbst. For Visvaldis, it was a humiliating experience. Prior to this, he considered himself an honest man. But this was a different life. As he said, when one hand washes the other, both are dirty.

Visvaldis refined his bribing skills over the next several months. Bribery was necessary for everything: putting baggage in the hold, getting a seat on the train, finding food. Once the group arrived in Zerbst, they discovered that the friend with the apartment was living in a single room. Furthermore, only Nazi Party members found jobs in the city. They decided to try their luck elsewhere. The friend in Zerbst contacted the minister of a Baptist church in Schönebeck, about one hundred eighty kilometers west of Berlin, who arranged for lodging. Once there, Visvaldis secured work as a technical draftsman at Weltrad, a factory manufacturing machine gun parts.

1945

Nearing the end of the war, Allied aircraft bombed German cities on a regular basis. German authorities divided the country into lettered quadrants of equal size, with each quadrant subdivided into twelve smaller quadrants numbered one through twelve. Schönebeck's quadrant numbers were HD-8, referred to as Heinrich-Dora 8 on the radio, to warn residents of incoming bombings. Increasingly, the city filled up with people displaced by the fighting. Living arrangements became cramped, and foreigners, like the Latvians, were often evicted from apartments by Germans who needed housing.

By the time the American Army entered Schönebeck, the city was a smoking, burning pile of rubble with no resistance offered by residents. Visvaldis' landlord confessed that he was terrified of the returning German Army. Hitler ordered defense of every German city to the last person standing. Since the Schönebeckians had not done that, the landlord feared they would all be shot in punishment. Chaos reigned in the city, as people looted warehouses containing army supplies or sifted through rubble for items of value. Bicycles were a particularly hot commodity. Across the Elbe River, Visvaldis saw Russian forces. Rumors circulated everywhere, even among United States servicemen, that Schönebeck would soon be assigned to the Soviet zone. Visvaldis decided to leave Schönebeck to avoid capture by the Russians. To do so legally required applying for a place in one of the Displaced Persons camps. Visvaldis headed to a United States command center, explaining that he was desperate to get away from Schönebeck before the Russians entered the city. The soldiers at the command center were perplexed. Why was he running away? The Russians were allies who helped defeat the Germans. They were the good guys....

A few days later, trucks arrived to transport Visvaldis and the other refugees to a large Displaced Persons camp near Meerbeck, in lower Saxony, part of the British occupation zone.

Simplified Choices

My sister, Maruta, got married in July 1975. Prior to the wedding, my mother was moody and nervous, often crying or shutting herself in her bedroom with headaches. There was a reason for this; Maruta and her future husband were moving to Wyoming right after the wedding. For my mother, this was another loss: her daughter would be living across the United States so far away that she was in a different time zone. She wrote to her father about it. His reply was characteristically pragmatic in the Latvian way: Skaidrīte, it is fate that when children grow up, they head out into the world. You write that Maruta is 2,000 kilometers away from you, but how many thousands of kilometers are you from where I live? It is something you will need to get used to.

As our home environment grew tenser in the days leading up to the wedding, we argued a lot. I remember exploding at my mother about something. As usual, the source of the disagreement is long forgotten, but I remember the shouting. After my mother left to go to her room again, Elvīra came to me, tears in her eyes. She scolded me harshly. It breaks my heart to hear you talk to your dear, beloved mother like that! How can you treat her so badly? You should honor her every day of your life. I lost my mother—what I wouldn't have given to have her with me like you do!

It did not matter how many years passed. For Elvīra and my mother, the wounds of loss did not heal.

Chapter 13

To Stop Was to Die

July 1944–January 1945

On a summer evening in Wellesley, Massachusetts, 1988, Aunt Elvīra finally broke her silence and spoke about leaving Latvia. In July 1944, she worked in Livonia, about sixty kilometers east of Riga. The 19th Latvian, including her brother Arnolds, was retreating across the eastern border, pursued by the Red Army. Most people still believed that the Latvian Legion would push back the Soviets, but as the front moved westward, fleeing refugees told a different story. Forty-four years later, as Elvīra sat with me on my father's porch, sipping a glass of wine, I asked how she left her country. She spoke softly but quickly, as if the memory burned her as the words left her mouth:

> There was panic and fear. It would be like 1940 again! I packed a suitcase with some clothes and food and headed out with everyone. Those with bicycles rode until the road became too full. Many just dropped their bicycles on the sides of the road. Farmers coming from Vidzeme [Livonia] and other areas had horse-drawn carts, some with one or two cows tied behind them. You cannot imagine the mess— horses, carts, old people, families, all trying to get out. The girls and women—we all wrapped shawls around our heads, hunched over,

and kept our faces down. We were trying to look like old women so that the Russian soldiers wouldn't rape us.

The Russian planes were flying low, looking for people to shoot at. When we heard their engines, we would jump into the ditches and lie there until the planes passed. To stop was to die—you would be left behind and killed by Russian soldiers. We walked at night to stay hidden. But there were air strikes at night. We would hear the planes in the distance, meaning that another airstrike was coming. The Russian planes dropped flares to light up the ground below. If they saw movement, they shot. They wanted to kill us. We would lie very still in the ditches, praying they would not see us.[1]

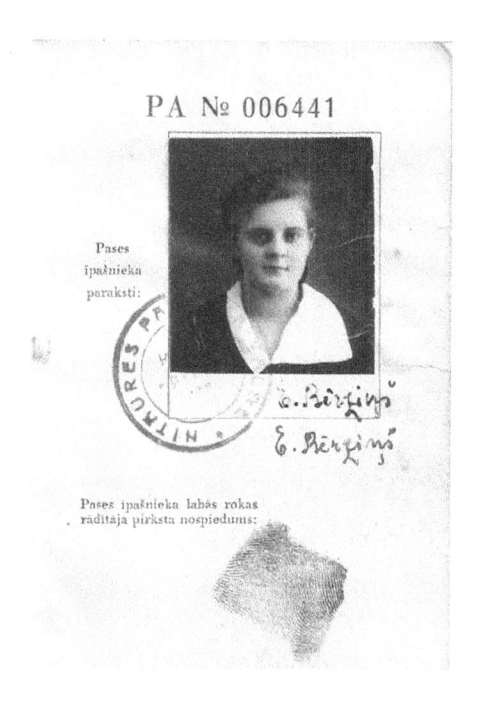

Elvīra's passport. Author's collection.

My mother shared few details about leaving Latvia. In 1944, she was working as a dairy inspector and living on her own. When I asked why her family stayed in Latvia, she told me that her father, stepmother, and younger siblings had packed up their belongings. Their plan was to meet up with my mother in Courland. The roads were filled with confused, frightened people, unsure of where they were going or for how long. When it was time to leave, her sister Aina was missing. She had gone to say goodbye to her boyfriend. By the time they found her and got to Courland, the borders were closed to civilian evacuations. With the exception of her older sister, Elvīra, her family remained in Latvia. She never saw her father or stepmother again.

My mother's passport. Author's collection.

In 2023, on her daughter's farm in Courland, my sister and I asked Aunt Aina about what happened. Aina was now ninety-six years old, vision impaired, and used a walker to get around, but she was mentally sharp, recalling names, dates, and places with no difficulty. Sitting in her bedroom with us, she told a completely different version of why the family did not get out of Latvia. By July 1944, refugees from the eastern part of Latvia arrived in Livonia. Two families from the Madona area camped out by the farm where her father, her mother Olga, and their younger children lived. The 19th Latvian was about forty kilometers away, when the Bērziņš family gathered their livestock and headed west, along with the two Madona families. The unfortunate group also included my grandfather Jānis' paramour. They stopped at a town eight kilometers away, and camped out for a few days. Hordes of refugees arrived, a sign that the 19th Latvian and the shifting front was nearby. Olga and Jānis argued incessantly, yelling and cursing each other, until Aina finally had enough. When the Madona families moved on to Courland, Aina left with them. She was seventeen years old. There was no boyfriend, as my mother told me, or a plan to meet up with her. My grandfather and the rest of the family stayed where they were, taking shelter as the front moved through, eventually returning to Nītaure after Riga was occupied by the Soviets. In fact, no one in the family knew that my mother fled to Courland. As Arnolds wrote home in his January 13, 1945 letter, "I gather you do not know anything about Skaidrīte either."

Aina's group traveled along with a 19th Latvian unit for protection. The unit was ordered to report to positions near the town of Džukste, not too far from the Baltic coast. Aina and the Madona refugees followed them and stayed there. They found an abandoned farm for shelter and picked the fields over to eke out enough food for subsistence. A cow wandering the road provided milk to supplement their forage. When the fighting drew too close for comfort, the group moved on and found another abandoned house. After the war, Aina remained in Courland.

I don't know why my mother told her alternate version of the story. Perhaps it was guilt, or a false memory brought on by wartime trauma. Perhaps she sent a message to Nītaure that never arrived. Memory can be deceiving, perspective shaped by events, distance, time, and even emotion. My mother longed to find her family but fled without knowing what happened to them. This may have been her attempt to rewrite her family narrative in a way she could bear. Once she got to Liepāja, she searched for her family. The back pages of the newspapers, *Tēvija* and *Kurzemes Vārds*, posted messages from refugees seeking lost family members, leaving information about where they were headed. Though she anxiously scanned the pages, she found no information about her family. Now I know why: her family never intended to leave their country.

In spite of the nearby fighting, the decision to leave their land was heart-rending for Latvian families. Our friend, Astrīda, was a girl when her family left their farm in Semigallia, just after the Red Army crossed the border. She, her sisters, and mother were terrified of the approaching soldiers. Her father shut himself in their bedroom for several hours, weighing their options. When he emerged, he agreed. It was best to leave before the Russians arrived. Packing to leave, Astrīda carefully tucked letters, a diary, and a few special photographs amongst her clothes. She hid other items in the house, fully expecting to return in a few weeks once the Red Army was driven out of Latvia. As she walked through the gardens and orchards, inhaling the scents of ripe cherries, currents, and blackberries, she never imagined that they were leaving the family farm forever.[2] Like thousands of other families, she had complete faith in the Latvian Legion, young men from their fields and cities, who would give their lives in defense of the fatherland: Latvia, not Germany. The legionnaires' courage and blood would keep the land safe for Latvians.

Their faith and hopes were rapidly dying. On September 29, 1944, Riga citizens awoke to a startling headline on the front page of the Nazi newspaper *Tēvija* [*Fatherland*]. Written in large, bold letters dominating the page were the inconceivable words, *"Riga Must Evacuate."* The sub headline further reinforced the message: *"Let no Latvian fall victim to the Bolshevik terror."*[3] Evacuation of Riga was mandatory, particularly for men, who would be conscripted by the Red Army. The Germans intended to send as many civilians to Germany as possible for a labor force. The process was streamlined from previous weeks; civilians were directed simply to take their passport to the Immigration Office and fill out an application. After this step, civilians reported to the Transportation Office to receive a free ship or rail ticket to Germany, along with a certificate stating that the traveler was free of lice and any contagious diseases. Up to one hundred kilograms of personal items were allowed in storage, up to thirty kilograms of hand-carried luggage, with an unlimited amount of food. Refugees could also bring five hundred Reichsmarks with the stipulation to deposit sums over the allotment in the Ostland Bank. German authorities demanded that refugees surrender their items for storage until they departed. Most of them did not see their belongings again.

As Soviet troops advanced across Lettgalia, they conscripted any remaining teenage boys or men into the Red Army. These new "recruits" were invariably sent directly to areas where the fighting was heavy, without any training or adequate equipment. The Soviets referred to these invaded areas as "liberated" and therefore treated the conscripts as Soviet citizens who could legally be forced to fight in their army. Anyone unable to fire a gun became a forced laborer. Anyone challenging the order was shot.[4] Soviet air strikes leveled the city of Jelgava, including houses, hospitals, schools, churches. The fighter planes also destroyed four trains filled with civilian refugees waiting to leave the train station.[5]

The Red Army advanced and cut off Courland from the rest of Latvia. The coastal cities of Liepāja and Ventspils remained the only possibilities for evacuation. Courland now had over 250,000 unsheltered people. Few were as fortunate as Visvaldis, who stayed in his friend's apartment. The majority of refugees slept in the parks, in the woods, in open air, suffering exposure, sickness, and hunger. Campfires were prohibited: with the approaching cold weather, a humanitarian disaster was imminent. Mothers with young children huddled together, going to the People's Aid stations for milk, clothing, and a hot meal. Farm animals overgrazed the land; eventually, their owners drove them out into the streets, where the livestock roved in search of food, usually ending up in a slaughterhouse. When I visited Liepāja in 2023, I was struck by the number of parks and green spaces in the city. While there were numerous parks, they were small. It is difficult to imagine thousands of people plus livestock seeking shelter here.

The People's Aid Office fed as many people as possible once a day, with soup made from horse meat. The German authorities provided no food due to shortages, and the situation grew worse as the weather turned from fall to winter. Bread, in particular, was unavailable; if farmers had grain, there was nowhere left to grind it. If they succeeded in grinding it into flour, there were no bakeries intact to bake it.

Ventspils, a northern coastal city, was the departure point for those fleeing to Sweden. Refugees hid from the German patrols charged with preventing an exodus to Sweden. If caught, the refugees were rounded up, forced to dig trenches, and threatened with imprisonment in a concentration camp if they refused. Transportation to Sweden was arranged covertly through a network of fishing boats and barges. The boats were small and could escape detection by either the Germans or the Soviets but the surf was often rough, increasing the likelihood of swamping and drowning those on board. By the end of December 1944, authorities forbade fishermen to sail into the Baltic without German soldiers on board. Any boats not used for fishing were either destroyed or guarded in a central storage location. Civilians living eight kilometers or closer to the coast were forcibly relocated inland so as to prevent emigration. German gendarmes patrolled the shoreline at points used by boats ferrying refugees to the barges. Emigration to Sweden stopped.[6]

As the bombings in Liepāja increased, so did the panic. Masses of refugees, desperate to board a ship to Germany, began shoving and pushing each other aside. Osvolds Freivalds, the head of the People's Aid office in Liepāja, witnessed a brutal tragedy, born of this desperation. A mother boarding a ship lost her young son when the surging crowd pushed him from the ship's dock. The child fell from the ship onto the street, and died instantly upon impact. Unable to push through the crowd to return to shore, the grieving mother was forced to sail away, leaving her small child where he fell. Freivalds and the People's Aid workers buried the boy in the Liepāja cemetery.[7]

In spite of the overcrowded, squalid conditions, German authorities continued to direct people in a forced evacuation to Courland. With the near-constant bombing attacks, a trip to get a bowl of horse meat soup could be fatal. People dove under carts, hid behind trees, or simply threw themselves into ditches or low-lying areas in an attempt to cheat death. At the beginning of December 1944, authorities ordered the division of refugees into two groups: able to work and unable to work. This effectively meant the separation of families, particularly young children, their parents, and the elderly. "Able to work" was a euphemism for forced labor; nearing the end of the war, the Reich was taking children as young as twelve years of age to fill the need. Forced laborers maintained and built railroads, dug trenches, following the given orders.[8]

By January 1945, all civilians, regardless of gender or age, were forced to dig fortifications. Ships no longer accepted refugees, so the people who had not secured passage to Germany remained in Latvia. The German Army requisitioned any available livestock or food. Starving, forced to labor under cruel conditions, these Latvian civilians remained in their homeland essentially as serfs, once again, serving their masters.

As my father aged into his nineties, his physical health began to decline. His twice broken left leg pained him. The cartilage wore down; bone rubbed against bone when he walked. Years of limping without orthotics to correct the discrepancy in the length of his legs curved his spine, the stress causing hairline fractures. He developed congestive heart failure, sometimes laboring for air. Though Karl lived with him, he wasn't there every moment of the day. What if Dad fell down the stairs while he was alone?

Maruta and I pleaded with him. Dad, won't you move to a smaller place? A condo with no stairs to climb? The house is too big for you and Karl to keep up. You'd be safer.

My father refused to consider this. Even in his late nineties, he would furniture-walk his way through the rooms and fix something to eat for lunch. On nice days, he would somehow make his way outside to the garden and pull up weeds or trim plants. Finally, even this life-long pleasure became too much for him, and he spent his days sitting on the porch, peering at the quiet street with his fading vision.

After one particularly tense conversation between him, my sister, and me, he laid down the final word. When I'm dead, you can blow the house up if you want. As long as I'm alive, I won't leave. The only way I'm going is when I'm carried out, feet first!

That is exactly what happened, though not quite like my father thought it would. It was his third fall that did it. As he lay on the floor, unable to get up, he begged Karl not to call the ambulance. He begged the paramedics to let him die at home. The hospital released him to a rehabilitation facility, but he did not recover his ability to walk. From there, he went into assisted living, where he lived for another year and a half.

He had already left one home, one country, and his family behind. Damned if he was going to leave this home without putting up a fight. To him, being safe meant staying in the home he and my mother made in the United States. Safety was an emotional, not a physical, state.

Chapter 14

Simplified Choices

September 1944–Spring 1945

My father was not called up during the first mobilization in March 1943. Born in 1918, he missed the cut-off by one year. The second mobilization called for younger men, again missing my father, but it was inevitable that he would run out of luck. The third mobilization, December 1943–January1944, called up men born 1917–1918 as well as those born 1922–1924. My father attended his physical screening as ordered but was rejected because of his pronounced limp; his twice broken left leg was shorter than the right, and he was deemed unfit for combat. He left the screening elated. As he later said, "If not for that limp, I would probably be lying somewhere in eastern Prussia now."

The German forces on the Eastern Front were now retreating. Desperately needing manpower, they overlooked frailties they rejected earlier. In the late summer of 1944, authorities called for total mobilization, including those once passed over: the old, the lame, and the visually impaired. My father said, "If you could still stand or barely see, you were drafted." Once again, he reported to the health office. The penalty for draft evasion was death. There was no thought of escape or avoidance; as he said on the porch in 1979, when someone points a gun at you, it simplifies your choices. This time his limp did not spare him; he was assigned to a logistics unit bound for Germany. His registration date was September 16 in the nearby city of Valmiera. Draftees received instructions to bring three days' worth of food.

The remaining days passed quickly. Is there ever enough time when awaiting deployment? September 16, a beautiful clear day, was the threshing bee at his family home, Pudas. Early that morning, my father, along with twenty hired men, harvested and threshed the wheat his father grew that season. He worked most of the day, but quit early, leaving the others to finish the work. Going home, he washed up, changed his clothes, and said goodbye to his mother. She lovingly wrapped up generous portions of ham and bread in a cloth. If you cannot protect your child from a bullet, at least you can feed him. Crying silently, she held onto him, getting her last look at her son, as he tucked the food into his rucksack and lashed it up. His father shook his hand and wished him well. Tears aside, they knew it was a case of die now with a bullet in your brain for draft evasion or taking your chances in battle. Looping the rucksack over his shoulder, he mounted his bicycle and pedaled away from his home. He was due to report at the registration office in Valmiera by 17:00.

Stopping briefly at his sister Alīne's house, he left his bicycle in her barn and walked to the train station. Boarding the narrow-gauge train that would take him to Valmiera, he watched out the window as Umurga slowly disappeared in the distance, the halcyon days of his youth along with it. Along the way, the train stopped as more conscripts climbed aboard. Night fell, indigo-soft and indifferent, as the narrow-gauge pulled into the train station at Valmiera. The conscripts deboarded, rucksacks filled with country staples of ham, bread, cheese, mother's love, and headed to the registration office. After registering, the conscripts were directed to a commanding officer. From there, they boarded another train bound for Riga, filling two carloads with the new recruits, and a few private citizens. Once filled, the train pulled out of Valmiera, in the darkness, lights out.

The train moved slowly along the tracks, no lights shining to guide its way. During the war years, no one traveled anywhere except by night with no lights. The Allies would fly overhead, dropping flares, to identify any kind of movement—train, car, or human—and bomb them.[1] Distinctions between soldiers and civilians were insignificant. Darkness became a way of life, paradoxically both dangerous and safe for what it concealed. The train moved slowly, stopping three or four times as Soviet planes flew overhead, searching for bombing targets. The recruits stayed silent, holding their collective breath, as they experienced their first time as enemy targets. Finally, early in the morning, the train pulled into Riga.

The conscripts boarded at a nearby high school. By now, the fighting was close to the city. The recruits spent two days in Riga as they awaited the arrival of more recruits from all over Latvia. Many were older men with poor vision, unfit for active duty, but still able to provide labor service. Sleeping quarters were non-existent; the recruits found space on the floor, using their rucksacks as pillows, for whatever sleep they could manage. My father, used to the relentless pace of work on the farm, was bored. He decided to visit a friend who still lived in Riga, and obtained a pass from his commanding officer. The pass specified the time he was due back at the temporary quarters.

Walking down Elizabeth Street, renamed Wolter von Plettenberg Ring by the Germans, my father felt like he could breathe again. He passed the familiar buildings, walking calmly, as he thought about reconnecting with his friend. Perhaps he could find a store to purchase some alcohol or food to bring as a gift.

Suddenly, he was surrounded by German gendarmes. Shouting in German, they grabbed his arms. A young man, not in uniform, walking the streets of Riga was surely a deserter or draft evader. Either way, it was a punishable offense by a bullet to the head, concentration camp, or immediate trip to the front. My father shouted back that he had a pass. His captors allowed him to withdraw it from his pocket. It was written in Latvian, which none of them spoke. They frog-marched him over to another officer. My father continued his protestations, and eventually they found a Latvian translator who confirmed that he already was in the army and on legitimate leave. By the time the miscommunication was cleared up, he was due to return to the high school, the time of leave having expired.

The next day, over 2,000 conscripts boarded an enormous German passenger ship, my father among them. Private citizens also boarded, many of them refugees fleeing the advancing Red Army. The boarding process began around noon and concluded at 17:00. It was a beautiful, sunny day, fairly warm for the end of September. The port was filled with relatives and friends of the people on board the ship—those who had been able to get to Riga. As the sun set, the ship pulled out of the port. Someone began to sing, and every Latvian on the ship or shore joined in, the words to the song known by all.

> Daugav', both shores
> Never divides.
> Kurzeme, Vidzeme, Latgale are ours.
> Fortune, reign over us,
> Protect our land.
> One language, one soul,
> One land of ours.[2]

Sixty years later, the memory was still vivid and emotional for my father. As he spoke of it, his voice broke, tears in his eyes. Wiping them with the back of his hand, he said softly, "It was truly moving, how we left. Everyone had tears in their eyes. It was a truly emotional moment, how I left my homeland. I will never forget." The next time he would see the shores of Latvia would be July 1989. He would never see his parents again.

The ship sailed out of the Daugava in the remaining daylight. Once it reached the mouth of the sea, they anchored and waited until darkness fell to reduce chances of being attacked. That night, the ship sailed through the Bay of Riga's narrows into the Baltic Sea. The following day, they sailed the Baltic slowly, watching for aircraft. Alerts were announced throughout the ship. There was one room where all the draftees slept, wherever they could find room on the metal floor. Two days later, they arrived in Danzig [known as Gdansk, Poland today] early in the morning. After deboarding, the military passengers were brought by truck to a large hangar. Still in civilian clothes, they climbed onto trucks that transported them to one of the barracks the Germans had for pilots, not far from Berlin.

My father and his fellow Latvians received a two-week training. It was rigorous, but they had some spare time in which to see nearby Wittenberg. Never much of a church-goer, my father visited the Wittenberg Castle Church, where Martin Luther nailed his 95 Theses to the door on October 31, 1517, thereby beginning the Protestant Reformation. He was impressed by the experience. Perhaps the proximity of war caused him to become more open to faith than during the two-hour long sermons he endured as a youth in Umurga. One night, the recruits felt the impact of bombs released over Berlin, which my father described as, "a huge, pressurized wind that crushed you." At the conclusion of the training, the trainees received their uniforms and deployed. They were now auxiliaries in the service of the Luftwaffe.

My father never identified his specific unit, mentioning only that he was with Latvian conscripts commanded by a German officer, serving as support soldiers to a field air force unit. This was the basis of his claim that he served with the Latvian Army. In truth, he served the Germans; there was no Latvian Army. He also did not know his exact location, only that he was in Germany, fairly close to the fighting. He first loaded kitchen supplies on trucks bound for the military field kitchens, hoisting heavy boxes and sacks of sugar weighing about one hundred pounds each. There were perks to this kind of work; he and a friend, Lībeks, each kept a spoon in their pockets. While positioning the sugar sacks on the trucks, they surreptitiously wiggled the spoon into the sack along its seams and pulled out some sugar that

Simplified Choices

immediately went into their mouths—as long as their supervisor was not looking—giving them some much-needed supplementary calories.

Later, his unit moved even closer to the fighting to load gasoline and munitions, including shells for artillery cannons, onto trucks. It was grueling work: "Those bombs were as heavy as the devil, about sixty pounds each. We worked only at night because the British and American planes were flying overhead all the time." They were legitimate targets; the Allies frequently bombed logistics trucks to interrupt the flow of supplies to the front lines. My father's unit stayed in a hastily constructed barracks behind a granite quarry. The trucks awaiting cargo and gas were parked on a road next to the barracks. Years later, sitting safely on his front porch in Wellesley, he recalled the night he survived a bombing:

> One night they gave us the canteen. Usually, they just gave you a pot with some soup, whatever they had, to eat. Canteen was when you sometimes got cigarettes and booze. This time we got one bottle of cognac for two people. My friend Lībeks and I thought, 'Now, this will be good!' We put the bottle of cognac on the table next to our beds and went to sleep. There were windows in the barracks. I pulled the blanket over my head and was already asleep. All at once, I heard smashing sounds. Glass was flying everywhere! We were getting bombed by either the British or the Americans, I am not sure which. I looked over immediately to see where the cognac bottle was to make sure it was safe [laughs]. See, in war, you lose your sense!

Fortunately for my father, the bombs released too early, with the majority exploding in the quarry. Once the aircraft disappeared, the men left the barracks to assess the damage. A few of the trucks were destroyed, with one blasted into a pine tree. A nearby meadow was completely torn up, littered with dead cows. It was a close brush with death, as was every day during war:

"The most insane thing was the phosphorus that the Allies released

Simplified Choices

on the Germans at night. It rained down, and whatever it hit, burned. The most horrible weapon was the phosphorus. You could not do anything. If you wanted to flee, they [Germans] shot you. If you stayed, they [Allies] bombed you."

During his wartime service, my father carried a small folded paper in his pocket with an invocation to protect him:

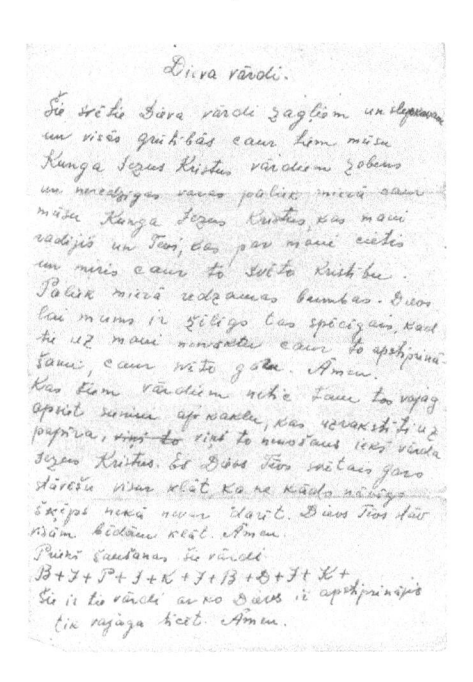

Soldier's Invocation. Author's Collection.

Brittle with age, the invocation was preserved in a file of his important papers and found after his death in 2019. Aigars Lielbardis of the Latvian Folklore Institute explained it as a combination of prayer and superstition, a charm intended to keep soldiers safe. Writing protective charms was a common practice among Latvians for centuries; the charms often combined elements of Christianity and superstition, a remnant from Latvians' pagan beliefs. The handwriting is almost illegible, and some phrases do not make much sense, most

Simplified Choices

likely the result of numerous attempts to copy it over and pass it along. I have added some words and punctuation in brackets to convey the meaning more clearly:

> These are the holy words of God for thieves and murderers and [, in] all hardships through the words of our Lord Jesus Christ, the sword and unseeing powers become peaceful through our Lord Jesus Christ, who created me and you, who suffered and died for me, through holy baptism. The visible bombs become still. May God have mercy on us, the almighty, that they may not fall on me through the reaffirmation of the holy spirit, Amen. Whoever does not believe these words, he must tie [next word is illegible] around his neck, what is written on the paper, he won't be shot [, protected] by the word of Jesus Christ. I God the Father the Holy Spirit, will stand by him so that no deathly spear can harm him. God, the Father, stands by during all troubles. Amen. For shooting [,] these words: B + J + P + J + K + J + B + D + J + K. These are the words with which God has confirmed [you] only need to believe.

The letters at the bottom probably represented the initial letter of a holy name: D for *Dievs* (Latvian for God), K for *Kristus* (Christ), or J for *Jesus*. My family donated the original document to the Latvian Folklore Institute's collection of charms in 2023.

Perhaps the charm worked. My father made it out of military service through a fortuitous accident. In the spring of 1945, he was delivering munitions at night when he was accidentally grazed by a bullet in his left leg, the same leg that snapped twice in his youth and saved him from active duty in the army. The unit's German doctor patched him up and said that he was fit to report for duty the following day. Then, lowering his voice, the doctor quietly offered to make the paperwork disappear for my father and a small group of his friends. True to his word, the doctor destroyed the paperwork; no record of his service exists in Latvia. My father rounded up four other Latvians and they walked five kilometers that night on crutches and canes. One of his injured companions had to be carried. Had they been stopped, they would have been shot as deserters. They made it to a British-occupied area near Hamburg, where they applied for sanctuary as refugees. My father had survived the war.

DISPLACED

Simplified Choices

September 20, 2018

    The dining room at The Falls Assisted Living is bedecked with mylar balloons, silver and gold streamers, and a small pitcher of gold and burgundy mums. I place a platter of fragrant saffron bread, the traditional sweet served at celebrations, in the center of the table. Carefully, I poke three wax digits into the pastry's golden crust: 100. Karl heads out to the parking lot to offer a steady, assisting arm over the uneven pavement to the arriving guests. On past birthdays, a roomful of friends gathered to laugh, toast my father's health, and sing. Now a dwindling number are able to come, and they have a slippery grasp on health.

    The guests enter, every one of them bearing flowers in the Latvian tradition. Nora arrives with her mother, Lilija, and Astrīda. Aina, who has known my father since the DP camps, comes with her caregiver. Miķelis and Brigita, their grown son Andris, and a few other friends complete the group. Once we are assembled, a staff member wheels in my father, wearing his old fraternity colors, as are all the male guests. One by one, his friends approach him with hugs. It is difficult to read his thoughts. He certainly recognizes his friends, grasping their hands with both of his, though he is unable to hear their greetings and can discern their faces only if they are within three feet of his. After some snacks and conversation, I light the candles, and we enthusiastically sing the Latvian celebratory song, "Many Blessed Days" (Daudz baltu dieniņu):

> *Many blessed days may Fate grant thee!*
> *Living robustly and bountifully!*
> *Many blessed days may Fate grant thee!*
> *Working robustly and bountifully!*
> *Many blessed days may Fate grant thee!*
> *Loving robustly and bountifully!*

    Fate has, indeed, granted my father many blessed days: a prosperous *life in the United States, a wife he adored, three children, four grandchildren, and a great-grandson he held in his arms just a few months before. But Fate also brought sorrow and many days of fear, danger, and uncertainty. For my father, the road to blessed days was long and difficult.*

Chapter 15

Little to Do But Wait

May 8, 1945–1946

Europe, V-E Day, 1945. The images are familiar, captured by photographers in Europe and the United States, reprinted in articles, history books, and web sites. Fireworks over the Kremlin...singing citizens waving flags as they marched down the Champs-Élysées... cheering crowds in front of Buckingham Palace...confetti drifting over jubilant crowds in Manhattan, and the iconic shot of the sailor kissing a white-clad dental assistant in Times Square. The overwhelming joy and relief that, for continental Europe, World War II was over. The tanks, bombs, and bullets finally stopped. But not everyone shared the purely celebratory emotions, something my history classes omitted. Years later, my father wrote an essay for his fraternity yearbook, reflecting on the frustration and sadness Latvians felt:

> Sunny and pleasant, the spring of 1945 arrived, and with it the end of war. The world received the long-awaited peace with mixed emotions. To some nations, it brought freedom, to others disappointment, defeat, and slavery. The fate of nations was decided at the conference table by the mighty world powers—guided by the

whims of the moment or state of the spirit, regardless of the will and rights to self-determination of small nations. These mighty powers rejoiced and celebrated victory at the expense of the defeated and small nations. Our people were among the unfortunate, who, because of the naiveté of the Allies, were handed over to destruction and slavery.[1]

I think about this within the context of my two identities: a citizen born and educated in the United States and as the daughter of displaced Latvians. In all of my history classes, V-E Day was presented with the joyous rush of victory, of stopping Hitler, of freeing people incarcerated in concentration and POW camps. The Western concept of World War II history is largely based on the Nuremberg Consensus, which presents Nazism as the dominant paradigm of evil. It is undeniably true that Nazism was evil.[2] But what of Stalin and his murderous actions against the people whose countries he annexed? What of the deportations and executions that followed? Stalin committed crimes against humanity, yet both Roosevelt and Truman formed a favorable impression of him as a reasonable ally. Truman believed that Stalin was honest and smart: a man who would honor his word. History is largely written by the victors; the Latvians were among the losers. The story of the losers was not written in the history books I read in high school or college. Liberating Allied forces witnessed the horrors of concentration camps. They did not see the horrors of Gulag camps. Perhaps if they had, the attitude toward "Uncle Joe" Stalin would have been different. Or would the Allies simply not have cared? Acquiescing to Stalin's demands ended the war on continental Europe. What did the fates of a few countries matter in light of this larger goal?

Lost and alone, my father longed for his homeland, his farm, his family. Now twenty-seven years old, he had expected to have his architecture degree and a practice in Latvia, maybe even a family.

Instead, he found himself in a crowded refugee camp. Europe was in ruins. Cities bombed beyond recognition, farmland burned, industries destroyed, and an estimated ten to twelve million people displaced by the war: unsheltered, traumatized, many ill, and near starvation. They had no idea where their families were or even if anyone was still alive. These people were labeled "displaced persons" or DPs for short. Like millions, my father, mother, Visvaldis, and Elvīra became known by this acronym. It became their identity, superseding their previous identification with childhood villages, schools, or vocations.

The Latvians in the camps referred to themselves as *dīpīši*, pronounced "D P shih," a common bond for the rest of their lives.

Many years later, a friend of my father's from the camps formed a trio and recorded the folk song *I Do Not Know Nor Understand*. My father played the album frequently, singing along with this song. It expressed the uncertainty and desperation of their lives during this time:

> I do not know nor understand,
> What is it Fate wants from me?
> For what criminal offense
> She has left me to suffer.
> I have no Fatherland or home,
> Nor a single heart that loves me.
> In the morning, I rise, put on my shoes,
> God only knows where I will be in the evening.[3]

The Supreme Headquarters Allied Expeditionary Force, known as SHAEF, inherited the responsibility of sheltering and feeding the DPs. In the early months of 1945, as Allied forces took over areas of Germany, the DPs were housed in temporary structures wherever they could be found. Many of these temporary structures lacked running water, toilets, beds, kitchens, or even walls in some cases. After capitulation, SHAEF workers registered the DPs at collection points and housed them in provisional camps set up wherever there was space: former military barracks, labor camps, appropriated civilian houses, or even concentration camps.[4] Visvaldis found himself in a repurposed village; as punishment for inhumane treatment of United States fighter pilots shot down in the area, the town of Meerbeck was emptied of German civilians and converted to a DP Camp.

SHAEF's primary goal was prompt repatriation. Everyone from the commander of SHAEF, General Eisenhower, on down through the organization assumed that European citizens forced to leave their countries would eagerly return. Repatriation began almost immediately. Responsibility for running the camps, registration, care, and repatriation was assumed by the United Nations Relief and Rehabilitation Administration (UNRRA).[5] In Germany, UNRRA dispersed three hundred forty-nine teams around the country, averaging eight employees each, to provide food, shelter, clothes, and medicine to DPs as well as facilitate their return to homelands. By September 1945, six million DPs were already repatriated.[6]

Nationality and type of persecution determined DP status: racial, political, or religious. Germans from the Eastern territories, soldiers and collaborators of the Axis countries were not granted DP status. Initially, Latvian legionnaires were incarcerated in prisoner of war camps for Nazi collaboration. This was a bitter pill to swallow for the men conscripted to fight under the Nazi banner, but who did not share their ideology. In their hearts, the fight was always for Latvia, not Germany. As two of my father's legionnaire friends wrote, "We gave our lives, health, and youth in the battles of Džukste, Lestene, in our nation's last island of hope—Courland...Once honored with beautiful songs, music, and garlands, we were now branded as criminals, shameful, forgotten, and despised."[7] On October 1, 1946, the Nuremberg Military Tribunal issued specific definitions for war criminals and SS members. The Tribunal ruled that soldiers forcibly conscripted were not considered war criminals or collaborators, provided they had not participated in war crimes. Since the majority of Latvian legionnaires fit this definition, they obtained DP status after this ruling.[8]

The largest category of DPs was forced laborers, deported by the Nazis as civilian workers. The second largest group was made up of concentration camp, ghetto, and Holocaust survivors. There were also Eastern European Jews, called infiltrees, who fled their homelands by going further east to escape Nazi persecution. Finally, there were groups of non-Germans, such as my mother, Elvīra, and Visvaldis, who arrived in Germany during the last months of the war, fleeing the fighting.[9]

Upon arriving at an assembly center, the refugees filled out a questionnaire identifying their reasons for seeking DP status. If approved, they were issued a DP registration card and a destination assignment. Nationalities were grouped together. Next, the refugees went through a disinfestation procedure that consisted of dusting their bodies and clothes with insecticide for delousing. Upon my mother's entrance to Schwarzenbeck Camp, workers separated the women and men, directing them to showers. This was their first opportunity to bathe in a long time. As soon as the women soaped up, the water turned off. Stranded naked and soapy, the women began shouting. The water turned on again, ice-cold, and they rinsed off the soap as quickly as possible. Given the crowded conditions, disinfestation was of paramount importance. Outbreaks of typhus, tuberculosis, smallpox, and diphtheria occurred frequently. At Meerbeck, Visvaldis contracted stomach typhus, spiked a high fever, and nearly died. His brother, Adis, held at a nearby POW camp due to his status as a former Latvian Legionnaire, received permission to donate blood. Using a primitive hand-pumping mechanism, the transfusion process was so slow that the blood began to congeal before it reached Visvaldis' veins. When Visvaldis awoke from his fever-induced semi-comatose state, he was given morphine to take the edge off of the stabbing, unbearable pain he felt in his arms and legs. Making their rounds, the doctors referred to him as a "morphinist," an addict. Morphine was his best option as the available pain pills were weak and did not control the pain. Eventually, he recovered and was well enough to return to Meerbeck.

After July 1, 1945, SHAEF divided Germany into four occupation zones, each of which treated the DPs differently.

Germany 1945 – Allied Occupation Zones

The Soviets, who controlled eastern Germany, did not set up DP camps; instead, the NKVD ran filtration camps, the purpose of which was to determine if the refugees were considered Nazi collaborators. DPs found to be collaborators were deported to Soviet Gulag forced labor camps. Approximately forty-two percent of refugees screened ended up in the Gulag, where the vast majority perished under harsh conditions. All others were repatriated immediately, regardless of their wishes or fears.[10] SHAEF memorandum #38, dated April 1945, spells out the policy clearly: "After identification by Soviet Repatriation Representatives, Soviet displaced persons will be repatriated regardless of their individual wishes."[11] There was a political reason behind the Soviet insistence of repatriation: groups of refugees living elsewhere in the free world would be able to keep the language and cultural identity of their pre-Soviet countries alive, as well as work for their eventual independence. Refugees who did not return to the Soviet Union, where they could be eliminated or controlled, posed a threat. The Soviet representatives assessed the situation accurately; this was, in fact, exactly what the diaspora Latvians did. My American-born peers and I attended Latvian school to preserve the language and cultural identity for the future, when Latvia would regain independence. The endless letters to politicians written by my father and his peers kept up awareness of Latvia's forced annexation and its desire for independence. He believed in Latvia's right to sovereignty and refused to give up and accept the Soviet Union's claim to his country. It was his only way to fight for his family still living there.

Initially, forced repatriation was the norm in other zones as well. The French repatriated refugees quickly rather than allowing them to relocate. Camps in the British zone did the same, but as details of the fate awaiting DPs returned to the Soviet Union emerged, forcible repatriation became an issue that conflicted with the British and American belief in the right to asylum. Camps in the United States zone were the first to abandon this practice. The United States camps were also the first to recognize that Jewish Holocaust survivors needed to be housed together rather than living with non-Jews from their former countries.[12]

For DPs who no longer had a place they could return to safely, repatriation was simply not an option. Several groups went to extremes to avoid this, chief among them Poles, Ukrainians, Latvians, Lithuanians, Estonians, and Jews from Central and Eastern Europe.

Groups of DPs, upon imminent repatriation, begged the soldiers to shoot them instead of sending them back to a worse fate in the Soviet Union. DP camp officials reported incidents of suicide prior to repatriation. Responding to the overwhelming empirical evidence that a substantial group of people could not safely return to their former homelands, the United Nations passed a 1946 resolution that DPs could not be forcibly returned to their country of origin against their will. Now the overworked UNRRA added to its initial duties; it provided religious, cultural, and educational programs to DPs, as well as facilitating relocation to another country. UNRRA officially stopped running the DP camps in June 1947, at which point the International Refugee Organization (IRO) took over. There remained 700,000 DPs in camps, unable to repatriate for fear of persecution, my parents, Elvīra, and Visvaldis among them.

After his unauthorized departure from the military service, my father ended up in a dormitory near Hamburg. Like many Latvian citizens, he hoped to return home once Great Britain and the United States forced the Soviet Union to give up its claim to his nation— something he truly believed would happen. His DP registration record, dated July 18, 1945, shows the desired destination as "Australija," written in a different color ink from the rest of the card. Although Latvia was his first choice, he could not admit this to officials or he would have been repatriated to Soviet Latvia, and undoubtedly sent to a Gulag. Australia seemed as good an option as any.

My father's DP Registration Record, Arolsen Archives

A later DP questionnaire cited his reason for leaving Latvia as "forced labor." He identified "political persecution" as his reason for seeking asylum, describing himself as a "slave laborer." While my father was forced to serve as a laborer during the war, he omitted the detail that he had been conscripted into the German forces as an auxiliary soldier, fearing he would be labeled a Nazi collaborator.

For DPs like my father and mother, the temporary state slipped into permanence, long days with little to do but wait. The alienation voiced in the song *I Do Not Know Nor Understand* was real and deeply felt. No wonder my father sang along to his friend's record. What did fate want from them? Where would they ultimately be able to go and begin life again? Most importantly, would they ever set foot on Latvian soil and see their loved ones again?

Simplified Choices

Given my father's involvement in his fraternity, it was inevitable that Maruta, Karl, and I would also join Latvian student organizations. Karl joined Gersicania, the fraternity my father cofounded. Knowing that she would be moving to Wyoming, Maruta picked one of the larger organizations. I chose to join Zintas because I liked the women. Some of them were close family friends I had known all my life, so I felt like I belonged.

Latvian sorority sisters join in a cohort. Each cohort selects a Latvian song to be their official song; at meetings, members of each cohort present stand in order of the year they joined and lead the song, just as my parents' friends did at those early parties. The Zintas founding members picked a song with a cheery, upbeat melody, but the words tell a different story:

> *Quietly, quietly the cart rumbles,*
> *Like a honeybee droning.*
> *Life, life, evening, morning,*
> *Life is woven from halcyon days.*
> *Smoothly, smoothly glides the yarn,*
> *Not so smoothly glides life.*
> *Only the cart rumbles quietly.*
> *The path to happiness is always difficult!*[13]

The founding sisters had fled their country, survived war, witnessed suffering and death. They had lost family and every material possession they ever owned. The song echoes the emotions: life is a struggle, but we must keep going on. Sometimes singing is the best way to heal.

Chapter 16

Possibilities in Life

March 1946–September 1949

To my father, life in the DP camps seemed meaningless, a series of interminable days of waiting. Most of the camps housing the Latvians were located in former German army barracks or work camps. Surroundings were typically dirty, lacking basic necessities, and overcrowded. Besides the trying physical conditions, my father found the absence of purpose demoralizing and depressing. Accustomed to the hard work of a farm, he was not alone. This was a common complaint among young people of all nationalities.

As the temporary stay in DP camps extended to an indefinite holding pattern, adult DPs took jobs in the camps or even outside in labor positions. Former teachers instructed students in their native languages. DPs formed sports teams, choirs, orchestras, folk dance groups, theaters: all the cultural pursuits and leisure activities they missed from their respective homes. Some of these were high-caliber performance groups, composed of professional musicians or actors. Classes in English and French were offered to DPs preparing for future emigration. In Meerbeck, Visvaldis chose French, and later regretted that he had not chosen English. At the time, he was interested in the cultural appeal of French, but English was the practical choice.

For students like my father, these distractions were inane. They did not wish to take jobs as manual laborers; they wanted to complete their education. In the British zone, authorities required nearby German universities to fill ten percent of enrollment with refugees. The need for higher education was great among all nationalities displaced by the war, so the quota filled up quickly. German universities faced their own challenges starting up: extensive property damage and a shortage of professors. Prior to the war, Jewish academics, like Albert Einstein, resigned or were fired. After the war, the Allied occupation powers prohibited professors who were active members of the Nazi party from working in their previous profession. Upon acceptance to a German university, students cleared rubble and rebuilt university structures to make classrooms accessible. Visvaldis, one of the lucky ones, matriculated in the Chemistry department of the University of Kiel.

For those not accepted, the waiting continued. A group of Latvian, Lithuanian, and Estonian professors collaboratively proposed a solution: founding a Baltic University enabling students to obtain advanced professional degrees. The group found support from the first UNRRA Welfare Officer, Robert C. Riggle, and, with his help, secured space for classes in the lecture halls of the partially destroyed Hamburg Museum of History.

The *Museum für Hamburgische Geschichte* before Reconstruction (Hamburg, Holstenwall 24)

The Museum after Reconstruction.
In this building classes were held from March to December 1946

Hamburg Museum of History before and after reconstruction. Source: Baltic University pamphlet, 1949. Author's collection.

Baltic University began accepting applications in the fall of 1945. Eager to finish his studies that began at the University of Latvia a lifetime ago, my father applied and received a spot in the Architecture and Engineering School.

Simplified Choices

My father's student identification card, Baltic University. Author's collection.

In February 1946, the students transferred to a new home: Number 17 Displaced Persons Assembly Centre in the Hamburg Zoological Gardens, informally known as Zoo. The camp's only advantage was proximity: a ten-minute walk from the Museum of History. Students described Zoo as severely run down, and that was putting it mildly. The flimsy barracks, made of thin wooden planks with no insulation, were built for summertime use only. Designated a "limited use" camp due to its university affiliation, Zoo residents did not receive supplies given to other camps, such as clothing. In cold weather, wind and snow whistled through the visible cracks between the wall planks of the unheated buildings. By March 1946, Zoo had no more space available, so new students and faculty boarded at the nearby Alsterdorf Camp. Both Zoo and Alsterdorf were in central Hamburg, surrounded by piles of rubble from bombings during the Battle of Hamburg.[1]

Hamburg 1945: The Museum of History (top); Amelungen Street
(bottom)
Source: Baltijas Universitāte 1946–1949

With the Museum of History sufficiently repaired to allow entrance, classes formally began March 14, 1946. There were eight schools: Architecture and Engineering, Philology, Chemistry, Agriculture, Mathematics and Natural Sciences, Medicine, Mechanics, Economics and Law. Since students from the three Baltic nations attended, professors conducted lectures and discussions in German. The university used wax dies and cheap paper to reproduce books, rendering the pages blurry and difficult to read. Paper shortages prevented the university from printing enough books for all students. The University of Hamburg extended library rights to Baltic University students, but required them to use all materials on premises.[2]

One of the biggest hurdles the university faced was the question of status. The university advisory board, comprised of representatives from refugee and military organizations, insisted that the university should be renamed Baltic DP Study Center: a short-term solution that provided instruction for students seeking to apply to a university, but unable to confer degrees. Given the qualifications of professors and demanding curriculum, this designation was unfair. The reason was political; a university could become a center of anti-Soviet agitation, an uncomfortable position for the British, who were still allies with the Soviet Union.[3]

The issue of recognition had further implications than just the question of a degree. Since the Baltic University was not formally recognized as a university, the students were considered non-workers, so their daily caloric portion was restricted to 1,550 calories. By contrast, workers in "light work" positions received 1,755 calories daily, while "heavy laborers" received 2,590 calories daily. With hunger constantly gnawing, students supplemented their caloric intake as best they could. In the summer of 1946, my father was walking with a friend when they came upon a small plum tree heavy with fruit, much like the trees back at Pudas. The young men reached up and plucked as many plums as they could carry. Later, in secrecy, they ate until their stomachs were full, licking the juice from their fingers. My father laughed as he recalled the excursion: "We ate all the plums we had taken. We hadn't eaten fresh fruit for a long time, so nothing ever tasted so good. A few hours later, we discovered what too many plums can do to the stomach! We were miserable—all that delicious fruit, wasted!" At the conclusion of the second semester, fifty random students were weighed and found to be significantly underweight. As a result, portions for all students were increased to "light work" levels, while teenage students were bumped up to 1,940 calories daily. The issue of university status would not go away; during its three years of operation, the Baltic University would be renamed a total of eleven times, with most administrators refusing to recognize its university status.[4]

My father (right) and a friend sunning themselves. Author's collection.

That fall, students learned that the university would relocate to Pinneberg, about twenty kilometers north of Hamburg. The late autumn weather was particularly harsh: scarce food, inadequate heating materials, and little opportunity to find warm clothes. Knowing that they would soon be vacating Zoo camp, students demonstrated their problem-solving abilities by disassembling the social hall barracks, board by board. Although technically guarded by the military, no students were caught helping themselves to the wooden planks. That December, the dormitory barracks became considerably warmer with fires lit from an unidentified source of wood. For Christmas, male DPs staying at Zoo each received two razors while the female DPs received a pair of stockings and two ounces of chocolate—about half the ration given to DPs staying at other camps.[5]

In January 1947, the Baltic University officially relocated to a former German pilot flight school training camp in Pinneberg. Here, the buildings were relatively intact, though still unheated, and the

SIMPLIFIED CHOICES

students and faculty were housed in the same area, facilitating frequent contact. Conditions remained trying: insufficient food, constant cold, and sporadic light, so lectures were held anywhere with windows, including attics and corridors.

In the tradition of European universities, students expressed interest in forming fraternities and sororities with a prescribed code of ethics, respected traditions, and dedication to intellectual development —quite different from how we think of fraternities and sororities in the United States. In order to save power, electricity was shut off for certain periods every day. During the hours of darkness, no studies could be completed, so students gathered in rooms to discuss their options. A core of twenty-four young men, my father among them, began seriously planning the formation of a fraternity. There were jokes; when discussing possible names, one student suggested that the brothers stop shaving and name their fraternity "Usonia Bardienzis," which roughly translates to "Mustachia Beardis." Eventually, the students decided to pick a name with historic importance. They chose the name of the first Latvian castle on the banks of the Daugava: Gersica. Using the Latin form, the fraternity would be called Gersicania.[6] Selecting and displaying symbolic colors was an important tradition from the University of Latvia. Gersicania chose the colors white for knowledge and honor, violet representing passion for Latvia, and green for friendship and fraternal spirit. The young men wrote the oath: "Open your heart to friends, keep silent to strangers. Serve higher knowledge, shed blood for the Fatherland."[7] Zintas, the sorority I joined, was founded a month later. The founding women chose the representative colors blue (the power of the eternal values of the Latvian people), black (our time in exile) and green (hope for the future).

The fraternal bond was of paramount importance to my father. His fraternity brothers remained his closest friends for life, and formed our circle of family friends. There were regular meetings, academic discussions with professors, song instruction hours and song evenings, beer nights, dances with sororities, and even fencing instruction. Fencing took place in the camp's garage; at times, when a British Army coal truck pulled in, the fencers put aside their gear and shoveled coal into the truck's bed. For my father, this was a happy time. He was continuing his studies, he had an active social life, and there was still hope of returning to a free Latvia. The Latvians continued to believe that Britain and the United States would not allow the Soviet Union to permanently occupy their country.

In June 1947, the International Relief Organization (IRO) assumed administration of DP camps. Life changed overnight. Almost immediately, new rules forbid students and faculty from leaving the campus for any reason without written permission, including attending practical courses at hospitals for medical students. DPs could not publish newspapers, books, or research summaries, all of which had been instrumental in gaining positive international press for the Baltic University. The IRO forbade the matriculation of any more students as the school was to be shut down soon. The university disregarded these orders, accepting students on the sly—or, as the students put it—"on the rabbit." These students lived illegally in attics and attended classes, but reported to their assigned DP camps for supplies and food.

Like my father, many of the students attending the university were completing degrees that were interrupted by war. In July 1947, the military administration forbade any students older than twenty-five-years from attending. Since my father was now twenty-nine, this would have meant the end of his college education. The university appealed formally, and the age restriction was relaxed, provided students received special "hardship case" exemptions from the military command. My father received the exemption and completed his architectural degree, graduating December 30, 1948. Eight years after beginning his studies in Riga, he had persevered and obtained his personal key to possibilities in life.

The Baltic University officially closed on September 20, 1949. The

Simplified Choices

university lasted only three and one-half years, with a total of about two thousand students in attendance. The DP camps were soon closing, and the western powers were not pressuring the Soviet Union to give up its claim to the Baltic region. It was time for everyone to find a new home.

Simplified Choices

In the summer of 1970, I was twelve years old. My biggest concerns were my upcoming transition to middle school, called junior high back then, and a spat I had with my friend, Genia. It seemed I was on the outs with her and the group we hung out with. I was a straight A student, a rule-follower, the kind of girl who could be teased. Genia and company were mediocre students, but they dressed in tight body suits and jeans that dragged behind their boots, and were popular with the boys. They were risk-takers and lots of fun, so I desperately wanted to be accepted. The possibility that I might be losing my friends before entering a large, unfamiliar school felt like impending execution.

I noticed that my father seemed unusually subdued. I said something to him, but he barely answered me, quietly walking into a different part of the yard to tend a plant. I was already feeling rejected by Genia, so this annoyed me. How dare he ignore me like that?

I went inside and complained to my mother, What's his problem? She looked at me and said, He just received a telegram from Latvia. His father died.

So what? I retorted. He hasn't seen him for years.

Well, my mother gently said, He lost his father. Even after all this time, he still loves him. Feelings don't go away.

It is to my mother's credit that she had such a gentle response to my callousness. In my self-absorbed pre-teen state, I was incapable of understanding that grief is not limited by distance or time. I'm ashamed of my response to his sorrow.

I hope I went back and told him I was sorry for the loss of his father, but I can't remember for sure. So, here it is now. I am sorry, Dad, truly sorry for your loss.

Chapter 17

Nothing Left at Home

After graduation, my father remained in Pinneberg. He still hoped to return to Latvia to rejoin his family, a hope that was slowly fading with each passing month. In Spring 1949, unwelcome news reached the DPs: on March 25, the Soviets arrested and deported 38,000 Latvians to the Gulag for being enemies of the state. Technically, minors under the age of sixteen were not subject to deportation, but could follow voluntarily; this was a political sleight of hand on the Soviet part, enabling them to claim that children were not being deported. In reality, no child would remain behind without their family or home.

The arrests occurred at night, with armed muscle banging on doors and breaking them down if necessary. Outer buildings, places of employment, and educational establishments were all searched for family members related to anyone on the arrest lists compiled by county executive committees and the Ministry of National Security. The arresting teams counted heads and read a perfunctory accusation of criminal charges, followed by an order to pack up in twenty minutes. People arrested could not speak in their defense at any time; they were forced onto trucks and transported to waiting cattle cars. Other than what the deportees took with them, the government seized the remaining belongings and confiscated all property.

As in the previous deportations of 1940–41, the Soviets targeted classes of people viewed as threats to the implementation of the Communist system. First among the targets was the *kulak* class: landowners who possessed enough land and wealth that they would resist the state seizure and collectivization of private property. USSR Council of Ministers Decision number 761 defined *kulaks* as: permanently employed in agriculture; systematically employing seasonal or day laborers for farming or livestock; receiving income in cash or kind from the use of agricultural machinery; or farmers who regained property that had been expropriated during the Latvia SSR land reform of 1940–41.[1] The Council was correct in its assessment of the threat posed by landowners. Pēteris Spīgulis consulted with a lawyer in an attempt to fight the seizure of Pudas. The lawyer informed him that he was a *kulak*, and therefore an enemy of the state. Pēteris was not a large landowner. The Spīgulis family owned three hundred sixty acres of land, not the largest concern in the area. But Pēteris was successful and hired workers to help with crops and livestock. Under the Soviet system, farms of this size were now state property. He lost Pudas and received no compensation.

Sometime that spring, my father received word from a friend that his parents and younger sister Valija were among the deported. His friend wrote, "There is nothing left at home for you. Everyone was sent to Siberia. There is no Pudas anymore."

Registered as case number 10376, my grandparents and Aunt Valija were arrested on March 25, 1949 and deported to the Tomsk district, Asina region. Tomsk is located on the eastern edge of western Siberia; a total of 15,584 Latvians were exiled there.[2] Upon arrival, they received manual labor assignments on *kolkhozes* that would break them physically. Only the deportees able to work received supplies; those unable to meet their quotas starved. Fortunately, my grandparents had my young, strong Aunt Valija with them. She was able to work hard and earn food for the family. Any attempt to escape was punishable by twenty years in prison. No mail correspondence with family or friends was allowed. The deportees were isolated from the rest of the world.

Pēteris, Kristīne, and Valija Spīgulis in front of their living quarters, village of Rassveta, Tomsk. Author's collection.

With this devastating news, my father moved forward with his plans to emigrate. At this point in his life, his "you can't change anything" attitude served him well. He could not return to Latvia. His family was in Siberia, though he did not know where. What else could he do? He resigned himself to evaluating his options.

The IRO had one goal: relocating the 700,000 DPs still in its care. Camps reduced rations and began a concerted effort to relocate DPs to England, Canada and Australia. The British Commonwealth needed industrial and agricultural workers for economic recovery. Other European countries, like Belgium, sought coal miners. The DPs willing

SIMPLIFIED CHOICES

to work in these fields had plenty of opportunities and received visas promptly. Educated professionals, like my father and Visvaldis, were not in high demand.

Many Latvians accepted offers and moved to these countries, where they formed tight-knit diaspora communities. This scattering of people from a small nation was deeply felt. Whenever my sorority gathered, we began our evenings with the song, *To Distant Warm, Sunny Lands*, remembering friends and family who lived far away or had died:

> To distant warm, sunny lands
> The birds have long ago flown.
> In the sky the sun shines low,
> The wind drives dry leaves into the fields.
> Refrain: How fare you, my faraway friend?
> How fare you,
> How fare you?
> Memories of you are in my heart,
> Like the fragrance of a *Jāņu* wreath.
> I think of you—can you hear?
> While dreaming and while awake.
> Already the short day comes to an end,
> Beyond the forest, the red sun sets,
> To that distant land's edge,
> I long to go to you.[3]

The majority of United States citizens vehemently opposed immigration, and wanted it severely limited or stopped altogether. The Immigration Act of 1924 defined a national origins quota system that protected the homogeneity of the United States population. The government provided visas to only two percent of the total number of people of each nationality in the United States per the 1890 census, excluding people from Asia entirely. The Act also required a literacy test in any language. The quotas heavily favored immigrants from Britain and western Europe, the dominant nationalities present in 1890. For eastern or southern Europeans, the low numbers reflected in this census made immigration to the United States almost impossible.[4]

The situation changed when President Truman sent Earl G. Harrison on a mission to determine the conditions and needs of DPs in Germany, particularly Jewish refugees. Harrison's report was distressing, leading Truman to call for the expansion of the Act. There was anti-immigration pushback, most notably from the American Legion, Veterans of Foreign Wars, and the Daughters of the American Revolution.[5] In April 1947, Congress introduced a bill to expand immigration. The resulting revisions allowed 200,000 DPs to immigrate over the next two years while still retaining the quota system. Even with later revisions, the law remained restrictive: DPs had to be in resettlement camps by the end of 1945 in order to receive American visas; relatives of United States citizens received preference; and applicants needed to show sponsorship guarantees of housing and a job that would not displace a United States citizen. In response to the universally acknowledged humanitarian need, voluntary accredited social service programs sponsored DP refugees; many of these were religious, such as the National Lutheran Council or the Catholic Welfare Council.[6]

My father's best option appeared serendipitously. While reading a Latvian magazine, *Daugava*, he came across an article written by his cousin Ernests Spīgulis. My father immediately dashed off a letter to the editor in Sweden, explaining that he was Ernests' cousin. The editor forwarded the letter to the United States, where Ernests had emigrated shortly before. My father received an airmail letter from Ernests, now living in Boston, Massachusetts, instructing him not to leave the DP camp: "You must come to America. I will sponsor you and get you the visa."

My father struck immigration gold. Ernests applied for a visa, the

Baptist Church where he worked signed it as a guarantee, and sent it to the DP camp administration. My father now waited for the British to begin releasing DPs to the United States. The British delayed the release of paperwork for United States-bound refugees in the hopes that they would reconsider and come to the British Commonwealth, where there was still a shortage of laborers. In 1949, Visvaldis located a former colleague who was willing to sponsor him in the United States. Visvaldis waited for months for the paperwork to come through. Finally, in March 1950, he traveled to the central IRO office in Munich. The city was in ruins. He found the IRO office, functioning in a damaged building, where he learned that his paperwork came through weeks ago and they were trying to reach him at the camp. His papers were held aside by the British. Once this was cleared up, Visvaldis received approval to emigrate and sailed for the United States at the end of April 1950.

While my father waited for his paperwork to clear, he attended a small birthday party for the girlfriend of one of his Gersicania brothers. When the fraternity brothers arrived at the party, there were only two women. Seeking to improve the male to female ratio, one of the ladies volunteered that a friend of hers was visiting for the weekend, and was currently sleeping in her room. The friend, a young woman named Skaidrīte Bērziņš, turned out to be an old schoolmate of one of the Gersicania brothers, Jānis, the future father of my friend, Nora. An ebullient fellow, Jānis exclaimed, "Skaidrīte? She is from Nītaure! My town! We can't let her sleep!" He sprinted up to the room, pounded on the door, and called, "Skaidrīte! Wake up! Come out to the party or I am coming in and carrying you out!" Knowing Jānis, my mother knew this was no idle threat. She got up, dressed, and joined the party. The group chatted and did what Latvians always did when they got together—sang songs late into the night. My mother's clear singing voice and gentle manner impressed my father.

My mother, 1949, Author's collection.

She liked his smile and sense of humor. At the end of the evening, they exchanged addresses with a promise to write.

My father's paperwork came through a few weeks later. He boarded a Transocean Airlines flight in Wentorf, arriving in New York on June 30, 1949. As he navigated to his Boston-bound train, a bird flew overhead and let loose a little birdie relief, landing squarely on his head. Fortunately, he was wearing a hat! My father laughed it off, considering this a harbinger of good fortune in his new country. In Boston, his cousin Ernests met him, and true to his promise, had a place in his apartment for him, along with a job as the custodian in the Baptist Church. With Ernests' encouragement, he applied for a job as an architectural draftsman and was hired at the firm Jackson and Moreland in the fall of 1949. He survived the war, earned a hard-won education, emigrated to a new country, and finally gained employment as an architect. At the age of thirty-one, life began anew.

SIMPLIFIED CHOICES

First day in the United States: My father on Ernests' apartment roof, Roxbury, MA. Author's collection.

Simplified Choices

My father's full name is Arvīds Alfreds Spīgulis. On the first day of his job as an architectural draftsman, he reported to his new boss. The boss took one look at my father's name and said, Too long! No one can pronounce that. We'll call you Al. From that point on, my father was known as Al to his co-workers and clients. He embraced the change fully, willing to put aside the most personal aspect of his ethnic identity in favor of easing the American discomfort of stumbling over an unfamiliar name.

My mother had a similar experience. The name Skaidrīte baffled everyone. Upon taking her first retail job, her supervisor suggested Rita, so that is what she used as her American name. In spite of her own adoption of an easily accessible nickname, she disliked my sister's choice to do the same.

When we went to Latvia in 1989, one of our uncles asked us how Americans pronounce our names. When he heard the American pronunciation of Spīgulis, he burst out laughing and asked us to repeat it several times so he could laugh some more. It seemed humorous, this idea that people in the melting pot of the world could not learn how to say someone's name correctly.

Chapter 18

Only One Homeland

1949–1957

Laima—Latvian goddess of fate, destiny, and fortune, frequently invoked in song and speech—appeared to have cursed the Latvians. The Soviets destroyed their homeland, incorporating it into the USSR, sealing relatives and friends behind the Iron Curtain. Those who fled faced a painful dilemma: what did it mean to be Latvian when Latvia no longer existed? My father took the pragmatic approach. His family's fate pained him, as did that of his homeland, but returning to Latvia was not an option. He accepted this as another simplified choice and moved on. My mother had a different outlook. Lonesome, depressed, and withdrawn, she was caught in an emotional purgatory, unable to return to her old home yet unable to accept a new one. She had no knowledge of her family's fate. Stalin's Soviet government did not permit communication with the annexed Soviet republics. What happened to them? Were they alive? As in her childhood, she felt alone in the world, a wartime orphan. My parents' respective attitudes toward their immigration continued to shape their identities.

Embracing his fate, my father set about making Boston his new home. After beginning his job as a draftsman, he moved to a small apartment. Once settled, he reached out to his friends from Pinneberg still awaiting emigration. That year, he sponsored several of them, always finding space for an old mattress or two in his cramped apartment. When a fraternity brother and his wife, one of my future sorority sisters, arrived, my father strung a sheet across a corner so the couple could have a little privacy. True to the Gersicania oath he swore in 1947, my father always opened his heart to a friend. Not only was he fulfilling his fraternal oath, he was building a Latvian community. As more fraternity brothers arrived in Boston, they met monthly at my father's place. He became the nexus for the Boston Gersicania organization.

In the spirit of helping others find their way to the United States, my father wrote to my mother at her DP camp, offering to sponsor her. He had not forgotten that beautiful soprano and shy smile. Her response found him some months later, and they began to correspond. Sponsored by the Lutheran Brotherhood, she was already living in Saginaw, Michigan with Reverend Knauer, a Lutheran minister, and his family. Through the Red Cross organization, she learned that her sister, Elvīra, also sponsored by the Lutheran Brotherhood, lived in a different part of Michigan. The kind minister wrote to her sister's sponsor, offering to provide housing for Elvīra so the sisters could be reunited. As Reverend Knauer said to my mother, "There are only two of your family in the free world. It would be criminal for you to be apart."

Elvīra (left) and my mother (right) in Michigan, 1950. Author's collection.

Drawing on his ingrained hard work ethic, my father spent his nights learning English and studying for his Massachusetts architectural certification to become a fully licensed architect. As the Boston DP community grew, he joined the folk dance group and Lutheran church. In a letter to my mother, he described his new city as "European." The winding one-way streets and alleys, source of chagrin to lost tourists, and open-air markets reminded him of Riga's charm. My mother, on the other hand, continued to mourn the loss of her family and homeland deeply. Though she had chosen to emigrate to the United States, she very much saw it as exile. Her DP identity meant she did not belong where she was, and perpetually wanted to return home. On the eve of November 18, 1950, the independence day of free Latvia, she wrote:

> With every day we find ourselves farther and farther from our homeland, and no one knows when we will be able to return. Will we really have to stay here? We do not want to think that way. It is painful to hear that some [Latvians] have decided never to return

home. Although we do not know what our future will hold, you still do not want to hear that.[1]

They corresponded regularly. My father continued his adjustment and explored American life. He learned to drive, saved his money, and bought a used 1948 Studebaker for $900. In 1950, he took a new job at the well-respected architectural firm Shepley Bulfinch, where he worked for the rest of his career.[2] He traveled about New England with friends. Aunt Elvīra shared my father's attitude. She joined a Latvian choir and attended parties or dances with other Saginaw Latvians. Even with Elvīra's company, my mother fought depression and loneliness. During a cold, snowy week, she remembered coming home from school as a girl, warming herself on the bricks before the stove:

> We were many brothers and sisters, so sometimes it was a fierce struggle for that warm spot. How gladly I would be there now, though I do not know if I would even find any of my family. Christmas is nearing, those delightful, warm holidays…and now, for a long time, I have not felt that happy holiday feeling. I think that I will not speak of that anymore, because most of us are separated and everyone's heart hurts, hurts because you cannot help those who stayed at home and those scattered in strange lands.[3]

During June 1951, my father drove out to visit my mother. Taking the winding back roads from Boston to Michigan, he shook hands and chatted with strangers at stop signs or red lights. In Michigan, my parents spent a few days together, in the company of Elvīra as chaperone, after which they agreed to wed. When I asked about the speed of this decision, my mother simply said, "We were getting on in years. We both wanted a family, so there wasn't much time left to start. We agreed that we would try, and if it didn't work out, we would divorce." They married on September 2, 1951, and remained happily so until my mother's death, sixty-three years later. My father became a

United States citizen in 1955; my mother obtained her citizenship in 1963.

———

Stalin died on March 5, 1953. In 1956, his successor Nikita Khrushchev gave a scathing speech to the 20th Communist Party Congress, truthfully denouncing Stalin as a dictator and mass murderer.[4] The following year, he revoked Stalin's decree on lifetime exile, allowing those still alive to apply for readmission to Latvia SSR. He also allowed contact with countries outside of the USSR. In 1957, after years of searching, my father discovered the Gulag resettlement village where his family lived and wrote to their address in Tomsk, Siberia, sending news and pictures of his family. His mother Kristīne wrote back, the first opportunity she had to communicate with her son since he rode off from Pudas on his bicycle on that sunny day in September 1944. I discovered this letter in that dusty box on the basement utility shelf of my parents' house. The sorrow my grandmother held in her heart for thirteen years, followed by the joy of finding out her son was alive, overwhelmed me as I read her words:

> Heartfelt thanks for your letter and photographs. I kissed them all and cried from surprise, and thought that I really was in the midst of your family after such long years when I no longer hoped to think that I would see my son with his family…Dear children, both of us old folk have walked a long life path and are standing close to the grave's edge when life's sun sets and the grave's bells will escort us to a quiet resting place. Only one longing in my heart—to see my loved ones once again, for now everything seems like a wonderful dream.[5]

Valija, Kristīne, and Pēteris returned to Latvia; their official release date was April 18, 1957. They received permission to live at Pudas, now a *sovkhoz* [state owned farm]. The three of them shared one room,

SIMPLIFIED CHOICES

with three other families living in the rest of the house. Assigned to feeding the *sovkhoz* pigs, Valija rose before dawn six days a week to perform the grueling job. Pēteris and Kristīne did what they could, gathering firewood, cutting it into shorter lengths, or other lighter tasks. The stay in Siberia had not helped their health, and they both suffered with chronic pain and digestive problems.

My father's older sister, Alīne, did not live at Pudas in 1949, so she was not deported. She stayed in Latvia, supporting herself and her children by hauling logs out of the forest for eighteen-hour shifts. Her husband, Arturs, a former legionnaire, was deported after the war, first to Amurai, then to Vorkuta Gulag, located ninety-nine miles above the Arctic Circle. Vorkuta was so cold he suffered frostbite and his hair froze to his bed. The prisoners found ways to supplement their thin clothes, stuffing them with bark and whatever dead grasses they could find for additional insulation. They also dug up and ate grass, when they could find it. Punitive work camps sought to get as much labor out of the prisoners as possible before they died; they received meager portions of food with insufficient calories for their work. Arturs was released in 1957, but returned home weighing less than one hundred pounds with a fraction of his former strength. While in Vorkuta, an accident involving heavy machinery crushed parts of his body. As he wryly noted, "If it had not been for that accident, they would have killed me."

For years, my father and his friends from Pinneberg sat together in our living room after dinners, trying to figure out what exactly happened during the war. Most of them did not know exactly where they had been stationed or what happened to their friends. In the 1960s, very little information was coming out of Soviet Latvia. Hungry for information, they searched for explanations as to why Latvia lost its freedom. They bought books written by diaspora authors that described similar wartime experiences. They wrote letters tirelessly to members of Congress, ambassadors, foreign secretaries, even the President, petitioning for formal sanctions against the Soviet Union on behalf of Latvia. All received polite form letters with the same response: the United States condemned the annexation of the peaceful Baltic nations. The sympathetic response letters were intended to appease the voting base of Latvians. My father saw through this, and understood that this was politician-speak for no action.

―――

My mother also wrote to Latvia and received a letter from her father, Jānis, on November 1, 1957. The news from home was not comforting. He split with her stepmother, Olga, and now lived with his lover, Emma, who gave birth to their daughter in 1945. Emma and the girl spent eight years in Siberia, rounded up in the same 1949 mass deportation as my father's family. Jānis, like my father's parents, never used the word "Siberia." Instead, they employed euphemisms like "that faraway place." Under Stalin, all deportees were criminals. To speak of Siberia or to admit to deportation was tantamount to acknowledging guilt. Years spent laboring in the Gulag did not count toward pensions and made it difficult to find jobs upon return to Latvia SSR. My mother's brother, Jānis Jr., was killed in 1954. Her father wrote that Jānis Jr. was drunk when he fell asleep in his two-yoke cart and dropped the reins, which wrapped around the wheel of the cart, turning the horses off the road. The cart hit a pile of stones and fell on top of him, killing him. Although Jānis Jr. was a taboo subject my mother did not discuss freely, in response to my questions, she once told me that he joined the Communist Party in an effort to better his life. She believed the Communists killed him when he became disillusioned and wanted to leave the Party. In 2023, Aunt Aina shared her suspicions about his death; the Latvian partisans murdered him and covered the incident up with a staged accident. The partisans, known as the *meža brāļi* (forest brethren) murdered Latvians they felt were betraying their country by collaborating with the Soviet apparatchiks. There was no investigation, no proof—just her conviction that a young man who grew up on a farm and knew his home village intimately would not have driven the cart off the road, even after he had a few drinks.

My mother continued to struggle with her identity as an émigré Latvian. Even my grandfather Jānis picked up on her depression, describing it as "fatigue toward life" in a letter to Elvīra. In 1968, my mother offered to sponsor her father to come and live with us. He refused, writing, "I do not want to do that because I need to keep busy each day, and what would I do at your house…We must make peace with our fate." She asked again in 1974, and, again, he declined. My mother wrote to him, "There is only one homeland." Jānis replied, "It may be that sometimes longing for your lost homeland overtakes you…And yet, you cannot be bitter about your fate."

With a successful architectural career, his family and friends, my father grew to love the United States as his home. My mother got used to life here, but the sadness and pain remained. The DP identity was permanently part of them. They were diaspora Latvians, and their homeland was the independent Latvia of their youth. Their homeland existed only in their memories.

RETURNING

Simplified Choices

When I was in college, I had a summer job in Boston. My father and I commuted together, parking at a garage near both of our offices. One evening, as was our usual custom, I met him after work was over to walk to our car. We chatted about our respective days, when I heard a woman's voice behind us say sharply, Speak English! We both heard it, but ignored the voice and kept going. Louder: speak English! A robust woman with shoulder-length bushy red hair walked abreast of us, an umbrella in her hand. She jabbed the umbrella directly at my father. SPEAK ENGLISH! THIS IS AMERICA, GODDAM IT! SPEAK ENGLISH!!!! People around us turned and stared, but kept their distance from the confrontation that was unfolding. My father simply looked at her and said politely, in his accented English, Lady, if you do not leave us alone, I will call the police. SPEAK ENGLISH!!!! She was shouting by now, blocking our path with her extended umbrella. We stopped. People rubbernecked, some even stopping to watch more closely. I took the low road, and shouted back at her to mind her own business, along with a few choice expletives sprinkled in. Apparently, I reached her on her level, because she abruptly turned around and walked off.

We resumed our walk to the garage. Shaken, I referred to her as unhinged and crazy. My father's response was more measured. You can't let people like that upset you, he said.

My father was an American citizen. He spoke fluent English and was an architect, well-respected by his clients, but she hadn't noticed his suit and professional demeanor—just that he spoke a foreign language. Had this happened to him before? Was he already used to being attacked for speaking another language? For having an accent? For being part of another world? For being different?

Chapter 19

Return to Latvia

July 1989

Forty-five years after leaving their homeland, my parents overcame their fear of reprisal and returned to Latvia. Gorbachev's policies of *Glasnost* and *Perestroika* reassured them that it was finally safe to visit. To quell any remaining unease, they opted to be part of a tour as this offered some degree of protection. Maruta, Karl, and I joined them on the trip. Our grandparents were deceased, but we would meet aunts, uncles, and cousins who, until then, existed simply as names on the back of the occasional photograph.

July 1, 1989, we stood on the Helsinki pier, watching as the *Georg Ots*, a passenger ferry with an enormous hammer and sickle painted on the side, approached. The ship was our passage to a new, unfamiliar, frightening world. On board, my parents discovered cause for concern; Karl, a vegetarian, packed along beans to sprout for a dietary supplement. They were sure he would be held up in customs for smuggling, so we spent a good portion of the ferry ride arguing about this. The bean sprout controversy proved to be nothing at all. Upon our arrival in Tallinn, we made it through customs without any suitcase checks or questions, the tour operators having conducted thorough background checks prior to the trip.

Simplified Choices

After lunch in Tallinn, we boarded a bus bound for Riga, estimated to be a five-hour trip. With each kilometer, my parents' excitement grew. When the bus stopped briefly at the Latvian border, my father ran into a nearby field like a young boy, picked a small bouquet of wildflowers, and presented them to my mother, saying, "Flowers from our homeland for my heart's flower!" To her, no professional floral arrangement could compete with that humble bunch of what most Americans considered weeds. She beamed as she accepted the gift.

Then the calamities began. We nearly ran out of gas near Salacgrīva and detoured to locate fuel, not a simple task during a time of gas shortages. After refueling, we resumed the trip, only to have the fan belt give out by the Baltic Sea. The delays did not dampen my parents' joy of being on Latvian soil once again. Whispering and giggling together, they strolled arm in arm, like two teenagers in love. We walked down to the shoreline, removed our shoes, and felt the soft, white sands of the Baltic coastline between our toes. Signs posted on the beach warned sunbathers against swimming. We later learned that the Baltic was now quite polluted with chemical run-off and therefore not safe for swimming. The Soviet Union had no EPA to enforce rules against discharging chemical by-products from nearby plants. Fan belt fixed, we reboarded. Amid a series of alarming knocks, groans, and occasional breakdowns, we lurched along, stopping periodically so that the driver could tinker with the engine and fix it up enough to keep going.

In July, the sun stays out until 23:00; all the same, it was dark when our bus finally rolled into the Hotel Riga parking lot. A crowd of Latvians, waving and bearing flowers, waited in front of the hotel. Among them were Alīne and Valija, clutching their faces and each other, mouthing my father's name, "Arvīdiņš," [diminutive of Arvīds, a term of endearment] as they caught their first glimpse of their brother since September 1944. My father leapt out of his seat and pressed his face against the window, so excited I thought he would jump off the bus before it came to a stop. As the crowd poured off the bus, I found myself hugging cousins I had never met but knew instantly by our shared facial features, crying as we introduced ourselves. I caught a glimpse of my mother, shyly extending her hand to her sisters-in-law, only to be engulfed in a huge hug. All around us in the parking lot, this scene was reenacted by other families, separated for decades by war and politics.

From left: Valija, my father, Alīne, reunion 1989. Author's collection.

Aunt Valija had baked a gorgeous torte, decorated with strawberries and whipped cream, that put anything offered by a patisserie to shame. For the first time ever, my extended family broke bread together as we sat in a hotel room and enjoyed the cake. I looked around the room, filled with laughing, eating people, and felt a hollow loss. I came from a large family. Those small holidays, cobbled together by my parents with other diaspora Latvians, should not have happened. I should have grown up with my whole family—lots of cousins, aunts, and uncles. I should have known my grandparents. The joy of meeting them was real, but so was the loss. The Nazis and the

Soviets stole my family from me.

My father was shocked at the condition of Riga and the effects of Soviet control. To him, Latvia SSR had become a foreign country. Riga, once beautiful, was in disrepair. Old Riga's colorful buildings listed, paint peeling, and the stench of sewage often emanated from doorways. In the country, indoor plumbing was rare. The tour guide warned us not to drink the tap water as filtration was poor. Bottled mineral water we purchased often tasted like a tablespoon of salt was dumped into each bottle, the varying levels of fluid reflecting a lack of quality control. Food at the hotel was limited to greasy pork cutlets, potatoes, and an anemic tomato or cucumber slice. For Karl, the fatty foods shocked his digestive system and he became sick. Visiting relatives in the countryside, however, gave us welcome luxuries not seen in Riga: fresh berries, vegetables, milk, eggs, smoked chicken, and sweets. As my Aunt Valija said, "We do alright here. We have a cow, chickens, vegetables, and fruit trees. I don't know how people in the cities can live."

Throughout Riga, store shelves were empty. My sister and I entered a store, looking for a bottle of wine to bring to an uncle's house. All we found were some bags of flour, canned tomatoes, and pickled pigs' feet. The "currency store" on the other hand, was fully stocked with coffee, alcohol, foods, even tires, for those paying in foreign currency instead of rubles. My father bought tires for our few relatives with cars. We used American cigarettes as a form of tipping the staff in the hotel. It did not matter if the recipients smoked; American cigarettes were currency on the black market.

Demonstrable animosity existed between Russians and Latvians. Walking down sidewalks in Riga, Russians did not make room for an approaching group of Latvians, forcing them to step off into the street. One evening, we attended a concert in the Dome Cathedral, and found some Russians sitting in our seats. My brother politely asked them to move in Latvian; they continued chatting and did not even acknowledge his presence. When he repeated the request in English, they moved immediately. Another evening, my sister and I purchased a nice bottle of wine at the currency store, and decided to walk to our cousin's apartment for dinner instead of taking a bus. As we rounded a corner, two drunken men stepped out and blocked our way, eyeing us greedily as one of them slurred out something in Russian. We stepped to the side to avoid them, but they immediately stepped in front of us. Nearby, a small group of men watched this encounter with interest. I raised the bottle of wine, staring at the Russian directly in front of me, ready to smash it over his head if necessary, and screamed, "Fuck off you drunken pig!" The English curse words worked their magic. Both men immediately retreated to their friends, and we continued on our way. My sister whispered, "I'm glad you thought to do that. I was terrified."

Everywhere, cracks in Soviet control were evident. Although forbidden, Latvians covered the steps leading to the Freedom Monument with flowers. My parents laid a bouquet of roses at the monument. Miraculously, the Soviet government had not destroyed the monument, believing that demolition would cause tension among ethnic Latvians.

Simplified Choices

My parents at the Freedom Monument, 1989. Author's collection.

Russian was the official administrative language, and technically the state encouraged all Latvian Soviet citizens to become bilingual. This policy was one-sided: Latvian speakers all learned Russian, but many Russian speakers spoke only that language. When my cousin Inga once boarded a city bus and asked for change in Latvian, the bus driver responded in Russian, "Use a person's language, not a dog's language," and threw the change at her. The government rewrote Latvian history according to Soviet historiography, so our cousins discouraged us from visiting the Museum of History. As Inga remarked, rolling her eyes, "Oh yes, you can learn all about how we were 'liberated!'" Soviet propaganda referred to all Soviet citizens as "one great family." It did not take long to see that the great family was dysfunctional.

With the exception of a few conversations like these, our relatives stuck to safe topics about their country. They volunteered little information about life under the Soviets. Our parents warned us against speaking openly in the hotel rooms, as they were undoubtedly bugged. Hotel workers were always present in the hallways, as if keeping an eye on us. There was no escape from a sense of unease; we were all being watched.

Pudas

We applied for and received permission to visit my father's former home, Pudas. On a sunny morning, we split up into two cars and drove out from Riga. A car tailed us for quite some time, turning around and disappearing just before we reached the outskirts of Umurga. "They were following us to make sure we didn't go anywhere else," said my cousin, Aivars, who was driving.

When my father last saw his childhood home, Pudas, it was meticulously cared for and thriving: well-maintained houses and outbuildings, apple orchards, berry bushes, fields of rye and wheat, potatoes, carrots, and beets, robust herds of cows, pigs, and sheep. Now, like a neglected grandmother, the house slumped and sagged in places, in need of the repair that comes with pride of ownership. The farm was part of the *sovkhoz* system: Soviet government property tended by workers without personal connection to the land. Soviet collectivization policy divided the house into four apartments, four families sharing the space once lived in by my father, his parents and two sisters. Looking at the deteriorated condition of the buildings, he paused for a minute or so, then remarked, "Well, everything changes over forty-five years."

In spite of this, he still had a deep connection to the land. He proudly posed for a photograph in front of the maple tree he planted as a boy, now standing forty feet tall, straight and strong. He recognized the buildings, and even recalled which crops were grown in the fields. For him, the place was still his childhood home, still beloved. After touring the farm, we headed to the Umurga cemetery. My father stood before his parents' graves silently for a few minutes, then asked which

SIMPLIFIED CHOICES

grave was his mother's and which one was his father's. Locked in a moment of private grief, he cried. My mother, Maruta, and I did too. I cried for the grandparents I never knew.

As foreign as the country now seemed, I saw how much being back in Latvia meant to my parents. I was beginning to understand the pain and loss they had kept from us all of our lives. The energy that both he and my mother applied to raising me, Maruta, and Karl with strong Latvian identities was the way they showed their love for their homeland. The reality of all the *nevers* they experienced—never seeing parents again, never sharing emotions or experiences—became enshrined in *forever*. Forever holding memories of Latvia in their hearts, forever keeping the language alive by teaching it to us, forever thinking of themselves as Latvians.

Prior to this trip, Latvian language and culture were what I called the essence of our Latvian identity. I knew that they longed to see Latvia again from conversations, the songs they sang, and the commemorations of important Latvian dates. I knew they missed their families from the packages, letters, and pictures they sent to Latvia. The part I lacked was a real understanding of their pain. At the time of this trip, I had not yet read the letters my mother wrote expressing her alienation and sorrow. The pain of leaving, of family separation, was not something they discussed openly with us. They kept silent about their pain. Being with them in a greatly changed Latvia, one so different from the country they left behind, made it impossible to hide their loss. Huddled around the table, my father and his sisters whispered intently to each other while the rest of us ate and conversed. I got the feeling that they were trying to compress forty-five years of separation and completely different experiences into the few meals we would share together during our stay. The expression *making up for lost time* comes to mind. But, of course, you never really do. The time that has passed, time spent apart, is gone forever.

My father at Pudas, July 1989. Author's collection.

The Bērziņš Reunion

We did not visit my mother's birthplace in the town of Nītaure. At the time, my mother felt that the stress and emotion of visiting her old home would be too much. Nor could we visit the homes of her sisters, Aina and Rita, in Courland, as the region remained off-limits to foreign visitors. My mother nervously faced a part of her family history she had been spared in the United States: meeting her half-sister Maija, the child of Jānis and Emma, for the first time. The family meeting was arranged at Maija's *kolkhoz* in the village Vidriži. By contrast to the Spīgulis clan, the Bērziņš family was reserved. My mother shook hands with each of her sisters. Aina and Rita were quiet and, at first, appeared a little uneasy. Maija was warm and forthcoming, welcoming us to her home with joy. When my mother's brother, Kārlis, arrived, he shook her hand, saying, "You are so small. I remember you as being so big."

He was seven years old when he last saw my mother. The distance between the siblings slowly dissolved as we ate and drank; by the time we left, I was relieved to see my mother finally let her defenses down and cry. She had made a connection with her sisters and brother, but, again, there was no making up for lost time.

From left to right: Maija, Rita, Aina, my mother. Author's collection.

By the time our two-week trip was over, we were all ready to leave. My parents, in particular, were distraught by what they had seen in Soviet Latvia. After decades of longing, they hoped to return to their homeland, but that was not possible. Under Soviet rule, their homeland changed. The low standard of living, the shortages, and the knowledge that every word, every movement was watched by informants wore them down. Latvia no longer felt like home. Even my mother, who for so long resisted thinking this way, agreed. Upon deplaning in Boston, my father exclaimed, "Thank God we are back home. I could fall to my knees and kiss the ground!" After hearing about how we were Latvian, not American, all of my formative years, I was surprised. My father had become both Latvian and American.

The end of repression was coming. On August 23, 1989, the Balts organized peaceful demonstrations, joining hands in a human chain that stretched between the three capital cities of the Baltic states: Tallinn, Riga, and Vilnius. Participants sang Estonian, Latvian, and Lithuanian songs as they stood with clasped hands, protesting Soviet rule. The picture of the human chain, miles long, made the news around the world. The singing protests are now known as the Velvet Revolution.

Latvia's legislature declared its independence from the Soviet Union on May 4, 1990, now known as "the Latvian Republic's Restoration of Independence Day." In response, the Soviet government rejected the declaration and increased political and military pressure to remain in the USSR. My parents returned to Latvia for the second time in August 1991. It was a trip with a purpose. My father searched township records, produced proof of his previous ownership, and completed the required paperwork to sign Pudas over to his sister Valija, restoring the land he loved and tended as a young man to his family. My mother joined her sisters in Nītaure to erect a gravestone on their father's grave. During this visit, right-wing forces in the Soviet Union attempted a coup against Gorbachev on August 19. Two days later, the Latvian parliament formally declared its independence from the Soviet Union. In response, Soviet military forces occupied government buildings and radio stations throughout the Baltic countries. When the coup failed, the troops withdrew. Once again, my parents' nightmare returned in the form of Soviet military vehicles driving through Riga's streets, helicopters buzzing overhead, bringing back the trauma of 1940. Fortunately, their flight back to the United States left as scheduled. They never returned to Latvia again.

As part of the dissolution of the Soviet Union, Latvia received official recognition as an independent republic on December 25, 1991. In order to vote in Latvian elections, my parents obtained dual citizenship, as did many other émigrés; they wanted a voice in the rebuilding process of sovereign Latvia. Some of their émigré friends purchased property in Latvia, splitting their time between the United States and their homeland. Others returned to live, taking jobs and helping Latvia make the difficult transition from Communism to democracy. My parents chose to remain exclusively in the United States. Latvia had changed, but so had they. Though they carried both passports, my parents—like me—were now half and half.

Chapter 20

May the Sands Rest Lightly

Years passed. Aunt Elvīra died in 1997, followed by Visvaldis two years later. Elvīra and Visvaldis chose to return to the soil of free Latvia for their eternal peace. They are buried in the Nītaure cemetery, sharing the Bērziņš family plot with my grandfather Jānis, his first wife Zelma, second wife Olga, son Jānis Jr., and daughter Velta. The plot is neat, carefully tended by my cousins who rake the gravel, weed the ground covers on the graves, and put fresh flowers in standing vases.

My mother spent seven years in a nursing home, where my father visited her every day, conversing with her and reading from the Latvian newspaper *Laiks*. As Alzheimer's stole her memories and personality, she still recognized my father, smiling and clapping her hands in delight when he appeared. After she died in 2014, I thought my father would die shortly afterwards, but he continued on for five more years. What else could he do but accept his fate to live out his final years without the comfort of his wife's love? She had been his soul mate for sixty-three years, navigating their transition as Latvian immigrants to American citizens together. He kept going, like Latvians always did.

My father died on August 19, 2019, one month shy of his 101st birthday, outliving many of his friends. Those still able to travel came to bid him farewell. After a memorial service in the same Lutheran church he joined in 1950, we gathered in the adjacent community hall. True to a Latvian gathering, we served Latvian breads, plenty of food, wine, and a beautiful torte. We sang his old favorite, *Pūt vējiņi*, with all the Latvians joining in, no lyric sheets required. Afterwards, one of my American friends remarked how moving and beautiful the song was. Another commented on how amazing it was that everyone joined in and knew the song. I replied, "Of course we know the song. We're Latvians. We sing. It's in our souls."

My parents chose the Latvian Memorial Park in New York as their final resting place. Though they did not return to Latvia, they are interred among their friends, the diaspora Latvians. These are the people who sfhared their fate, their sorrows, their hardships, and joys. These are the people who understood their choices.

Vieglas smiltis. May the sands rest lightly.

Chapter 21

Return to Latvia

June 2023

Maruta and I returned to Latvia in June 2023, our first visit since 1989. We arrived on June 14: Deportation Day. Public buildings flew the Latvian flag at half-mast. Everywhere else, Latvian flags were displayed in front of buildings, draped with translucent black mourning banners. Latvians still remembered and honored the thousands who lost their lives in the Gulag. Many buildings also displayed Ukrainian flags, demonstrating solidarity with the Ukrainians fighting to keep their country and freedom.

We found a transformed country. Latvia is now a thriving democracy and member of the European Union. Stores are fully stocked with anything you could possibly need or want. Given Latvia's numerous farms, the food is all farm to table, fresh and delicious. Old Riga is restored and beautiful once again, restaurants and shops tucked in the winding cobblestone streets. Our relatives live in comfortable homes and apartments, not cramped conditions shared with multiple families. But the biggest change, by far, is the people. In 1989, they gave guarded terse answers to our questions. As several cousins remarked, "Our parents taught us that the walls had ears." Constantly watched and censored, Latvians could not trust anyone, even other members of the family. People would potentially inform on anyone to better their lives. The less they shared, the safer they felt. Silence protected them. Now unafraid, our relatives spoke freely about their country, the government, and their challenges.

We had a full agenda, visiting cousins and traveling the small country. Topping the list of our destinations was our mother's home village of Nītaure. By this time, Maruta and I had both read our mother's letters from Latvia. We knew how much she missed Latvia and longed for her family. But who was she really? What made her transition to a new country so much more difficult than our father's? Our mother was still an enigma, having kept so much to herself.

One sunny hot day, our cousin Daiga and her husband Aivars drove us out from Riga to search for our mother's past. Even today, Nītaure remains a tiny village. Though the main road was now paved, other roads were still hard-packed dirt, and the center of town had only a few houses and one small store. Looking around, we saw a couple of Soviet era apartment buildings, recognizable by exposed concrete construction, with little sign of life, other than laundry drying on a clothesline. After laying flowers on the family graves, we drove to the church our mother attended, deserted except for a cow grazing around the building, cowbell clanking as she moved. Driving on, we stopped at her elementary school, an imposing stone building that was originally built as a German baronial manor. A large, sloppy stork's nest sat atop the chimney, considered a good luck omen for the inhabitants of the building. As I walked around to the front of the building, the school director, a woman with short, spiked purple hair, poked her head out of a window and greeted me. I approached, introduced myself, and explained that we were visiting sites from our mother's childhood. She enthusiastically invited us in and gave us a tour of the entire building. Classrooms contained smart boards and computers, but, other than that, little had changed since our mother walked the halls. Latvia is a small country; while walking the grounds, through rows of tall, twisted, ancient trees, we discovered that she knew someone named

Spīgulis, undoubtedly one of our more distant relatives. Before we left, the school music director sat down at a piano located by the front entrance and played a beautiful melody for us. Looking around the school, listening to the music, I felt closer to my mother than I had for years. It was almost as if she was still there: a girl, running through the trees, laughing and singing with the innocence of those who have not yet experienced war.

At the director's suggestion, we stopped in at the library to look at some old Nītaure pictures. As things go in a small village, the librarian had already heard of our arrival and was awaiting us. It turned out that she was the unofficial Nītaure archivist. For years, she had collected the names of all the residents deported during both Soviet occupations. We found Emma and Maija's names on the list. While speaking with her, we learned the exact location of our mother's old home, Kubļi, that had burned down in the 1980s. Back in the car, we followed her directions and found the fields and woods where the house once stood. Two deep ruts leading to the former location of the house still remained, filled in with tall grasses and tiny purple wildflowers. Trees and shrubs surrounded the fields, but there was no sign of the buildings that my mother called home. I thought about Arnolds' letters and his descriptions of the area during wartime. What a shock it would have been to see it treeless, like the palm of a hand, as he described. The wind, birds, and stridulating insects were the only sounds we heard. Had the front really come through here? It was almost impossible to believe. Breathing in the stillness of the fields and woods, I realized what a country girl my mother had been. I imagined her standing in a field, singing orphan songs to the songbirds in the trees. The land showed me who she really was. Finally I understood just how miserable and jarring the adjustment to American cities like Saginaw and Boston must have been for her. She needed the land of Latvia to feel complete.

Driving back to Riga, we stopped in Sigulda. Aivars recalled the first time he set foot in a church: Christmas Eve 1991. He was part of an army unit stationed in the town. A group of soldiers went into the local church and stayed for a candlelight Christmas service, probably the first held here in forty-five years. As they entered, the worshippers sang *Silent Night*. Aivars was moved; he had never heard the hymn, nor any other Christmas music. Religious thought and practice were forbidden under the Soviet occupation, so Christmas was not observed. Children born during that time were not christened; they had "naming celebrations" of a secular nature. Anyone worshipping God or praying had to do this in secret. The Soviets closed churches and repurposed them as concert halls, museums, or community centers. Not surprisingly, church attendance in Latvia today is fairly low.

We spent the remaining two weeks visiting more cousins, who outdid themselves with hospitality, driving us across Latvia to visit with family members, see local sights, and taste regional specialties. Seeing our aunts, Aina and Maija, we had the chance to fill in our family tree and ask questions about what really happened during the war. Both welcomed us lovingly, as if we had grown up a few villages away. We asked Maija why she and her mother were deported in 1949: "We were deported by accident. There was a list of deportees, but two people had bribed officials to let them disappear. The gendarmes had to find two bodies to replace them, so they came to our house." Maija added, "Even though it was a mistake, no one ever got sent back once they got to Siberia."

On the Summer Solstice, we drove out to our cousin Aivars' house and visited Pudas. His brother, Ilmārs, now manages the forest around the farm. Fields are rented out to a local farmer, and a distant relative now lives in the old house. After visiting the cemetery where our grandparents and aunts are laid to rest, we returned to Aivars' home and celebrated the solstice with a feast and large bonfire. Maruta and I were exhausted from the travel, so we did not await the sunrise, taking our chances with the mischievous spirits that might have escaped from the underworld through the open gates.

We were nearing the end of our trip, but still had more cousins to see. Over lunch in her backyard gazebo, our cousin Inga described the Soviet era as bleak, gray, and hopeless. Back then, Latvians felt that they did not deserve anything, that they had to save and conserve because there would never be enough. They lived in crowded apartments and struggled to obtain necessary supplies to live. The packages my parents sent were the only way they obtained medicines and necessities, like quality eyeglasses or good shoes. Interestingly, the letters I read insisted that they could get anything in Latvia SSR, mentioning the needed items in a casual postscript. This was staged for the Soviet censors; Latvians dared not suggest that the mighty Soviet Union had less than optimum living conditions. As a child, Inga joined the Young Pioneers, the Communist version of Scouts. She came home proudly wearing her red scarf one day; grandfather Pēteris simply turned away without saying a word. As she said, with the retrospective wisdom of age, "How must he have felt, having spent eight years in Siberia, then seeing his grandchild wear the red scarf!"

The day before we left, we met our childhood friend, Viktors, for lunch. The son of my godfather, Viktors was a member of our exile family. We grew up together, celebrating holidays, going to Latvian school, and spending hours playing games like flashlight tag while our parents visited. His father was one of the Gersicania brothers my father sponsored back in 1950. Viktors came to live in Latvia by way of a career in the United States Army. In 1991, the United States government opened offices in all of the newly independent former Soviet republics. Given his fluency in the language, Viktors was a natural selection to open the United States military office in Riga. As soon as he set foot on Latvian soil, he felt at home. Latvia was a special place, his fatherland. He met his future wife, got married, and applied for dual citizenship. As he said, "I love the United States. I love Latvia. I feel at home in both places."

Simplified Choices

I began this search seeking answers about my identity: what did it mean to be Latvian? Love of land, the almost sacred bond between the land and people is still evident. Several of our cousins had beautifully tended gardens, filled with flowers and vegetables. Our relatives all shared the same work ethic as my parents. What has changed, is their acceptance of fate, the *as the master commands* mentality of my parents' generation. Our contemporary relatives now feel possibility and hope. They know they have choices to make a different kind of life, even challenging their government, if necessary. They no longer have to accept what fate hands them.

Tension still exists between Russians and Latvians. Today, about twenty-five percent of Latvia's inhabitants are ethnic Russians, the result of the Soviet Union's aggressive Russification efforts. While some regard Latvia as their home, marrying Latvians and learning the language and culture, many have not. Latvians recently voted to begin closing publicly funded Russian schools in a phase-out program. In the future, ethnic Russians opting to send their children to Russian-speaking schools will have to pay private tuition. Following Putin's invasion of Ukraine, Latvia is shoring up its defense and reducing its dependence on Russian energy and products. As a defensive move, Latvia's transportation department is changing the width of its train tracks so that they are no longer the same as those used in Russia. Recently, the *Saeima* voted to increase the percentage of Latvia's gross national product devoted to military spending to 4%. Prior to this, Latvia and the other Baltic nations consistently met the NATO requirement of spending at least 2% of their gross national products on defense. Latvians are acutely aware of Russia's denial that the Baltic countries were forcibly annexed. Vladimir Putin has repeatedly referred to the loss of the Baltic territories as a geopolitical disaster. Latvia has no intention of allowing Russia to annex their country again. The former master no longer commands.

The most important part of being Latvian I discovered was one I had not fully appreciated before: the collective pain my parents, their families, and friends felt. For my parents and other diaspora Latvians, it was the Year of Terror, the Nazi occupation and Holocaust, the war, the second Soviet occupation, emigration, and beginning a new life far away from their families. My grandparents, aunts, and uncles who remained in Latvia shared the pain of the three occupations and the war. They had the additional pain of living under the Soviet master, suffering repressions, denied their language and culture, forbidden to teach their children about religion or Latvian history. My parents had freedom but lost their families, their country, and had to create their own community in a foreign land. My relatives remaining in Latvia lacked freedom but had each other. Those of us who grew up in the diaspora share the pain of Latvia's history, our parents' experiences, and the loss of family. We are products of that history, those experiences, that loss.

My father used the term "simplified choices" to describe decisions made under threats, during occupations, in wartime, or in refugee camps. "Simplified" does not mean simple. The choices my parents made may have seemed to them like the best ones at the time, but they were complex and painful. Even if they believed in fate, they still made choices they believed increased their chance of survival. When survival is at stake, the importance of evaluating wrong versus right diminishes.

After the research, the interviews, the letters, and returning to Latvia, I understood what it meant to be Latvian better than I did while growing up. Latvians have experienced collective sorrow and overwhelming loss. Centuries of living under foreign occupations and rules that change with each regime. Wars. Holocaust. Mothers losing husbands and children. Brothers fighting brothers. Terrified children and their parents taken at night, forced onto cattle cars bound for concentration camps, or exiled to Gulag camps. Refugees fleeing the land they loved in an attempt to have a chance at life. People never seeing their loved ones again. The loss of freedom for a nation that had known it for only twenty-one years but had craved it for centuries.

I understand why Latvians sing. To speak would be to let the pain in, to recognize it individually, and it would be crushing. A song is a community experience. Through songs, my parents and their friends shared their losses, their grief, but also their hopes and joys. The songs were medicine. The songs healed.

In 1989, Latvia felt like a frightening, foreign country. Freed of the Soviet occupation, it now feels familiar and comfortable. The warm welcome from my relatives, the ease of conversing in Latvian, the beauty and peace of the land, all fit. My ancestors are buried here. My cousins and family history live here. Like Viktors said, I feel at home in both places.

Mr. Thomson, our old friend with the chocolates, was right. I can't split myself in half. I am not half and half. I am one hundred percent American. I am also one hundred percent Latvian. I am both. Forever.

Acknowledgments

Almost six years ago, it was my good fortune to have dinner with Thomas Crew, military historian, author, and friend. I had recently found my uncle's letters from the Eastern Front. Intrigued, Tom asked me about my uncle, the letters, and my parents. By the end of our dinner, he said, "You have a book here, Anita. You have to write it." At the time, I thought the book would be a history of Latvia, weaving in my family story. Tom encouraged and advised me during years of research conducted through the Covid pandemic, answered countless questions, and edited the drafts of that version of my book. He also introduced me to Chris Robinson, cartographer, who created precise maps to support my narrative. Thank you, Tom. I would never have gotten there without your support and help.

I thought I was done. Then my dear talented friend, Kate Youngdahl, a seasoned writer, filmmaker, teacher, and poet, read the manuscript and called me, saying, "Do you want to hear what I have to say?" Kate immediately saw that the book should be a memoir; her invaluable suggestions helped me switch the focus to my family history. Thank you, Kate. This book would not exist without your guidance.

Kate also introduced me to Baron Wormser, poet, author, teacher, and editor, who sensitively edited the book, offering suggestions as to where I could deepen the story. Thank you, Baron—it is a much better book with those additions.

Thank you to my brother, Karl Spīgulis, and sister, Maruta Litus, for translation assistance and countless discussions about our family history. Together, we pieced together a family story that was missing information. Maruta traveled to Latvia with me in June 2023, seeking answers, taking notes, and trying to make sense of the new information we gained, particularly about our mother. Thank you, Marty—our trip enabled me to complete this book, and will remain one of the fondest memories of my life.

As all authors do, I imposed upon my family and friends to read the manuscript in its various stages of development. Maruta Litus, Chuck DeSnyder, Lisa Tannenbaum, Erin Anderson, and Martha Tripp, thank you for your careful reading and feedback. Thanks to my friend Eve Berne, speech and language pathologist, who listened patiently while I explained Latvian pronunciation, offering her suggestions as to how to create a key for non-Latvian speakers.

In Latvia, there are many people to thank. Jānis Tomaševskis of the Latvian War Museum filled in the gaps and shared information about my Uncle Arnolds. Aigars Lielbārdis of the Latvian Folklore Institute explained my father's invocation and provided historical information about Latvian charms. The Latvian Occupation Museum graciously gave permission to use photographs of Riga during the first Soviet invasion. On a personal note, thank you, Aunt Aina, for sharing painful memories. Thanks to my cousin, Daiga, and her husband, Aivars, who arranged our schedule and facilitated our quest to discover our mother. I am also grateful to all of our Latvian cousins who welcomed us and introduced us to independent Latvia.

Finally, thank you to Chuck, Ben, Eric, and Erin for cheering me on, offering encouragement when I needed it, and listening to my ideas as I sought clarity. Your support kept me going. I love you all.

Appendix A: Latvian Pronunciation Guide

A pronunciation guide to key Latvian names, places, or terms appearing by chapter is provided below. Latvian words are almost always accented on the first syllable.

<u>Vowels</u>

- Vowels can be short or long, indicated by a macron over a long vowel.
- /a/ (short) is pronounced "u" (up); /ā/ (long) is pronounced "ah"
- /e/ is pronounced as in English (Ed); /ē/ draws the sound out long (eh) or /ai/ in /**ai**r/
- /i/ is pronounced as in English (it); /ī/ is pronounced /ee/
- /o/ is quite different from its English counterpart, pronounced as a vowel diphthong, gliding the sounds /oo/ and /aw/; /ō/ is pronounced /oh/
- /u/ is pronounced as a cross between /oo/ and /ŭ/, a blend of "moon" and "mun." In the guide below, this is indicated as /oo/

Appendix A: Latvian Pronunciation Guide

- /ū/ is pronounced /oo/ as in "moon." In the guide below, this is indicated as /ōō/
- Short /a/ endings of words are pronounced /uh/ as in "Atlanta"
- Latvian has several vowel diphthongs. Commonly encountered is /ie/ pronounced /eeya/ blended together quickly so it is one syllable, not two

Consonants

Most consonants are similar to their English counterparts, with a few notable exceptions (others exist but are not found in this text):

- /c/ is pronounced as the /ts/ sound in /i**ts**/
- /g/ is always a hard sound, as in /**g**ate/ unless it has a diacritic above it: /ġ/ pronounced /j/ as in /**j**ump/
- /j/ is pronounced as /y/ in /**y**es/; there is no /y/ in the Latvian alphabet
- /l/ is pronounced as in English; /ļ/ is /ly/ as if pronouncing both the l and y (**y**es) blended together, quite different from the English sound
- /r/ is rolled more than in English, /rr/
- Diacritics indicate digraph sounds
- /š/ is /sh/
- /č/ is /ch/
- /ņ/ is pronounced like the /ny/ in "ca**ny**on", or the /ng/ in "hi**ng**e," depending on the speaker's accent

Pronunciations are approximate and based on the author's accent, which is a blend of the Livonian accent and American English.

Appendix A: Latvian Pronunciation Guide

Family Names				
Name	**Pronunciation**	**Name**	**Pronunciation**
Arvīds	Ar/veeds	Skaidrīte Bērziņš	Sky/dree/teh Bear/zinsh (n like canyon)
Pēteris Spīgulis	Peh/ter/iss Spee/ghoul/iss	Kristīne Ārgalis	Kris/teen/eh Are/gull/iss
Alīne	Al/een/eh	Valija	Vull/ee/yuh
Visvaldis Bišs	Viss/vull/dis Bish	Elvīra	El/vee/ruh
Aina	Eye/nuh	Jānis	Yah/niss
Kārlis	Car/liss	Maija	My/uh
Sīpols	See/pols		

Appendix A: Latvian Pronunciation Guide

\multicolumn{4}{c}{Half and Half}			
Latvian Word	**Pronunciation**	**Latvian Word**	**Pronunciation**
Trimda	Trim/duh	Pīragi	Pee/rah/gih (like git)
Pūt Vējiņi	Poot Vay/ih/nyih (canyon)	Zintas	Zin/tuss
\multicolumn{4}{c}{As the Master Commands}			
Vieglas smiltis	Veeya/gluss smill/tiss	Pērkons	Par (like **Pa**ris)/koo awns
Laima Laime	Lie/muh Lie/meh	Auseklis	Ow/sek/liss
Saule	Sow/leh	Jāņi	Yah/ny/ih (canyon)
Kā kungs pavēl	Kah koongss puh/vehl		
\multicolumn{4}{c}{Masters of Their Land}			
Izsūtīsanas Diena	Iz/soo/tee/shun/us Dee/yen/uh	Tautas Padome	Tow/tuss Pud/oh/meh
Dievs svētī Latviju	Deeyavs (runs together in one syllable) Sveh/tee Lut/vee/yoo	Kurzeme	Cour/zem/eh
\multicolumn{4}{c}{Kulak Son}			
Bērzlejas	Bears/ley/us	Katvari	Cut/var/ih
Andrejs	Un/drays	Umurga	Oo/moor/gah
Pudas	Poo/dass	Kreišmanis	Kraysh/mun/iss
Limbažu/Limbaži	Lim/bazh/oo or Lim/bazh/ih (zh pronounced like /s/ in pleasure	Sapraša	Sup/rush/uh
Nepraša	Neh/prush/uh		
\multicolumn{4}{c}{Orphan Girl}			
Nītaure	Nee/tow/reh	Laģi	Luh/jih (j like in jump)
Kubļi	Koo/blyih	Žigurmāte	Zhih/goor/mah/teh
Cēsis	Tseh/sis	Vaidava	Vy/duh/vuh

Appendix A: Latvian Pronunciation Guide

\multicolumn{4}{c	}{**Latvia For Latvians!**}
Kārlis Ulmanis	Car/liss Ool/mun/iss	Saeima	Sigh/muh
Čakste	Chuck/steh	Kviesis	Kv/eeya/sis
Vadonis	Vud/o/niss (short o)	Saimnieks	Sigh/m/neeyks/
		Saimniece	Sigh/m/neey/tseh
\multicolumn{4}{c	}{**The Year of Terror**}
Baigais Gads	Buy/guys Guds (rhymes with cuds)	Kirhenšteins	Keer/hen/shteins
Vilnis Zirdziņš	Vil/niss Zir/dzinysh (canyon)	Stūru Māja	Stoo/roo My/yuh
Lat	lut	Vilnis Zirdziņš	Vill/niss Zir/dzinysh (canyon)
Stūru Māja	Stoo/roo My/uh	Lāčplēsis	Lawch/pleh/sis
Lāčplēšu dziesma	Lawch/pleh/shoo dz/eeya/smuh	Zābaks	Zah/bucks
Astrīda	Us/tree/duh		
\multicolumn{4}{c	}{**Trading One Master For Another**}
Liepāja	Leeya/paw/yuh	Daugavpils	Dow/guv/pills
Krustpils	Kroost/pills	Pašpārvalde	Pash (/a/ like up/) par/vul/deh
\multicolumn{4}{c	}{**Forever No Peace Beneath Latvia's Birches**}
Biķernieki	Bich/err/nyeey/kih (canyon)	Mežaparks	Mezh/uh/parks
Rumbula	Room/boo/lah	Arājs	Ar/eyes
Vagulāns	Vug/oo/lahns	Teidemanis	Tay/deh/mahn/iss
\multicolumn{4}{c	}{**Life is a Struggle**}
Daugava	Dow/guv/uh	Kurzemes cietoksnis	Cour/zem/ehs Tseeya/too-ock/sniss
Remte	Rem/teh	Leonīds	Leh/o/needs

Appendix A: Latvian Pronunciation Guide

Every Man For Himself			
Īle	Ee/leh	Vaiņode	Vy/nyooaw/deh
To Stop Was to Die			
Madona	Mud/oo awn/uh	Džukste	Jook/steh
Tēvija	Teh/vee/yah	Jelgava	Yell/guv/ah
Ventspils	Vents/pills		
Simplified Choices			
Valmiera	Vull/meer/uh	Vidzeme	Vidz/em/eh
Latgale	Lut/gull/eh	Lībeks	Lee/beks

Appendix B: Letters from Arnolds Bērziņš

Adolf Hitler's 144-9

    1943 21st November

    Greetings!!!

    My sincerest thanks for the package and letter that I received. But I delayed in my response, and good that I did. If I had written, you would have sent the package and I would not have received it, because see I am already in Rīga. Tomorrow I may still be here, but then after that probably to Germany. The trip to Germany turned out to be completely unexpected, and that is why there was no time to write home. Yesterday at three I received the news, and at 18:00 had to drive to Rīga. We arrived in Rīga this morning at 10:00 and by the time all was settled and we arrived here it was already afternoon. Things did not go badly for me in Liepāja and they will not go badly in Germany either. We will be in Germany about a month or maybe longer. The service there will be tough but after that when I return again I will have more free time. I will probably have to go to southern Germany.

    Most of all I needed soap because that was not distributed to us. If Aina you have already sent something already that is too bad but eventually I will get it. Too bad that my suitcase cannot be packed full with food because that will be harder to get in Germany. But all has to be overcome. Life is a struggle.

Until now, the service has been much easier for me than at home, for at home I did not have as much free time. I had lived comfortably among my company so much that I was sorry to leave.

With my health, things are also going well except that I lost my voice from Liepāja's climate. Sometimes if I want to say something my mouth opens and closes but I cannot get any sound out. When you receive this letter then call home and tell everyone not to send anything. This evening I will try to call home.

With greetings,
Arnolds

Appendix B: Letters from Arnolds Bērziņš

1945 13th January

Dear greetings!

First of all, thank you for the New Year's wishes. For us here, Christmas was spent during fierce battles, so understandably it was impossible to have the holiday spirit. All ended fortunately, although the entire time was spent in bigger or smaller battles. We were all prepared to celebrate the holidays, but those cursed Russians began their attack December 23rd. Where that happened you may have read in the newspapers, because a lot was written about the third Kurzemes [Courland] battle.

We spent New Year's in a stable because if you do not want to freeze to death on the field you have to get used to that kind of living. I am lucky that I was safe and healthy and able to greet the New Year.

September 26th I went through Nītaure, but as it was late I could not go home, because the night front was already in Nītaure, and in that event I might have stayed with the Russians. On top of this, I returned from ???[illegible] and was searching for my unit, which I caught only by Eglīniem at the last possible moment. Nītaure was empty and I did not meet anyone and therefore I know nothing about home…On the windowsill, I wrote that I had been there and if later some of the people meet up with them they can say that I am safe and healthy. I was standing further along on the road to Lagi when I heard from a boy that my unit was stationed behind Ratnieki [another village] and was getting ready to drive further, so I did not go further into Lagi. From Zavadas looking toward Lagi was like looking at a palm [of a hand] because the forest that had been between them was chopped down and trenches were dug along the swamp's edge. That is why I cannot believe that Lagi remained intact, because the front was there for about a week. We spent one more night in Peļņos and then stopped Mālpilī not far from that high tower and road that led to Siksni. All the way to Rīga we met many refugees from many different townships, just not from Nītaure. I knew absolutely nothing about any of you. I only now received your letter. You cannot imagine the happiness I felt that at least I know where you are. At the end of October, I also received the letter that I guess you wrote August 27th.

 I gather you do not know anything about Skaidrīte either, I think perhaps she stayed there, because there were rapid changes. For that reason, I beg you to write quickly if you hear any news about the rest of them. With longing, I will await every one of your letters. I will write back more frequently as much as possible, at least every week I will try to write a letter. Maybe you could correspond with some of my friends, who have no one who can write to them, because they remained on the Russian side. Maybe there are some other Latvian women [who would be willing to write]. Give them this address. If you write to someone, please do not tell them that you are my sister. Do not take offense at my suggestions, but you cannot imagine how every one of us waits for just a line. Their names: Corporal O. Caune and helmsman J. Lukstiņš. Now we have a new number [Feldpost], but letters arrive also at the old number. Now it is #57966. Wishing you a happy New Year and maybe this year I will return to my homeland.

 Arnolds

Appendix B: Letters from Arnolds Bērziņš

Feldpost #57966
1945. 1. March
In the bunker, [illegible]
Greetings Sister!!

Thank you very much for your letter, which I received 23. February. I could not answer right away because we were plagued by fierce fighting. Now everything is quiet and calm again. There were pretty wild days, but all the same, everything went luckily. This commotion, compared with Christmas, was a cinch!

Regarding Nītaure, I can say that I guess no one has been driven out. On 27 September I was in Mālpils. Then events happened quickly and I did not get a chance to get there [to Nītaure]... I also have not gotten newspapers from Valmiera. I think that many did not get out of that corner. Fate is dreadful but we cannot do anything about that. Let us hope that, in the end, it will not be that horrible...

For me personally, I am truly doing well and can be quite satisfied with myself. I have plenty of everything, I have shoes and have also eaten well. At least I feel well-fed. I am also satisfied with the life of a soldier. It is not pleasant, but all the same, it has its own beauty and attractiveness. Sometimes thinking about the old peacetime life, after this kind of life it would be difficult to get used to the old life again. Living here, we have gotten spoiled, like soldiers do. We are no longer used to work. Personally, I cannot imagine that I could work like I used to work back at home. Thus far, I have not learned how to drink and smoke, and I do not plan to do those things. We can get together with civilians frequently, because there are also civilians in the houses where we are staying. The kinds of parties that are held here, you cannot imagine. Even women are still possible to meet, and so with our unit are two prostitutes.

Maybe this seems strange to you, but what can a soldier do, he has to find some kind of distraction. I usually do not participate in those orgies, because my [girl]friend is quite respectful. There are still lots of civilians in Kurzeme.

A few days ago we forced back the Russians in one place and some horrible sights were revealed. We found seven women and all had gunshots to the head. After this sight, our hatred for the Russians increased. You cannot imagine the feelings we had seeing all of that. I think that you are somewhere in Prussia and that is why the beginning battles resulted in a small break. As of January 30, I have been awarded the Iron Cross, 2nd class. Otherwise all is the same. I will await your response.

With greetings,
Arnolds

Appendix B: Letters from Arnolds Bērziņš

1945. 14th March

In the bunker, "Rādi redzīt"

Greetings from the homeland!

After such a long time has passed, I will try to write tonight. I would have written sooner, but on account of heavy fighting, it was not possible. On account of the frequent relocations, I just did not have the desire to write. During the days, it is nonstop work, and the nights are spent under the open skies or in a stable if we find one. The last several days were very cold and that is why I did not want to write. Now I am back in the fighting region, now it is calmer, but things could flare up again at any moment. During the last few days, the thaw has set in, and, with that, I think that spring will arrive. During the summer, all the hardships will be much easier to bear than they are in winter. My clothing is very good and there is no reason to worry about freezing. Food is also very good, because we have the chance to look for something ourselves. In a word, I am very good friends with the service. I am sure you will have heard and read a lot about our 19th division. Our commander has said that the Kurzemes soldiers are the best in the world, and we are the best in Kurzeme, in other words, the best of the best. Therefore, sister, you can be proud that your brother is fighting here. Dreiliņš and Strūka are also with me. Dreiliņš father is also somewhere in the Mecklenburg area. There are a lot of civilians and refugees in Kurzeme and those that are close to the front get to witness all the horrors of war.

As of late, I have something new and interesting for you. One day, that is the fourth of March, I received a letter from Aina. The surprise was so great that I walked around completely dizzy all day. I could not think clearly anymore. I had given her my address, but the next day I was not there anymore because we had to head to the battlefield. Three of my colleagues stayed at that address, and then Aina went and saw them, but she did not have a lot of time, because in the evening even she had to move. In that place, we were only about three kilometers from each other, but even so, it was not possible to meet, now we are probably about ten kilometers apart. I will try to get to see her when it is possible. Aina is working in some place that is only about three kilometers from the front. Truthfully, she is much closer to the horrors than I am. During battle, we are closer, but otherwise during calmer times, I am twice as far away [from wartime horrors]. Aina, however, has courage, and she undoubtedly has seen a lot. Even so, it is not safe for such a young girl to be living by herself so close to soldiers, but there is not anything we can do about it for now. The rest [of the family] have also apparently left home and landed somewhereby Inču Kalns, but where they are now, I do not know. Whether they are in Germany, Kurzeme, or Vidzeme. By Inču Kalns, the front stopped for a bit, and if they did not delay too much, it would have been possible to cross the Daugava. Hard, hard to know, but what can we do. Maybe you could put an advertisement in "Tēvija" that you and I are looking for them. Truly, I do not know what to do.

I will try to get Aina to me, so if you want to write to her then write to me and I will forward the letter to her. Do not be afraid for me, sister, I am very sorry for everyone else.

Until we meet again,
Arnolds

Notes

1. Half and Half

1. A pronunciation guide to key Latvian terms appears in Appendix A.
2. *Daugavas Vestnesis* Nr. 135, Saturday, 15 June 1940.
3. Latvian folk song, "Pūt vējiņi," first verse. Popular Latvian songs are credited as "folk songs" because they belong to the people, not the original composer or lyricist, whose names are lost over time.

2. As the Master Commands

1. Pie tēvu zemes dārgās," first verse, Auseklis words adapted by Schiller, music by E. Dārziņš.
2. Daina Bleiere, Ilgvars Butulis, Inesis Feldmanis, Aivars Stranga, and Antonijs Zunda, editors, *History of Latvia, the 20th Century* (Riga: Jumava, 2006), 39. Andrejs Plakans, *The Latvians: A Short History* (Stanford: Hoover Institution Press, 1995) 25.
3. Plakans, *The Latvians*, 63-65.
4. Plakans, *The Latvians*, 86. Bleiere, et al., *History of Latvia*, 39.

3. Masters of Their Land

1. Plakans, *The Latvians*, 105; Bleiere, et al., *History of Latvia*, 70.
2. Bleiere, et al., *History of Latvia*, 75-76.
3. Bleiere, et al., *History of Latvia*, 78-79; Prit Buttar, *Between Giants: The Battle for the Baltics in World War II* (New York: Osprey Publishing, 2015), 20-21; Edgars Dunsdorfs, *Latvijas vēstures atlants: skolām un pašmācībai* (Melbourne: Kārļa Zariņa Fonds, 1976), 210.
4. Bleiere, et al., *History of Latvia*, 193.
5. Kārlis Baumanis, "Dievs, svētī Latviju," Latvian national anthem (1873).
6. Following the October Revolution of 1917, Lenin and the Bolshevik Party assumed power in Russia, renamed the Russian Socialist Federative Soviet Republic, often abbreviated as Soviet Russia. It was not until the Russian Civil War ended in 1922 that it was known as the Union of Soviet Socialist Republics (USSR), comprised of Russia, Ukraine, Belarus, and Transcaucasia.
7. The Consul General at Moscow (Summers) to the Secretary of State, "Article Three," in *Foreign Relations of the United States: 1918 The Conclusion of the Peace of*

NOTES

    Brest–Litovsk, (New Haven, CT: Yale Law Library, The Avalon Project: Foreign Relations), accessed May 31, 2021. https://avalon.law.yale.edu/20th_century/bl34.asp.
8. Nigel Jones, *The Birth of the Nazis: How the Freikorps Blazed a Trail for Hitler*,(New York, Carroll & Graf Publishers, 2004), 124-125.
9. Jones, *The Birth of the Nazis*, 130.
10. Jānis Bērziņš letter to Elvīra Bišs, March 3, 1965.
11. "Article II. Peace Treaty Between Latvia and Russia, August 11, 1920, Riga," in *League of Nations Treaty Series* (WWII Databases: 1920 LNT Ser 63; 2 LNTS 195, posted December 20, 2009), *http://www.worldlii.org/int/oth-er/treaties/LNTSer/1920/63.html.*
12. Bleiere, et al., *History of Latvia*, 135–142; Plakans, *The Latvians*, 119–120.
13. Plakans, *The Latvians*, 122–123.
14. Bleiere, et al., *History of Latvia*, 51–55.

5. Orphan Girl

1. Augusts Briedis, "Gaišais rīts," hymn, fourth verse.
2. Jānis Bērziņš letter to Skaidrīte Spīgulis, June 15, 1968.
3. Ulmanis, Kārlis, 1923, as qtd in Siliņš, Zigurds, editor, *Redzu jaunu dienu nākam* (Riga: Avots, 1992) 17.

6. Latvia for Latvians!

1. Jordan Tyler Kuck, *"The Dictator Without a Uniform: Kārlis Ulmanis, Agrarian Nationalism, Transnational Fascism, and Interwar Latvia,"* (PhD Dissertation, University of Tennessee, 2014, https://trace.tennessee.edu/utk-graddiss/2895), 115-121.
2. Edgars Dunsdorfs, *Latvijas vēsture* (United States: Amerikas Latviešu Apvienība, 1980), 256.
3. Latvijas Republikas Saeima, "History of the Legislature: The People's Council," *About the Saeima*, accessed June 7, 2021, https://www.saeima.lv/en/about-saeima/history-of-the-legislature.
4. Constitutional Assembly, "Latvijas Republikas Satversme" [Constitution of the Republic of Latvia], (adopted February 15, 1922), part VIII, accessed June 7, 2021, "Cilvēka pamattiesības likumi" [Fundamental human rights laws], likumi.lv/ta/id/57980-latvijas-republikas-satversme.
5. Plakans, *The Latvians*, 138.
6. Bleiere, et al., *History of Latvia*, 167.
7. Vita Zelče, ""Bēgšanas no brīvības: Kārļa Ulmaņa režīma ideoloģija un rituāli," in *Reiz dzīvoja Kārlis Ulmanis* (Agora No. 6, Zinātne), 325-326.
8. *Aizsargs*, 1937. G. 9 burtnīca, 30, as qtd in Bērziņš, *Ulmanis*, 223-225.

9. Bleiere, et al., *History of Latvia*, 172-175; Dunsdorfs, *Latvijas vēsture*, 279; Zelče, *"Bēgšanas no brīvības,"* 328.
10. Bleiere, et al., *History of Latvia*, 163-164.
11. Plakans, *The Latvians*, 138.
12. 1935 Census.
13. Plakans, *The Latvians*, 135-138.
14. Declassified and released by Central Intelligence Agency Sources Methods Exemption 3B2B Nazi War Crimes Disclosure Act Date of release: 2007; date of memo: 5 August 1955.
15. Dunsdorfs, *Latvijas vēsture*, 281.

7. The Devils' Pact

1. Latvian folk song, "Sarkandaiļa roze auga."
2. Esther B. Fein, "Soviets Confirm Nazi Pacts Dividing Europe," *The New York Times*, August 19, 1989, Section 1, page 1.
3. "Papers Relating to the Foreign Relations of the United States, The Paris Peace Conference 1919, Volume XIII," *The Covenant of the League of Nations, Articles 1-26,* Joseph V. Fuller, ed., (Washington, DC: Government Printing Office, 1947), history.state.gov/historicaldocuments/frus1919Parisv13.
4. Office of the Historian, United States Department of State. *The League of Nations 1920.* https://history.state.gov/milestones/1914-1920/league
5. Inesis Feldmanis and Aivars Stranga, *Destiny of the Baltic Entente 1934-1940*, (Latvian Institute of International Affairs, 1994), 8-9, 14.
6. Feldmanis, and Stranga, *Destiny of the Baltic Entente*, 33-34.
7. Donald Cameron Watt, *How War Came—The Immediate Origins of the Second World War, 1938-1939*, (New York: Pantheon Books, 1989), 224, 365.
8. Cameron Watt, *How War Came*, 113; Zara Steiner, *The Triumph of the Dark: European International History 1933-1939* (Oxford University Press, Oxford, United Kingdom, 2011), 884-886.
9. Cameron Watt, *How War Came*, 363-364.
10. Cameron Watt, *How War Came*, 447-448; 457-458; Steiner, *The Triumph of the Dark*, 910.
11. Cameron Watt, *How War Came*, 458-459. The English translation of the secret protocol appears in Appendix C.
12. Teske, Koestring, as qtd. in Cameron Watt, *How War Came*, 462.
13. Steiner, *The Triumph of the Dark*, 915.
14. Valters Nollendorfs, Ojārs Celle, Gundega Michelle, Uldis Neibergs, and Dagnija Staško, eds., *The Three Occupations of Latvia, 1940-1941: Soviet and Nazi Takeovers and Their Consequences* (Riga: Occupation Museum Foundation, 2005), 11.
15. Nollendorfs et al., *The Three Occupations of Latvia*, 11.

8. The Year of Terror

1. Irēne Šneidere, "The Occupation of Latvia in June 1940: A Few Aspects of the Technology of Soviet Aggression,"in *The Hidden and Forbidden History of Latvia Under Soviet and Nazi Occupations, 1940-1991*, Caune, et al., eds., (Riga: Latvian Institute of History, University of Latvia, 2005), 44-45.
2. Buttar, *Between Giants*, 43.
3. Šneidere, "Technology of Soviet Aggression," in *Hidden and Forbidden*, Caune, et al., eds., 46-47.
4. Šneidere, "Technology of Soviet Aggression," in *Hidden and Forbidden*, Caune, et al., eds., 48.
5. U. S. House of Representatives, Select Committee on Communist Aggression, *Communist Takeover and Occupation of Latvia*. Special Report No. 12, 83rd Congress, 2nd Session (Washington, DC: U. S. Government Printing Office, December 30, 1954), 10.
6. Krasnovodsk is in present-day Turkmenistan, bordered by Afghanistan and Iran. At the time of Ulmanis' imprisonment, it was known as the Turkmen Soviet Socialist Republic. "History of the Presidency, Former Presidents: Kārlis Ulmanis," President of the Republic of Latvia website (published online March 16, 2021), accessed January 15, 2022, https://www.president.lv/en/karlis-ulmanis.
7. Šneidere, "Technology of Soviet Aggression," in *Hidden and Forbidden*, Caune, et al., eds., 33.
8. Bohlen, Charles, *Minutes of Roosevelt–Stalin Meeting, December 1, 1943*, Report No.378 (Foreign Relations of the United States: Diplomatic Papers, The Conferences at Cairo and Tehran, 1943).
9. "Die, But Do Not Retreat," in *Time* (January 4, 1943), content.time.com/subscriber/article/0,33009,790648-1.00.html.
10. Bleiere, et al., *History of Latvia*, 249-254; Select Committee on Communist Aggression, *Communist Takeover and Occupation of Latvia*, 12-16.
11. Jānis Riekstiņš, "The 14 June 1941 Deportation in Latvia," in *Hidden and Forbidden*, Caune, et al., eds., 64.
12. Ben-Cion Pinchuk, as qtd. in Senn, "Baltic Battleground," in *Hidden and Forbidden*, Caune, et al., eds., 23.
13. Levin as qtd. in Senn, "Baltic Battleground," in *Hidden and Forbidden*, Caune, et al., eds., 24.
14. Bleiere, et al., *History of Latvia*, 249.
15. Vīksne, "Soviet Repressions Against Residents of Latvia," in *Hidden and Forbidden*, Caune, et al., eds., 60.
16. J. Graubiņš, V. Plūdons, "Lāčplēšu dziesma,"1934.
17. Šneidere, "Technology of Soviet Aggression," in *Hidden and Forbidden*, Caune, et al., eds., 39-40; Riekstiņš, "14 June 1941 Deportation," in *Hidden and Forbidden*, Caune, et al., eds., 68-70.
18. Šneidere, "Technology of Soviet Aggression," in *Hidden and Forbidden*, Caune, et al., eds., 39-42.

9. Trading One Master for Another

1. Alfred Rosenberg, as qtd. in Buttar, *Between Giants*, 57–58.
2. Inesis Feldmanis, "Latvia Under the Occupation of National Socialist Germany, 1941–1945," in *Hidden and Forbidden*, Caune, et al., eds., 77.
3. Buttar, *Between Giants*, 55-57.

10. Forever No Peace Beneath Latvia's Birches

1. Aivars Stranga, "Holocaust in Occupied Latvia," in *Hidden and Forbidden*, Caune, et al., eds., 164–165.
2. Office of the United States Chief of Counsel For Prosecution of Axis Criminality, *Nazi Conspiracy and Aggression, ("Red Series"), Vol VII*, 986.
3. Andrew Ezergailis, *The Holocaust in Latvia 1941-1944: The Missing Center*, (Riga: The Historical Institute of Latvia, 1989), 239-241; 245.
4. Bleiere, et al., *History of Latvia*, 283–284.
5. Ezergailis, *The Holocaust in Latvia*, 5.
6. Snyder, Timothy, *Bloodlands: Europe Between Hitler and Stalin*, (New York: Basic Books, 2010), 344.
7. Stranga, "Holocaust in Occupied Latvia," in *Hidden and Forbidden*, Caune et al., eds, 168-169.
8. Ezergailis, *The Holocaust in Latvia*, 67-69.
9. Rudīte Vīksne, "Members of the Arājs Kommando in Soviet Court Files: Social Position, Education, Reasons for Volunteering, Penalty," in *Hidden and Forbidden*, Caune et al., eds., 200-201.
10. Arturs Žvinklis, "Photo and Film Documents on the Holocaust in Latvia," in *Holocaust Research in Latvia*, Symposium of the Commission of Historians of Latvia, Vol. 12, (Riga: Materials of an International Conference, 12–13 June 2003, and 24 October 2003, and the Holocaust Studies in Latvia, 2002–2003), 164.
11. Vīksne, "Arājs Kommando," in *Hidden and Forbidden*, Caune et al., eds., 193.
12. Emīls Dārziņš, composer, and Kārlis Skalbe, lyrics, "Mūžam zili ir Latvijas kalni," verses 1-2, (1909-1910). A kokle is a traditional Latvian plucked stringed instrument, similar to the zither.

11. Life is a Struggle

1. Convention (IV) respecting the Laws and Customs of War on Land and its annex: Regulations concerning the Laws and Customs of War on Land," adopted October 18, 1907 at the International Peace Conference, The Hague, in *Treaties, States, Parties and Commentaries* (International Committee of the Red Cross database), Ihl-databases.icrc.org/ihl/INTRO/195.

Notes

2. Latvian folk song, "Tev dzīvē laimes nav," first verse.
3. Latvian National Archives, LVVA–6.2.2./5/7794, accessed July 8, 2020.
4. Latvian National Archives, LVVA–6.2.2./5/7794, accessed July 8, 2020.
5. All quotations in this paragraph are taken from Arnolds Bērziņš, letter dated November 21, 1943
6. Lieutenant Zegner's Field Service Report, November 28, 1943, in *Karavīrs otrā pasaules kara laikā*, 161–162.
7. P-71 fonds, 1. Apraksts, 3. Lieta, 35, p. 71. Latvian Historical Archives.
8. Archival database, Latvian War Museum, accessed July 21, 2020; Karl-Heinz Frieser, Klaus Schmider, Klaus Schönherr, Gerhard Schreiber, Krisztián Ungváry, and Bernd Wegner, *Germany and the Second World War, Vol. VIII. The Eastern Front 1943–1944: The War in the East and on the Neighboring Fronts* (Oxford, UK: Oxford University Press, 2017), 281; Silgailis, *Latvian Legion*, 62–67; Buttar, *Between Giants*, 163–164.
9. The 19th Latvian took up positions adjacent to the Latvian Legion 15th Division. This was the only time during the entire war that both divisions of the Latvian Legion fought together under Latvian command. Both divisions supported the German VI SS Corps.
10. Arthur Silgailis, *Latvian Legion* (San Jose, California: R. James Bender Publishing, 1986), 94–100.
11. Silgailis, *Latvian Legion*, 103-107
12. Arnolds Bērziņš, letter dated January 13, 1945.
13. Silgailis, *Latvian Legion*, 124; Buttar, *Between Giants*, 271.
14. Edgars Dunsdorfs, *Mūžīgais Latviešu karavīrs* (Melbourne, AU: Latvian Scout President General Karl Gopper Fund, 1966), 261.
15. Alberts Eglītis as qtd. in Osvalds Freivalds, *Kurzemes Cietoksnis I* (Copenhagen: Imanta, 1984), 150.
16. Arnolds Bērziņš, letter, January 13, 1945.
17. Alberts Eglītis as qtd. in Freivalds, *Kurzemes Cietoksnis I*, 150.
18. Silgailis, *Latvian Legion*, 123, 143; Freivalds, *Kurzemes Cietoksnis I*, 144.
19. Arnolds Bērziņš, letter dated January 13, 1945.
20. Silgailis, *Latvian Legion*, 147-149.
21. Arnolds Bērziņš, letter dated March 1, 1945.
22. *Latvijas Kareivis*, 26 January 1945 issue, Latvian War Museum, Riga.
23. Arnolds Bērziņš, letter dated March 14, 1945
24. Bleiere, et al., *History of Latvia*, 291-293; Buttar, *Between Giants*, 319.
25. Leonīds (surname unknown), letter to Skaidrīte Spīgulis, July 10 (year unknown).

12. Every Man for Himself

1. Gotenhafen refers to a Polish port city, known as Gdynia. It was renamed Gotenhafen by the Nazis during their occupation of Poland.

13. To Stop Was to Die

1. Elvīra Bišs, July 1988.
2. Astrīda Straumanis Ramrath, *Where Do I Belong? The Journey of a Country Girl*, (self-published, 2016), 51–53.
3. *Tēvija, Nr. 231,* (Riga: September 29, 1944), 1.
4. Buttar, *Between Giants,* 274–275.
5. Dagnija Neimane, *Flight From Latvia: A Six-Year Chronicle*, (self-published, 2016), 32.
6. Osvalds Freivalds, *Kurzemes Cietoksnis II* (Copenhagen: Imanta, 1954), 29–32; 30–35; 55.
7. Freivalds, *Kurzemes Cietoksnis II,* 27.
8. Freivalds, *Kurzemes Cietoksnis II,* 38.

14. Simplified Choices

1. In the 1930s, both the United States and Great Britain condemned the act of targeting civilians. During World War II, the Germans were the first to bomb civilian targets during their invasion of Poland. The Allies responded in kind, justifying the actions as necessary to stop the Nazis. Since my father lived under Nazi occupation, he may not have been aware of the fact that the Germans actually started the practice.
2. J. Norvilis, composer and J. Rainis, lyrics, "Mūsu zeme."

15. Little to Do But Wait

1. Arvīds Spīgulis, "Vide un Laiks," in *Gersicania,* Gunārs Grūbe, Arvids Spīgulis, Valfrīds Spuntelis, and Ilgonis Zariņš, eds., (New York: Grāmatu Draugs, 1963), 11.
2. Inesis Feldmanis, "Nazi Occupation Policy in Latvia (1941-1945): Current Problems of Research and Solutions" in *Latvia Under Nazi German Occupation 1941-1945,* eds. Andris Caune, Inesis Feldmanis, Heinrihs Stods, Irēne Šneidere, Rita Kļaviņa, Vija Stabulniece, com. Dzintars Eglītis, Symposium of the Commission of Historians of Latvia, Volume 11, (Riga: Institute of Latvian History, University of Riga, 2004), 70.
3. Latvian folk song, "Es nezinu un nesaprotu," first and second verses.
4. Mark Wyman, *DP: Europe's Displaced Persons, 1945–1951,* (Associated University Presses, 1989), 43–44.
5. The United Nations Relief and Rehabilitation Administration was created by an agreement between 44 nations on November 9, 1943. Its creation precedes that of the United Nations, which was formed in October 1945. Source: United Nations Archives, https://search.archives.un.org/united-nations-relief-and-rehabilitation-administration-unrra-1943-1946.

NOTES

6.6. Arolsen Archives, *"Background Information on Displaced Persons Documents,"* E-Guide, accessed November 3, 2020, https://eguide.arolsen-archives.org/en/additional-resources/background-information-on-displaced-persons-documents/.
77. Jānis Piksis, and Valfrīds Spuntelis, "Latvju Karavīri," in *Gersicania*, 80.
88. Inesis Feldmanis, and Kārlis Kangeris,*The Volunteer SS Legion in Latvia,* (Prague: Embassy of the Republic of Latvia in the Czech Republic, February 12, 2014), par. 7.
9.. Christian Höschler, *Displaced Persons in Postwar Europe: History and Historiography,* (Arolsen Archives), 14 - 19, accessed 12/15/2020, arolsenarchives.org/content/uploads/200215_aafundstuecke_web_en_rz.pdf.
10.. *Background Information on Displaced Persons Documents, E-Guide,* Arolsen Archives, https://eguide.arolsen-archives.org/en/additional-resources/background-information-on-displaced-persons-documents/, accessed November 3, 2020.
11. SHAEF Memorandum #38, Arolsen Archives, 6.1.1/82495546/ITS Digital Archive, accessed December 15, 2020.
12. *Background Information on Displaced Persons Documents, E-Guide,* Arolsen Archives, accessed December 15, 2020.
13.1. Latvian folk song, "Klusi, klusi, ratiņš rūc," verses 1, 3, 6, 7

16. POSSIBILITIES IN LIFE

1. Arnolds Grāmatiņš, "Universitātes Vēsture," in *Baltijas Universitāte: 1946–1949* (Germany: PBLA Kultūras fonds, 1989), 13.
2. Grāmatiņš, "Universitātes Vēsture,"in *Baltijas Universitāte,* 10–13.
3. Grāmatiņš, "Universitātes Vēsture,"in *Baltijas Universitāte,* 14–16.
4. Grāmatiņš, "Universitātes Vēsture," in *Baltijas Universitāte,* 18–19; Edgars Dunsdorfs, "Mīļam bērnam daudz vārdu," in *Baltijas Universitāte,* 56–58.
5. Grāmatiņš, "Universitātes Vēsture," *Baltijas Universitāte,* 19–21.
6. Jekabs Ziedars, "Jaunās korporācijas," from *Memoir* manuscript, E-mail correspondence with author, October 22, 2018.
7. Pauls Grūbe, "Gersicanias Devīzes un Simboli," in *Gersicania,* 8.

17. NOTHING LEFT AT HOME

1. Spridzāns, "On the Blackest Day of Latvia," in *Latvijas Vestnesis*
2. Latvijas Iedzīvotāju 1949. gada 25. marta deportācija, Latvijas Valsts Arhīvs, accessed March 26, 2020, http://www.archiv.org.lv/dep1941/meklesana49.php
3. Latvian folk song, "Uz tālām siltām saules zemēm." *Jāņi* is the Latvian summer solstice celebration when young women wove wreaths of flowers for their hair, a night of singing, dancing, and young romance.
4. Office of the Historian, Foreign Service Institute, United States Department of State. *"The Immigration Act of 1924,"* accessed February 5, 2021, https://history.state.-

gov/milestones/1921–1936/immigration-act.
5. Wyman, *DP*, 194.
6. Wyman, *DP*, 195–199.

18. Only One Homeland

1. Skaidrīte Bērziņš, letter to Arvīds Spīgulis, November 16, 1950, author's collection
2. Founded in 1874, Shepley Bulfinch Richardson and Abbott is one of the oldest, most respected architectural firms in the United States. My father was one of the architects who started the firm's hospital design division.
3. Skaidrīte Bērziņš, letter to Arvīds Spīgulis, December 8, 1950, author's collection.
4. Francis X. Clines, "Soviets, After 33 Years, Publish Khrushchev's Anti-Stalin Speech," *New York Times*, April 6, 1989, 12.
5. Kristīne Spīgulis, letter to Arvīds Spīgulis, April 9, 1957, author's collection.

Bibliography

Books and Articles

Arolsen Archives. *Background Information on Displaced Persons Documents.* E-Guide. https://eguide.arolsen-archives.org/en/additional-resources/background-information-on-displaced-persons-documents/. Retrieved November 3, 2020 and December 15, 2020.

Baltais, Mirdza Kate. *The Latvian Legion: Selected Documents.* Toronto, ON: Amber Printers and Publishers,1999.

Balodis, Alfreds. "Alma Mater—Baltijas Universitāte." In *Gersicania: 1947–1962*, edited by Gunārs Grūbe, Arvids Spīgulis, Valfrīds Spuntelis, and Ilgonis Zariņš,13–15. New York: Grāmatu Draugs, 1963.

Bērziņš, Alfreds. *Kārlis Ulmanis: cilvēks un valstvīrs [person and statesman],* Second Edition. Brooklyn, NY: Grāmatu Draugs, 1974.

Bleiere, Daina. "Repressions Against Farmers in Latvia 1944 - 1953." In *The Hidden and Forbidden History of Latvia Under Soviet and Nazi Occupations: 1940–1991.* Symposium of the Commission of Historians of Latvia, Volume 14. Edited by Andris Caune, Inesis Feldmanis (1941–1945), Irēne Šneidere (1949–1941), Aivars Stranga (Holocaust), Heinrihs Strods (1944–1991), Valters Nollendorfs, and Erwin Oberläner. Translated by Eva Eihmane. Riga: Latvian Institute of History, University of Latvia, 2005: 242 - 255.

Bleiere, Daina, Andris Caune, Inesis Feldmanis, Heinrihs Strods, and Irēne Šneidere, editors. *History of the Baltic Region of the 1940s to the 1980s.* Symposium of the Commission of Historians of Latvia, Volume 24. Riga: Latvian Institute of History, University of Latvia, 2009.

Bleiere, Daina, Ilgvars Butulis, Inesis Feldmanis, Aivars Stranga, and Antonijs Zunda. Translated by Valdis Bērziņš, Filips Birzulis, Pēteris Cedriņš, and Rihards Kalniņš. *History of Latvia: the 20th Century.* Riga: Jumava, 2006.

Buttar, Prit. *Between Giants: The Battle for the Baltics in World War II.* New York: Osprey Publishing, 2015.

Cameron Watt, Donald. *How War Came—The Immediate Origins of The Second World War, 1938–1939.* New York: Pantheon Books, 1989.

Citino, Robert M. *The Wehrmacht's Last Stand: the German Campaigns of 1944–1945.* Lawrence: University Press of Kansas, 2017.

Clines, Francis X. "Soviets, After 33 Years, Publish Khrushchev's Anti-Stalin Speech." *The New York Times.* April 6, 1989: 12.

Daugavas Vestnesis Nr. 135. Saturday, 15 June 1940.

Bibliography

"Die, But Do Not Retreat." Time, January 4, 1943. Accessed February 25, 2021. Content.time.com/subscriber/article/0,33009,790648-1.00.html.

Dunsdorfs, Edgars. "Mīļam bērnam daudz vārdu" [Beloved child many names]. In *Baltijas Universitāte, 1946–1949*, edited by Arnolds Grāmatiņš, 56–59. Germany: PBLA Kultūras fonds, 1989.

Dunsdorfs, Edgars. Latvijas vēsture. United States: Amerikas Latviešu Apvienība, 1980.

Dunsdorfs, Edgars. *Latvijas vēstures atlants: skolām un pašmācībai [Atlas of Latvian history: for schools and self-study]*. Melbourne, AU: Karļa Zariņa fonds, 1976.

Dunsdorfs, Edgars*Mūžīgais Latviešu Karavīrs* [The Eternal Latvian Soldier.] Melbourne, AU: Latvian Scout President General Karl Gopper Fund, 1966.

Ērglis, Dzintars. "A Few Episodes of the Holocaust in Krustpils: A Microcosm of the Holocaust in Occupied Latvia." In *The Hidden and Forbidden History of Latvia Under Soviet and Nazi Occupations: 1940–1991*. Symposium of the Commission of Historians of Latvia, Volume 14. Edited by Andris Caune, Inesis Feldmanis (1941–1945), Irēne Šneidere (1949–1941), Aivars Stranga (Holocaust), Heinrihs Strods (1944–1991), Valters Nollendorfs, and Erwin Oberländer. Translated by Eva Eihmane. Riga: Latvian Institute of History, University of Latvia, 2005: 175–187.

Evacuation Orders in Riga. *Tēvija*. Number 231. 29 September 1944.

Evarts, Edvīns. "Economic Policy of the German Occupation Rule in Latvia During World War II." In *Latvia Under Nazi German Occupation, 1941–1945. Materials of an International Conference, Volume 11, 12–13 June 2003*, edited by Andris Caune, Inesis Feldmanis, Heinrihs Strods, Irēne Šneidere, Rita Klaviņa, and Vija Stabulniece. Compiled by Dzintars Ērglis. Riga: Institute of Latvian History, University of Latvia, 2004: 101–107.

Ezergailis, Andrew. *The Holocaust in Latvia 1941-1944: The Missing Center*. Riga: The Historical Institute of Latvia, 1989.

Fein, Esther B. "Soviets Confirm Nazi Pacts Dividing Europe." In *The New York Times*. August 19, 1989: Section 1, page 1.

Feldmanis, Inesis. "Latvia Under the Occupation of National Socialist Germany 1941–1945." In *The Hidden and Forbidden History of Latvia Under Soviet and Nazi Occupations: 1940–1991*. Symposium of the Commission of Historians of Latvia, Volume 14. Edited by Andris Caune, Inesis Feldmanis (1941–1945), Irēne Šneidere (1949–1941), Aivars Stranga (Holocaust), Heinrihs Strods (1944–1991), Valters Nollendorfs, and Erwin Oberländer. Translated by Eva Eihmane. Riga: Latvian Institute of History, University of Latvia, 2005: 77–91.

Feldmanis, Inesis. "Waffen SS Units of Latvians and Other Non-Germanic Peoples in World War II: Methods of Formation, Ideology, and Goals." In *The Hidden and Forbidden History of Latvia Under Soviet and Nazi Occupations: 1940–1991*. Symposium of the Commission of Historians of Latvia, Volume 14. Edited by Andris Caune, Inesis Feldmanis (1941–1945), Irēne Šneidere (1949–1941), Aivars Stranga (Holocaust), Heinrihs Strods (1944–1991), Valters Nollendorfs, and Erwin

BIBLIOGRAPHY

Oberläner. Translated by Eva Eihmane. Riga: Latvian Institute of History, University of Latvia, 2005:122–131.

Feldmanis, Inesis, and Kārlis Kangeris. *The Volunteer SS Legion in Latvia*. Embassy of the Republic of Latvia in the Czech Republic. Ministry of Foreign Affairs, Republic of Latvia. February 12, 2014.

Feldmanis, Inesis, and Aivars Stranga. *The Destiny of the Baltic Entente 1934-1940*. Latvian Institute of International Affairs, 1994.

Freivalds, Osvalds. *Kurzemes Cietoksnis I [The Courland Fortress I]*. Copenhagen: Imanta, 1954.

Freivalds, Osvalds.*Kurzemes Cietoksnis II [The Courland Fortress II]*. Copenhagen: Imanta,1954.

Freivalds, Osvalds, and Oskars Caunītis. *Latviešu Karavīrs otrā pasaules kara laikā I–IV [The Latvian Soldier During World War II]*. Daugavas Vanagu centrālās valde, 1970.

Frieser, Karl-Heinz, Klaus Schmider, Klaus Schönherr, Gerhard Schreiber, Krisztián Ungváry, and Bernd Wegner. Translated by Barry Smerin and Barbara Wilson. *Germany and the Second World War, Volume VIII. The Eastern Front 1943-1944: The War in the East and on the Neighboring Fronts*. Oxford, UK: Oxford University Press, 2017.

Grāmatiņš, Arnolds. "Universitātes vēsture" [University history]. In *Baltijas Universitāte: 1946-1949*, edited by Arnolds Grāmatiņš, 8–44. Germany: PBLA Kultūras fonds, 1989.

Grūbe, Pauls. "Gersicanias devīzes un simboli" [Gersicania's mottos and symbols]. In *Gersicania: 1947-1962*. Edited by Gunārs Grūbe, Arvids Spīgulis, Valfrids Spuntelis, and Ilgonis Zariņš, 8. New York: Grāmatu Draugs, 1963.

Höschler, Christian, and Isabel Panek. *Two Kinds of Searches: Findings on Displaced Persons in Arolsen After 1945*. Arolsen Archives, 2019. https://arolsen-archives.org/content/uploads/200215_aa_fundstuecke_web_en_rz.pdf

Hunt, Vincent. *Blood in the Forest: The End of the Second World War in the Courland Pocket*. Warwick, EN: Helion & Company, 2017.

Ivanovs, Aleksandrs. "Sovietization of Latvian Historiography 1944-1959: Overview." In *The Hidden and Forbidden History of Latvia Under Soviet and Nazi Occupations: 1940-1991*. Symposium of the Commission of Historians of Latvia, Volume 14. Edited by Andris Caune, Inesis Feldmanis (1941–1945), Irēne Šneidere (1949–1941), Aivars Stranga (Holocaust), Heinrihs Strods (1944–1991), Valters Nollendorfs, and Erwin Oberläner. Translated by Eva Eihmane. Riga: Latvian Institute of History, University of Latvia, 2005: Latvian Institute of History, 2005: 256 - 270.

Jones, Nigel. *The Birth of the Nazis: How the Freikorps Blazed a Trail for Hitler*. 1987. New York: Carroll & Graf Publishers. 2004.

Kangeris, Kārlis. "'Closed' Units of Latvian Police—LettischeSchutzmannschafts - Bataillone. Research Issues and Pre-History." In *The Hidden and Forbidden History of Latvia Under Soviet and Nazi Occupations: 1940-1991*. Symposium of the

Bibliography

Commission of Historians of Latvia, Volume 14. Edited by Andris Caune, Inesis Feldmanis (1941–1945), Irēne Šneidere (1949–1941), Aivars Stranga (Holocaust), Heinrihs Strods (1944–1991), Valters Nollendorfs, and Erwin Oberländer. Translated by Eva Eihmane. Riga: Latvian Institute of History, University of Latvia, 2005: 104–121.

Kangeris, Kārlis. "Latvian Legion: A Dictation of the German Occupation Power or Fulfillment of the Latvian Hopes?" *History of the Baltic Region, 1940s–1980s*. Research of the Commission of the Historians of Latvia, 2007, and Proceedings of an International Conference, "Baltics During the Second World War." Edited by Bleiere, Daina, Andris Caune, Inesis Feldmanis, Heinrihs Strods, and Irēne Šneidere. Riga: Latvian Institute of History, University of Latvia, 2009: 62–94.

Klētiņš, Ž. Article about 19th Latvian artillerists. *Ventas Balss (Voice of the Venta)*. May 4, 1945.

Kovaļevskis, Pauls, and Oskars Norītis, editors. *Baigais gads*. Riga: Zelta ābele [Golden Apple Tree], 1942. Reissued 2003. https://latvietis.lv/BaigaisGads.

Kuck, Jordan Tyler. *The Dictator Without a Uniform: Kārlis Ulmanis, Agrarian Nationalism, Transnational Fascism, and Interwar Latvia*. 2014. University of Tennessee, PhD dissertation. https://trace.tennessee.edu/utk-graddiss/2895.

Lai atskan dziesmas: dziesmu krājums [Let songs ring out; a song collection]. United States: Grāmatu draugs, 1972.

Latvijas Kareivis [The Latvian Soldier]. 26 January 1945. Copy provided by Latvian War Museum, Riga.

Museum of the Occupation of Latvia. "Soviet Mass Deportations from Latvia," *Briefing Paper 04*. Riga: Ministry of Foreign Affairs in Latvia, August 2004.

Naimark, Norman M. *Stalin's Genocides*. Princeton, NJ: Princeton University Press, 2012.

Neiburgs, Uldis. "Western Allies in Latvian Public Opinion and Nazi Propaganda During the German Occupation, 1941 - 1945." In *The Hidden and Forbidden History of Latvia Under Soviet and Nazi Occupations: 1940-1991*. Symposium of the Commission of Historians of Latvia, Volume 14. Edited by Andris Caune, Inesis Feldmanis (1941–1945), Irēne Šneidere (1949–1941), Aivars Stranga (Holocaust), Heinrihs Strods (1944–1991), Valters Nollendorfs, and Erwin Oberländer. Translated by Eva Eihmane. Riga: Latvian Institute of History, University of Latvia, 2005: 132–147.

Neimane, Dagnija. *Flight From Latvia: A Six-Year Chronicle*. Self-published, 2016.

Nollendorfs, Valters, Ojārs Celle, Gundega Michele, Uldis Neibergs, and Dagnija Staško, editors. *The Three Occupations of Latvia 1940-1991: Soviet and Nazi Takeovers and Their Consequences*. Riga: Occupation Museum Foundation, 2005.

Pavlovičs, Juris. "Change of Occupation Powers in Latvia in Summer 1941. Experience of Small Communities." In *The Hidden and Forbidden History of Latvia Under Soviet and Nazi Occupations: 1940-1991*. Symposium of the Commission of Historians of Latvia, Volume 14. Edited by Andris Caune, Inesis Feldmanis (1941–1945), Irēne Šneidere (1949–1941), Aivars Stranga (Holocaust), Heinrihs Strods (1944–1991),

BIBLIOGRAPHY

Valters Nollendorfs, and Erwin Oberläner. Translated by Eva Eihmane. Riga: Latvian Institute of History, University of Latvia, 2005: 92–103.

Piksis, Jānis, and Valfrīds Spuntelis. "Latvju karavīri" [Latvian Soldiers]. In *Gersicania: 1947-1962*, edited by Gunārs Grūbe, Arvids Spīgulis, Valfrīds Spuntelis, and Ilgonis Zariņš, 80. New York: Grāmatu Draugs, 1963.

Plakans, Andrejs. *The Latvians: A Short History*. Stanford: Hoover Institution Press, 1995.

Podolsky, Anatoly. "Problems of Collaboration and Rescuing Jews on Latvian and Ukrainian Territories During Nazi Occupation: An Attempt at Comparative Analysis." In *The Holocaust Research in Latvia. Materials of an International Conference in Riga, 12-13 June and 24 October 2003, and the Holocaust Studies in Latvia, 2002-2003*. Edited by Andris Caune, Aivars Stranga, Marģers Vestermanis, Margita Gūtmane, Rita Kļaviņš, and Vija Stabulniece. Compiled by Dzintars Ērglis. Riga: Latvian Institute of History, University of Latvia, 2004: 87–91.

Ramrath Straumenis, Astrida. *Where Do I Belong? The Journey of a Country Girl*. Self-published, Amazon, 2016.

Riekstiņš, Jānis. "Colonization and Russification of Latvia 1940 - 1989." In *The Hidden and Forbidden History of Latvia Under Soviet and Nazi Occupations: 1940-1991*. Symposium of the Commission of Historians of Latvia, Volume 14. Edited by Andris Caune, Inesis Feldmanis (1941–1945), Irēne Šneidere (1949–1941), Aivars Stranga (Holocaust), Heinrihs Strods (1944–1991), Valters Nollendorfs, and Erwin Oberläner. Translated by Eva Eihmane. Riga: Latvian Institute of History, University of Latvia, 2005: 228–241.

Riekstiņš, Jānis. "The 14 June 1941 Deportation in Latvia." In *The Hidden and Forbidden History of Latvia Under Soviet and Nazi Occupations: 1940-1991*. Symposium of the Commission of Historians of Latvia, Volume 14. Edited by Andris Caune, Inesis Feldmanis (1941–1945), Irēne Šneidere (1949–1941), Aivars Stranga (Holocaust), Heinrihs Strods (1944–1991), Valters Nollendorfs, and Erwin Oberläner. Translated by Eva Eihmane. Riga: Latvian Institute of History, University of Latvia, 2005: 62–76.

Saliniece, Irēna. "Wehrmacht Soldiers in the Memory of the People of Latvia (according to oral sources of history). In *Latvia Under Nazi German Occupation: 1941-1945. Materials of an International Conference, Volume 11, 12-13 June 2003*, edited by Andris Caune, Inesis Feldmanis, Heinrihs Strods, Irēne Šneidere, Rita Klaviņa, and Vija Stabulniece. Compiled by Dzintars Ērglis. Riga: Institute of Latvian History, University of Latvia, 2004: 40–46.

Senn, Erich. "Baltic Battleground." In *The Hidden and Forbidden History of Latvia Under Soviet and Nazi Occupations: 1940-1991*. Symposium of the Commission of Historians of Latvia, Volume 14. Edited by Andris Caune, Inesis Feldmanis (1941–1945), Irēne Šneidere (1949–1941), Aivars Stranga (Holocaust), Heinrihs Strods (1944–1991), Valters Nollendorfs, and Erwin Oberläner. Translated by Eva Eihmane. Riga: Latvian Institute of History, University of Latvia, 2005: 17–32.

BIBLIOGRAPHY

Silgailis, Arthur. *Latvian Legion*. San Jose, California: R. James Bender Publishing, 1986.
Šneidere, Irēne. "The First Soviet Occupation Period in Latvia. 1940-1941." In *The Hidden and Forbidden History of Latvia Under Soviet and Nazi Occupations: 1940-1991*. Symposium of the Commission of Historians of Latvia, Volume 14. Edited by Andris Caune, Inesis Feldmanis (1941-1945), Irēne Šneidere (1949-1941), Aivars Stranga (Holocaust), Heinrihs Strods (1944-1991), Valters Nollendorfs, and Erwin Oberländer. Translated by Eva Eihmane. Riga: Latvian Institute of History, University of Latvia, 2005: 33-42.
Šneidere, Irēne. "The Occupation of Latvia in June 1940: A Few Aspects of the Technology of Soviet Aggression." In *The Hidden and Forbidden History of Latvia Under Soviet and Nazi Occupations: 1940-1991*. Symposium of the Commission of Historians of Latvia, Volume 14. Edited by Andris Caune, Inesis Feldmanis (1941-1945), Irēne Šneidere (1949-1941), Aivars Stranga (Holocaust), Heinrihs Strods (1944-1991), Valters Nollendorfs, and Erwin Oberländer. Translated by Eva Eihmane. Riga: Latvian Institute of History, University of Latvia, 2005: 43-52.
Snyder, Timothy. *Bloodlands: Europe Between Hitler and Stalin*. New York: Basic Books, 2010.
Spīgulis, Arvids. "Gersicanias pirmie gadi" [Gersicania's first years]. In *Gersicania: 1947-1962*, edited by Gunārs Grūbe, Arvids Spīgulis, Valfrīds Spuntelis, and Ilgonis Zariņš,18-22. New York: Grāmatu Draugs, 1963.
Spīgulis, Arvids. "Vide un laiks" [Life and time]. In *Gersicania: 1947-1962*, edited by Gunārs Grūbe, Arvids Spīgulis, Valfrīds Spuntelis, and Ilgonis Zariņš,11. New York: Grāmatu Draugs, 1963.
Spridzāns, Benedikts. "On the Blackest Day of Latvia". *Latvijas Vestnesis*, April 21, 1995, Number 62.
Steiner, Zara. *The Triumph of the Dark: European International History 1933-1939*. Oxford, United Kingdom: Oxford University Press, 2011.
Stranga, Aivars. "The Holocaust in Occupied Latvia: 1941-1945." In *The Hidden and Forbidden History of Latvia Under Soviet and Nazi Occupations: 1940-1991*. Symposium of the Commission of Historians of Latvia, Volume 14. Edited by Andris Caune, Inesis Feldmanis (1941-1945), Irēne Šneidere (1949-1941), Aivars Stranga (Holocaust), Heinrihs Strods (1944-1991), Valters Nollendorfs, and Erwin Oberländer. Translated by Eva Eihmane. Riga: Latvian Institute of History, University of Latvia, 2005:161-174.
Stranga, Aivars. "Problems in the Holocaust Research." In *The Holocaust Research in Latvia. Materials of an International Conference in Riga, 12-13 June and 24 October 2003, and the Holocaust Studies in Latvia, 2002-2003*. Edited by Andris Caune, Aivars Stranga, Marģers Vestermanis, Margita Gūtmane, Rita Kļaviņš, and Vija Stabulniece. Compiled by Dzintars Ērglis. Riga: Latvian Institute of History, University of Latvia, 2004: 17-31.
Strods, Heinrihs. "Sovietization of Latvia 1944-1991." In *The Hidden and Forbidden*

BIBLIOGRAPHY

History of Latvia Under Soviet and Nazi Occupations: 1940–1991. Symposium of the Commission of Historians of Latvia, Volume 14. Edited by Andris Caune, Inesis Feldmanis (1941–1945), Irēne Šneidere (1949–1941), Aivars Stranga (Holocaust), Heinrihs Strods (1944–1991), Valters Nollendorfs, and Erwin Oberländer. Translated by Eva Eihmane. Riga: Latvian Institute of History, University of Latvia, 2005: 209–227.
"Die, But Do Not Retreat." *Time.* January 4, 1943.
Treisman, Daniel. "Why Putin Took Crimea: The Gambler in the Kremlin." *Foreign Affairs,* May/June 2016.
Urtāns, Aigars. "An Insight into the Holocaust Research in Bauska, Valmiera and Ludza Districts." In *The Holocaust Research in Latvia. Materials of an International Conference in Riga, 12–13 June and 24 October 2003, and the Holocaust Studies in Latvia, 2002–2003.* Edited by Andris Caune, Aivars Stranga, Marģers Vestermanis, Margita Gūtmane, Rita Kļaviņš, and Vija Stabulniece. Compiled by Dzintars Ērglis. Riga: Latvian Institute of History, University of Latvia, 2004: 188–192.
Vestermanis, Marģers. "Riga-Kaiserwald Concentration Camp (A Few Aspects of the Camp's History." In *The Holocaust Research in Latvia. Materials of an International Conference in Riga, 12–13 June and 24 October 2003, and the Holocaust Studies in Latvia, 2002–2003.* Edited by Andris Caune, Aivars Stranga, Marģers Vestermanis, Margita Gūtmane, Rita Kļaviņš, and Vija Stabulniece. Compiled by Dzintars Ērglis. Riga: Latvian Institute of History, University of Latvia, 2004: 32–39.
Vīksne, Rudīte. "Extermination of Jews in Latvian Towns: Problems and Results of Research." In *The Holocaust Research in Latvia. Materials of an International Conference in Riga, 12–13 June and 24 October 2003, and the Holocaust Studies in Latvia, 2002–2003.* Edited by Andris Caune, Aivars Stranga, Marģers Vestermanis, Margita Gūtmane, Rita Kļaviņš, and Vija Stabulniece. Compiled by Dzintars Ērglis. Riga: Latvian Institute of History, University of Latvia, 2004: 41–46.
Vīksne, Rudīte. "Members of the Arājs Kommando in Soviet Court Files: Social Position, Education, Reasons for Volunteering, Penalty." In *The Hidden and Forbidden History of Latvia Under Soviet and Nazi Occupations: 1940–1991.* Symposium of the Commission of Historians of Latvia, Volume 14. Edited by Andris Caune, Inesis Feldmanis (1941–1945), Irēne Šneidere (1949–1941), Aivars Stranga (Holocaust), Heinrihs Strods (1944–1991), Valters Nollendorfs, and Erwin Oberländer. Translated by Eva Eihmane. Riga: Latvian Institute of History, University of Latvia, 2005: 188–208.
Vīksne, Rudīte. "Soviet Repressions Against Residents of Latvia in 1940–1941: Typical Trends." In *The Hidden and Forbidden History of Latvia Under Soviet and Nazi Occupations: 1940–1991.* Symposium of the Commission of Historians of Latvia, Volume 14. Edited by Andris Caune, Inesis Feldmanis (1941–1945), Irēne Šneidere (1949–1941), Aivars Stranga (Holocaust), Heinrihs Strods (1944–1991), Valters Nollendorfs, and Erwin Oberländer. Translated by Eva Eihmane. Riga: Latvian Institute of History, University of Latvia, 2005: 53–61.

Bibliography

Wyman, Mark. *DP: Europe's Displaced Persons, 1945-1951.* Associated University Presses,1989.

Zandbergs, Mārtiņš, editor and compiler. *Mārtiņa dziesma grāmata I.* United States: self-published, 1972.

Zegner. "Field Service Report, November 28, 1943." *Latviešu karavīrs otrā pasaules kara laikā, 4. sējums* [*The Latvian Soldier During World War II, 4th Volume*]. Freivalds, Osvalds, and Alfrēds Berziņš. Daugavas Vanagu Centrālā Valde, 1976: 161-162.

Zegner. "Field Service Report, March 1, 1944." *Latviešu karavīrs otrā pasaules kara laikā, 4. sējums* [*The Latvian Soldier During World War II, 4th Volume*]. Freivalds, Osvalds, and Alfrēds Berziņš. Daugavas Vanagu Centrālā Valde, 1976: 163.

Zelče, Vita. "Bēgšana no brīvības: Kārļa Ulmaņa režīma ideoloģija un rituāli" [Flight from freedom: Karl Ulmanis' regimes' ideology and rituals]. In *Reiz dzīvoja Kārlis Ulmanis. Agora* No. 6. Zinātne: 325-250.

Zunda, Antonijs. "Resistance Against Nazi German Occupation in Latvia: Positions in Historical Literature." In *The Hidden and Forbidden History of Latvia Under Soviet and Nazi Occupations: 1940-1991.* Symposium of the Commission of Historians of Latvia, Volume 14. Edited by Andris Caune, Inesis Feldmanis (1941-1945), Irēne Šneidere (1949-1941), Aivars Stranga (Holocaust), Heinrihs Strods (1944-1991), Valters Nollendorfs, and Erwin Oberländer. Translated by Eva Eihmane. Riga: Latvian Institute of History, University of Latvia, 2005: 148-160.

Zunda, Antonijs. "The Policies of the German Occupation Rule in Latvia (1941-1945): Opinions in Historiography." In *Latvia Under Nazi German Occupation: 1941-1945. Materials of an International Conference, Volume 11, 12-13 June 2003*, edited by Andris Caune, Inesis Feldmanis, Heinrihs Strods, Irēne Šneidere, Rita Klaviņa, and Vija Stabulniece. Compiled by Dzintars Ērglis. Riga: Institute of Latvian History, University of Latvia, 2004: 17-28.

Žvinklis, Arturs. "Photo and Film Documents on the Holocaust in Latvia." In *The Holocaust Research in Latvia. Materials of an International Conference in Riga, 12-13 June and 24 October 2003, and the Holocaust Studies in Latvia, 2002-2003.* Edited by Andris Caune, Aivars Stranga, Marģers Vestermanis, Margita Gūtmane, Rita Kļaviņš, and Vija Stabulniece. Compiled by Dzintars Ērglis. Riga: Latvian Institute of History, University of Latvia, 2004: 165-184.

Bibliography

Government Memos, Reports, Treaties, and Laws

U. S. Department of State, and Charles Bevans, compiler. "Armistice with Germany, November 11, 1918." In *Treaties and Other International Agreements of the United States of America: Volume 2, Multilateral Treaties, 1918–1930.* Washington, DC: Law Library of Congress. Accessed February 21, 2021. https://www.loc.gov/law/help/us-treaties/bevans/m-ust000002-0009.pdf.

Bohlen, Charles. "Minutes of Roosevelt–Stalin meeting, December 1, 1943. Report #378." In *Foreign Relations of the United States: Diplomatic Papers, The Conferences at Cairo and Tehran, 1943.* Washington, DC: U. S. Government Printing Office, 1943. https://history.state.gov/historicaldocuments/frus1943CairoTehran/d378

The Consul General at Moscow (Summers) to the Secretary of State. "Article Three," in *Foreign Relations of the United States: 1918 The Conclusion of the Peace of Brest-Litovsk.* New Haven, CT: Yale Law Library, The Avalon Project: Foreign Relations. Accessed May 31, 2021. https://avalon.law.yale.edu/20th_century/bl34.asp.

"Convention (IV) respecting the Laws and Customs of War on Land and its annex: Regulations concerning the Laws and Customs of War on Land," adopted October 18, 1907 at the International Peace Conference, The Hague. *Treaties, States Parties and Commentaries.* International Committee of the Red Cross database. Ihl-databases.icrc.org/ihl/INTRO/195.

Fuller, Joseph V., editor. "Papers Relating to the Foreign Relations of the United States, The Paris Peace Conference, 1919. Volume XIII." *The Covenant of the League of Nations, Articles 1–26.* Washington, DC: U. S. Government Printing Office, 1947. history.state.gov/historicaldocuments/frus1919Parisv13.

Harrison, Earl G. *Report of Earl G. Harrison: Mission to Europe to Inquire Into the Condition and Needs of Those Among the Displaced Persons in the Liberated Countries of Western Europe and the SHAEF Area of Germany—With Particular Reference to the Jewish Refugee.* August 24, 1945. Truman Harry S. (4); Principal Files, 1916 - 1952; Collection DDE-EPRE: Eisenhower, Dwight D: Papers, Pre-Presidential. Abilene, KS: Dwight D. Eisenhower Library. Online Version, https://www.docsteach.org/documents/document/harrison-report-concerning-conditions-displaced-persons-post-ww2.

"*History of the Presidency, Former Presidents: Kārlis Ulmanis.*" President of the Republic of Latvia website. March 16, 2021. Accessed January 15, 2022. https://www.president.lv/en/karlis-ulmanis.

Joint Four-Nation Declaration, The Moscow Conference, October 1943. *A Decade of American Policy: Basic Documents, 1941–1949.* Prepared at the request of the U. S. Senate Committee on Foreign Relations by the Staff of the Committee and the Department of State (Washington, DC: Government Printing Office, 1950).

Constitutional Assembly. "*Latvijas Republikas Satversme*" [*The Republic of Latvia's Constitution*]. Adopted February 15, 1922. Published online by Latvijas Vēstnesis on July 1, 1992. Accessed on February 27 and June 7, 2021. https://likumi.lv/ta/en/en/id/57980.

Bibliography

"Article II. Peace Trety Between Latvia and Russia, August 11, 1920, Riga." *League of Nation Treaty Series.* World War II Databases: 1920 LNT Ser 63. 2 LNTS 195. Posted December 20, 2009. http://www.worldlii.org/int/other/treaties/LNTSer/1920/63.html Molotov, Vyacheslav, and Joachim Ribbentrop. "Secret Supplementary Protocols of the Molotov-Ribbentrop Non-Aggression Pact, 1939." September 1939. *Nazi-Soviet Relations, 1939–1941: Documents from the Archives of the German Foreign Office.* History and Public Policy Program Digital Archive. https://digitalarchive.wilsoncenter.org/document/110994.

Office of the Historian, Foreign Service Institute, U. S. Department of State. *Summary of The Immigration Act of 1924.* Accessed on February 5, 2021.

Office of the Historian, U. S. Department of State. "The League of Nations 1920." https://history.state.gov/milestones/1914–1920/league.

Office of the U. S. Chief of Counsel For Prosecution of Axis Criminality, *Nazi Conspiracy and Aggression,* ('Red Series'), Volume I.Washington, DC: U. S. Government Printing Office, 1946.

Office of the U. S. Chief of Counsel For Prosecution of Axis Criminality, *Nazi Conspiracy and Aggression,* ('Red Series'), Volume VII. Washington, DC: U. S. Government Printing Office,1946.

U.S. House of Representatives, Select Committee on Communist Aggression. *Communist Takeover and Occupation of Latvia. Special Report Number 12 of the Select Committee on Communist Aggression.* 83rd Congress, 2nd session. Washington, DC: U. S. Government Printing Office, December 30, 1954.

U.S. Senate Committee on Foreign Relations and the Department of State. "The Moscow Conference, October 1943. Joint Four-Nation Declaration." *A Decade of American Foreign Policy: Basic Documents, 1941-49.* Washington, DC: U. S. Government Printing Office, 1950.

BIBLIOGRAPHY

Archives
Abajian, A. N. Memo to U. S. Department of State, Office of Investigations, Refugee Relief Program. Subject: Teidemanis, Herberts. December 12, 1955.CIA Library, CIA.gov.

Arolsen Archives: Arvids Spīgulis, Displaced Person Registration Record. June 28, 1946. https://collections.arolsen-archives.org/en/archive/69245905/?p=1&s=Spigulis,%20Arvids&doc_id=69245905.

Arolsen Archives: Arvids Spīgulis, Displaced Person Registration Record. July 18, 1945. https://collections.arolsen-archives.org/en/archive/79756751/?p=1&s=Spigulis,%20Arvids&doc_id=79756752.

Arolsen Archives: Arvids Spīgulis Displaced Persons Resettlement Questionnaire https://collections.arolsen-archives.org/en/archive/81732604/?p=1&s=Spigulis,%20Arvids&doc_id=81732604

Arolsen Archives: Skaidrīte Berziņš Displaced Person Registration Card, August 6, 1946. https://collections.arolsen-archives.org/en/archive/66580019/?p=1&s=Berzins,%20Skaidrite&doc_id=66580019.

Arolsen Archives: Skaidrite Berziņš Displaced Person Registration Card, August 6, 1945. https://collections.arolsen-archives.org/en/archive/66580020/?p=1&s=Berzins,%20Skaidrite&doc_id=66580020.

Central Intelligence Agency. *Sources, Methods, Exemption 3B2B Nazi War Crimes Disclosure Act*. Date of memo: 5 August 1955. Date of release: 2007.

Constitutional Assembly. "Latvijas Republikas Satversme" [Constitution of the Republic of Latvia]. Part VIII. Accessed June 7, 2021. Likumi.lv/ta/id/57980-latvijas-republikas-satversme.

The Consul General at Moscow (Summers) to the Secretary of State. *Foreign Relations of the United States: 1918 The Conclusion of the Peace of Brest–Litovsk, Article Three*. The Avalon Project: Foreign Relations. Accessed May 31, 2021. https://avalon.law.yale.edu/20th_century/bl34.asp.

The Covenant of the League of Nations. The Avalon Project: Documents in Law, History, and Diplomacy. Lillian Goldman Law Library. Yale Law School.

Latvian Historical Archives. P-71 fonds, 1. Apraksts, 3. Lieta, 35.

Latvian Legion Archival Database. Latvian War Museum. Accessed November 27, 2018 and July 21, 2020.

Latvian National Archives. LVVA-6.2.2/5/7794. Accessed July 8, 2020.

Latvijas Iedzīvotāju 1949. gada 25. marta deportācija [Latvian citizens deported 25 March 1949]. Latvijas Valsts Arhīvs [Latvian State Archives]. http://www.archiv.org.lv/dep1941/meklesana49.php

Latvijas Republikas Saeima. "History of the Legislature, The People's Council." Accessed June 7, 2021. https://www.saeima.lv/en/about-saeima/history-of-the-legislature.

"Peace Treaty Between Latvia and Russia, August 11, 1920, Riga, Article II." *League of Nations Treaty Series*. WWII Databases: 1920 LNT Ser 63; 2 LNTS 195, posted

Bibliography

December 20, 2009. Accessed June 8, 2021. http://www.worldlii.org/int/other/treaties/LNTSer/1920/63.html.

"The Peace Treaty of Brest-Litovsk." 3 March 1918. *WWI Document Archive*, edited by Richard Hacken. Brigham Young University Library, July 7, 2009. https://wwi.lib.byu.edu/index.php?title=The_Peace_Treaty_of_Brest-Litovsk&oldid=8392

SHAEF Memorandum #38. Arolsen Archives, 6.1.1/82495546/ITS Digital Archive.

State Statistical Office. Prepared and edited by Marģers Skujenieks. *Third Population and Housing Census in Latvia, 1930*. Riga: January 2, 1930. Accessed February 3, 2020. https://www.csb.gov.lv/en/statistics/statistics-by-theme/population/census/search-in-theme/185-third-population-and-housing-census-latvia1930

State Statistical Office. Prepared by V. Salnītis and edited by Marģers Skujenieks. *Fourth Population Census in Latvia, 1935*. Riga: May 15, 1936. Accessed February 8, 2020. https://www.csb.gov.lv/en/statistics/statistics-by-theme/population/census/search-in-theme/186-fourth-population-census-latvia-1935-latvian-and

U. S. Department of State. Foreign Service Institute. Office of the Historian. "*The Immigration Act of 1924.*" https://history.state.gov/milestones/1921-1936/immigration-act.

U. S. Department of State. Foreign Service Institute. Office of the Historian. *The Potsdam Conference, 1945*. https://history.state.gov/milestones/1937-1945/potsdam-conf.

U. S. House of Representatives, 83rd Congress. *Communist Takeover and Occupation of Latvia*, Special Report No 12 of the Select Committee on Communist Aggression Second Session, December 30, 1954.

U. S. National Archives & Records Administration. Transcript of President Woodrow Wilson's 14 Points (1918). http://www.ourdocuments.gov/doc.php?doc=62&page=transcript.

United Nations Archives and Record Management Section. Summary of AG-018 United Nations Relief and Rehabilitation Administration (UNRRA) (1943 - 1946). Accessed February, 25, 2021. https://search.archives.un.org/downloads/united-nations-relief-and-rehabilitation-administration-unrra-1943-1946.pdf.

Bibliography

Unpublished Material

Gertners, V., et al. Pamphlet describing the history of the Baltic University. Baltic University Student Council. 1949.

Baltic University in Figures and Pictures. Baltic University. 1949.

Bērziņš, Arnolds. Letter to Rita Bērziņs. November 21, 1943. Translated by Anita Spigulis-DeSnyder, Author's collection.

Bērziņš, Arnolds. Letter to Rita Bērziņs. January 13, 1945. Translated by Anita Spigulis-DeSnyder, Author's collection.

Bērziņš, Arnolds. Letter to Rita Bērziņs. March 1, 1945. Translated by Anita Spigulis-DeSnyder, Author's collection.

Bērziņš, Arnolds. Letter to Rita Bērziņs. March 14, 1945. Translated by Anita Spigulis-DeSnyder, Author's collection.

Bērziņš, Jānis. Letter to Elvīra Bišs. March 3, 1965.

Bērziņš, Jānis. Letter to Skaidrīte Spīgulis. June 15, 1968.

Bērziņš, Skaidrīte. Letter to Arvids Spīgulis. November 16, 1950. Translated by Anita Spigulis-DeSnyder, Author's collection.

Bērziņš, Skaidrīte. Letter to Arvids Spīgulis. December 8, 1950. Translated by Anita Spigulis-DeSnyder, Author's collection.

Bišs, Visvaldis. *Memoir.* Unpublished manuscript. Typewritten file. Author's collection.

Lielbārdis, Aigars. E-mail to author. July 13, 2020.

Spīgulis, Kristīne. Letter to Arvids Spīgulis. April 9, 1957. Translated by Anita Spigulis-DeSnyder, Author's collection.

Spīgulis, Vallija. Letters to Arvids Spīgulis. 1957. Translated by Anita Spigulis-DeSnyder, Author's collection.

Tomaševskis, Jānis. E-mails to author. October 22, 2018, November 27–29, 2018, and July 24, 2020.

Ziedars, Jēkabs. E-mail to author with enclosed chapter from memoir about Baltic University, October 22, 2018

Bibliography

Films

Latvian Legion. Directed by Inara Kolmane, and written by Uldis Neiburgs. Republic of Latvia, Ministry of Defense, Soros Fund. March 2012. https://latvianlegion.org/index.php?en/content-90-additional.ssi.

Sarkanā Migla [The Red Mist]. Directed by Konstantin Tumil-Tumilovich, narrated by Artūrs Dimiters. 1942.

Songs

All translations by Anita Spigulis-DeSnyder.

Baumanis, Kārlis. "Dievs svētī Latviju."

Briedis, Augusts, hymn. "Gaišais rīts, gaišais rīts."

Dārziņš, Emīls, composer, and Kārlis Skalbe, lyrics. "Mūžam zili ir Latvijas kalni," 1909-1910.

Dārziņš, Emīls, composer, and Auseklis, lyrics, adapted by Schiller. "Pie tēvu zemes dārgās."

Graubiņš, J., composer, and V. Plūdons, lyrics. "Lāčplēšu dziesma," 1934.

Latvian folk song. "Daudz baltu dieniņu."

Latvian folk song. "Es nezinu un nesaprotu."

Latvian folk song. "Klusi, klusi ratiņš rūc."

Latvian folk song. "Pūt vējiņi."

Latvian folk song. "Sarkandaiļa roze auga."

Latvian folk song. "Tev dzīvē laimes nav."

Latvian folk song. "Uz tālām siltām saules zemēm."

Norvilis, J., composer, and J. Rainis, lyrics. "Mūsu zeme." Composed 1935. Lyrics written circa 1918.

Milton Keynes UK
Ingram Content Group UK Ltd.
UKHW030101081124
450874UK00001B/155

9 798330 501755